Salman Rushdie

MANCHESTER
1824

Manchester University Press

CONTEMPORARY WORLD WRITERS

SERIES EDITOR   JOHN THIEME

Salman Rushdie

ANDREW TEVERSON

Manchester University Press
Manchester and New York

distributed exclusively in the USA by Palgrave

Published by Manchester University Press
Oxford Road, Manchester M13 9NR, UK
and Room 400, 175 Fifth Avenue, New York, NY 10010, USA
www.manchesteruniversitypress.co.uk

Distributed exclusively in the USA by
Palgrave, 175 Fifth Avenue, New York, NY 10010, USA

Distributed exclusively in Canada by
ubc Press, University of British Columbia, 2029 West Mall,
Vancouver, BC, Canada v6T 1z2

British Library Cataloguing-in-Publication Data
A catalogue record for this book is available from the British Library

Library of Congress Cataloging-in-Publication Data applied for

ISBN 978 0 7190 7050 1 *hardback*
ISBN 978 0 7190 7051 8 *paperback*

First published 2007

16 15 14 13 12 11 10 09 08 07   10 9 8 7 6 5 4 3 2 1

Typeset in Aldus
by Koinonia, Manchester
Printed in Great Britain
by CPI, Bath

823
Rushdie

For Simone, Dominic and Tristan, with love

I refuse to see literature as a purely aesthetic enterprise ... the use of form is not purely technical. It has meaning. You change the way in which you write and you change the things it's possible for you to say and therefore what is possible to think and therefore what is possible to do. So to shift forms is to act in all those ways. (Salman Rushdie, 1983, SRI, 49)

Contents

Series editor's foreword

Contemporary World Writers is an innovative series of authoritative introductions to a range of culturally diverse contemporary writers from outside Britain and the United States or from 'minority' backgrounds within Britain or the United States. In addition to providing comprehensive general introductions, books in the series also argue stimulating original theses, often but not always related to contemporary debates in post-colonial studies.

The series locates individual writers within their specific cultural contexts, while recognising that such contexts are themselves invariably a complex mixture of hybridised influences. It aims to counter tendencies to appropriate the writers discussed into the canon of English or American literature or to regard them as 'other'.

Each volume includes a chronology of the writer's life, an introductory section on formative contexts and intertexts, discussion of all the writer's major works, a bibliography of primary and secondary works and an index. Issues of racial, national and cultural identity are explored, as are gender and sexuality. Books in the series also examine writers' use of genre, particularly ways in which Western genres are adapted or subverted and 'traditional' local forms are reworked in a contemporary context.

Contemporary World Writers aims to bring together the theoretical impulse which currently dominates post-colonial studies and closely argued readings of particular authors' works, and by so doing to avoid the danger of appropriating the specifics of particular texts into the hegemony of totalising theories.

Acknowledgements

I am indebted to Bart Moore-Gilbert and Robert Clark for their support and advice at all stages of this project; without their valued input this book would not exist. I am also grateful to all those who commented on sections of the work in progress, particularly John Thieme, my series editor, and Margaret Coxall, who read most of the draft manuscript and who distracted me by noticing Rushdie's fascination with nipples. Thanks must also go to a small but invaluable band of fellows: to Christopher Warne for keeping me company with his book on Aristotle, to Anna Johnson for parachuting in from Tasmania with 'tales from the archives', to Mum and John for their unfailing confidence, to Max Coxall for his unhesitating generosity, to Brenda and Andrew for consistently finding exquisite holiday locations for me to work in, to Marie and Michael for finding argumentative friends with strong opinions about Rushdie, to Jade and May for entertaining Dom, and to Ada for 'not annoying Tev' with a butterfly net in the early stages. My supreme thanks is reserved for Simone, Dominic and Tristan. The latter two were forced to share their first months and years with this book and so deserve some recompense. The former has made everything possible by supplying generous quantities of patience, encouragement, intellectual inspiration, emotional reinforcement and red wine. This book is for them.

Quotations from *Imaginary Homelands: Essays and Criticism, 1981–1991* by Salman Rushdie, copyright © 1991 by Salman Rushdie, are used by permission of Penguin Books Ltd, and Viking Penguin, a division of Penguin Group (USA) Inc. Quotations from *Salman Rushdie Interviews: A Sourcebook of His Ideas*, ed. Pradyumna S. Chauhan, copyright © 2001 by Pradyumna S. Chauhan, are reproduced with permission of Greenwood Publishing Group,

Inc., Westport, CT. Lines from Sujata Bhatt's 'A Different History', *Brunizem* copyright © 1988 Sujata Bhatt are reproduced with permission of Carcanet Press.

Abbreviations

Chronology

19 June 1947   Ahmed Salman Rushdie born in Bombay (now Mumbai) to Anis Ahmed Rushdie and Negin Rushdie (neé Butt). His early education is at the Cathedral and John Connon School for Boys.

1961–5   Attends Rugby School in England.

1964   Rushdie's family moves to Karachi, Pakistan. Rushdie remains in England.

1965–8   Reads history at King's College, Cambridge.

1968   Lives briefly in Pakistan, working for the television service in Karachi.

1968–81   After a brief flirtation with acting, works in London as an advertising copywriter. This supports his early writing career.

1975   *Grimus* is published by Victor Gollancz.

1976   Marries Clarissa Luard.

1979   Son Zafar born.

1981   *Midnight's Children* is published by Jonathan Cape. It wins the Booker Prize for Fiction and the James Tait Black Prize.

1983   *Shame* is published by Jonathan Cape. It wins the French *Prix du Meilleur Livre Etranger*.

1984–85   Travelling in Australia with Bruce Chatwin. Begins a relationship with Robyn Davidson. Separated from Clarissa.

1986   Visits Nicaragua as a guest of the Sandinista Association of Cultural Workers.

1987   The travelogue *The Jaguar Smile: A Nicaraguan Journey* is published by Jonathan Cape.

1988   Marries Marianne Wiggins. *The Satanic Verses* is published by Viking/Penguin. It is awarded the Whitbread Prize for

Best Novel. Some Muslim groups begin to protest against the depiction of the Prophet Muhammad in the novel and it is banned in several countries including India. Muslim demonstrations against *The Satanic Verses* take place in Bolton and copies are publicly burned.

Jan.–Feb. 1989   There are further protests and book burnings in Bradford and London. Five demonstrators are killed by police in Pakistan during an attack on the American Cultural Centre in Islamabad.

14 Feb. 1989   The Ayatollah Khomeini issues a *fatwa* that demands the execution of Rushdie and his publishers. The following day the Iranian cleric, Hassan Sanei, offers a reward for Rushdie's murder. Rushdie goes into hiding with Marianne Wiggins, but Wiggins soon leaves him.

1990   *Haroun and the Sea of Stories* is published by Granta. It wins the Writer's Guild Award.

1991   The essay collection *Imaginary Homelands* is published by Granta.

1992   The British Film Institute pamphlet *The Wizard of Oz* is published.

1993   *Midnight's Children* wins the 'Booker of Bookers' – a special award for the best winner in the twenty-five year history of the prize.

1994   The short story collection *East, West* is published by Jonathan Cape.

1995   *The Moor's Last Sigh* is published by Jonathan Cape. It wins the Whitbread Novel of the Year Award.

1997   Marries Elizabeth West. Son Milan born.

24 Sept. 1998   After extended diplomatic negotiations, Iran's Foreign Minister, Kamal Kharrazi, announces that Iran does not intend to pursue the death sentence imposed by Khomeini and disassociates his government from the reward. Rushdie begins to conduct a more high-profile public life, though the threat is not entirely removed.

1999   *The Ground Beneath Her Feet* is published by Henry Holt. Rushdie moves to New York and begins a relationship with Padma Lakshmi. Separated from Elizabeth West.

2001   *Fury* is published by Jonathan Cape.

2002   The essay collection *Step Across This Line* is published by Jonathan Cape.

PART I

Contexts and intertexts

Introduction

For every text, a context. (Salman Rushdie, 1984, IHL, 92)

It is not hard to establish Salman Rushdie's fame: his novels have sold in their millions and been translated into multiple languages; the MLA international bibliography lists over seven hundred journal articles and book chapters written about his fiction; and there are currently in excess of thirty published monographs on various aspects of his life and work. Rushdie himself makes regular appearances at major international conferences and literary events, he gives frequent interviews and lectures, he is the subject of a number of documentaries and has appeared in films – both as a performer (a comical cameo in *Bridget Jones's Diary* in 2001) and as a character (a cartoon villain in the propaganda piece *International Guerrillas*).[1] His works have also enjoyed an extended life in other media: stage shows and musicals have been made based upon his novels, Bono from U2 has written a song using lyrics from *The Ground Beneath Her Feet* (1999), and a film based on one of his short stories entitled *The Firebird's Nest* is planned by the director Apoorva Lakhia. Perhaps most revealingly, the name of Salman Rushdie has become so familiar internationally that even those who do not generally read literary fiction have heard of him and know something about the subjects concerning which he writes.

Whilst Rushdie's prominence as a writer is everywhere apparent, however, it is harder to establish what it is precisely that he is famous for – his writings, or the 1989 *fatwa* in which the Ayatollah Khomeini demanded his execution for blasphemy. It is almost certainly the case that, had the threat to Rushdie's life not made him headline news in the late 1980s, 746,949 copies of *The Satanic Verses* (1988) would not have sold in 1989, and tabloid newspapers would not now make Rushdie's complicated love life the subject of double-page 'exclusives'. As Rushdie is quick to point out, however, he was already a well-known writer long before the passage of the Ayatollah's headline-grabbing decree, albeit for different and somewhat quieter (though not always uncontentious) reasons. By 1989 Rushdie had published three novels, the latter two of which, *Midnight's Children* (1981) and *Shame* (1983), had been widely applauded by the literary world. Rushdie had also, already, been the revered object of some of the media's most superlative praise, gleaning journalistic sound-bites for himself that may still be seen gracing the covers of his novels. In both the countries that Rushdie claimed as home in the early 1980s, moreover, *Midnight's Children* had, long before the *fatwa*, been greeted not only as a work of startling originality but as one that was destined to become a landmark text in the emergent counter-canon of 'post-colonial' (then 'commonwealth') fiction. In Delhi Anita Desai, upon attending a reading of Rushdie's fiction, remembers thinking that she was listening to 'the voice of a new age'.[2] Likewise, in London, the award of the Booker Prize to *Midnight's Children* in 1981 led Rushdie's near contemporary Kazuo Ishiguro, later a winner of the Booker Prize himself for *The Remains of the Day* (1989), to conclude that the publication of this novel represented 'a real symbolic moment', a 'milestone' for English-language authors living in Britain whose origins were not British. 'It so happened that around this time I brought out *A Pale View of Hills*', Ishiguro recalls. 'Usually first novels disappear ... without a trace. Yet I received a lot of attention, got lots of coverage, and did a lot of interviews.' The reason: 'everyone was suddenly looking for other Rushdies'.[3]

A novel that had such an impact on the literary world, it is safe to assume, would have ensured, *fatwa* or no *fatwa*, that its author remained studied in universities, negotiated by other writers, read by readers across the globe, courted by publishers, and nominated for major literary prizes. It is even arguable that the *fatwa* has actually served to damage Rushdie's reputation as a writer. In the first place, it has had the effect of turning Rushdie, in the public imagination, into a writer who writes exclusively and bombastically about Islam, when in fact Rushdie's interest in religion is only one aspect of a much more complex body of writing that engages with subject areas as diverse as the role of the occult in the countercultures of 1960s London, institutionalised racism in the police force in Thatcherite Britain, the conquest of Moorish Spain by Queen Isabella in the fifteenth century, Christian fundamentalism in contemporary America, Hindu fundamentalism in contemporary Mumbai, the Indian visual arts, European avant-garde cinema, the global phenomena of popular music and the impact on culture of the World Wide Web (to cite a few examples).

In the second place, the *fatwa* may be seen to have damaged Rushdie's reputation as a writer to the extent that the 'seriousness' of the 'Rushdie Affair', the gravity of the issues that it raised, has tended to create a general perception of his fiction that is more likely to have prevented readers discovering and appreciating his work than to have attracted them to it. Rushdie's fiction, it is sometimes felt by those approaching it for the first time, is going to be 'heavy', obsessed with theological detail and hampered by political argumentativeness. Readers with such expectations, however, are invariably surprised to discover that he is a comic writer, capable of approaching political and religious issues with levity, irreverence and humour. Indeed, it was Rushdie's habit of treating sacred subject matters with irreverence that angered some Islamic groups in the first instance.

To defend Rushdie against the accusation that he benefited from the *fatwa* is not, however, to imply that different and more pertinent questions cannot be raised about the social and political motives for his fiction being valorised in the ways that it has been. The *fatwa* may be discounted as the principal motivation for what Aijaz Ahmad has called the 'exorbitant celebration of Salman Rushdie', but harder to discount are arguments that his fiction has been so widely feted because his books satisfy a Western commercial appetite for the 'exotic'.[4] This aspect of the reception of Rushdie's works is not lost on Ishiguro who, even as he expresses gratitude that the success of Rushdie's second novel helped bring his own fictions into the limelight, is aware that the enthusiastic welcome accorded to works like *Midnight's Children* is not purely aesthetic in character. After the award of the Booker Prize to *Midnight's Children*, Ishiguro notes with a hint of disapproval, 'It was one of the few times in the recent history of British arts in which it was an actual plus to have a funny foreign name and to be writing about funny foreign places'.[5] In an early, assassin's essay on *Midnight's Children*, the Indian critic Aparna Mahanta reformulates this criticism in more extreme terms, arguing that Rushdie's novel did well in Britain because it was the latest in a long line of fictions to pander to Western desires to see India as a strange, sensual, tyrannical, fantastical other-place. 'In the lack-lustre world of postwar British fiction, Salman Rushdie's exotic fantasies have made a deep impact,' she writes; but not because 'exotic fantasia is alien to the tradition of British fiction'; rather because 'it has a very respectable lineage going back to Swift and Sterne and coming down to Waugh and Greene, a patrimony which … Rushdie has been able to emulate very successfully'. 'Naturally with the passing of the empire, this strain has waned,' she goes on, but 'Rushdie now steps into the gap, coming in the wake of the reigning nostalgia for the Raj, and decked with all the trappings of wit, humour and satire, that were the hallmarks of British fiction in the grand old days'. Rushdie's fiction, so far as Mahanta is concerned, effectively demonstrates that 'the Raj isn't dead after all', but lives on in 'The pseudo-sons, the Saleem Sinais' who have taken over from the heroes of Rudyard Kipling and of E. M. Forster.[6]

Ironically, Rushdie himself, in the same year that Mahanta penned this article, was engaged in a fierce critique of the popularity of what he calls 'Raj revivalist' fictions and films in the United Kingdom. These fictions, Rushdie argues (which include Richard Attenborough's film *Gandhi* and the television serialisations of *The Far Pavilions* and *The Jewel in the Crown*), are engaged in 'the creation of a false orient' which – like mulligatawny soup – 'tries to taste Indian, but ends up being ultra-parochially British, only with too much pepper' (IHL, 88–90). Such fictions are, Rushdie argues, politically suspect for a number of reasons: they revive the stereotypes of India inherited from the Orientalist tradition, they make Indians 'bit-players in their own history', and they imply that the British, rather than the Indians, are *'the ones whose stories matter'* (IHL, 90). Primarily, however, Rushdie insists that these fictions 'must be quarrelled with, as loudly and embarrassingly as possible' because they pedal 'a number of [false] notions about history', notably:

> the view ... that the British and Indians actually understood each other jolly well ... that the end of Empire was a sort of gentleman's agreement between old pals at the club ... and, above all, the fantasy that the British Empire represented something 'noble' or 'great' about Britain; that it was, in spite of all its flaws and meannesses and bigotries, fundamentally glamorous. (IHL, 101)

Evidently, so far as Rushdie is concerned, his own *Midnight's Children* represents, not an effect of this 'Raj revival' but an antidote to it: a fiction that depicts India from an Indian point of view, that places Indians centre stage, and that is overtly hostile to, rather than celebratory of, British imperial activities within India. Critics like Mahanta, however, seek to question the very basis for this defence, firstly by suggesting that *Midnight's Children* was successful in the West not because it resisted the 'Raj revival' but because it coincided with it, and secondly by denying that *Midnight's Children* can be described as a novel that is written from or represents the Indian point of view. As Mahanta goes on to argue in her article, *Midnight's Children*, as a novel written in English that draws substantially on European literary forms, cannot be said to be pitched at ordinary Indians, but only at Westerners and at:

> a tiny stratum of India's and Pakistan's elite, inheritors of the British mantle, the deracinated, speaking English, thinking English, dreaming English, Indians terrified,

horrified, revolted by Indians and India, yet unable to
escape the umbilical bonds.[7]

Mahanta's argument here is a touch overstated, particularly in
its sensationalist contention, repeated twice in the article, that
Rushdie is 'revolted by Indians'. She does, however, identify a
'problem' with Rushdie's socio-cultural location that subsequent
critics have also foregrounded. Timothy Brennan, for instance, in
the first published monograph on Rushdie's fiction, argues that
Rushdie cannot be said to speak from the perspective of, or on
the behalf of, the generality of 'Third World' citizens because his
fiction is addressed primarily to a metropolitan intellectual elite.
Likewise Aijaz Ahmad and M. Keith Booker (in his later work at
least) have argued that Rushdie has been globally successful as a
novelist because his privileged class location and his preference
for sophisticated modernist and postmodernist narrative forms
ensures that his work conforms to the kinds of discourses authorised by the Anglo-American academy.[8] Whilst the formula of
Rushdie's fictions has ensured that he has been extremely well
received in the Western (and Westernised) world, such critics
contend, it is not a formula that is politically enabling for the
non-West because it is not, as Brennan puts it, 'addressed to
them'.[9]

   It is one of the aims of this book to examine the intellectual basis of Rushdie's politicised aesthetic in detail and, in
so doing, to explore such criticisms further. It is worth noting
from the outset, however, that one of the characteristic features
of Salman Rushdie's writing is its self-consciousness, and its
willingness to incorporate an analysis of the cultural locations
from which it is written. The result of this is that the criticisms
that can be (and have been) made of Rushdie as a writer are
frequently anticipated, if not entirely defused or 'answered',
in his own writing – a fact that makes any simplistic judgements about his political locations difficult. Rushdie occupies,
as already suggested, a privileged position as a migrant intellectual, commenting, in a number of his works, upon political
situations that are viewed from a geographical (and we might
add emotional and ideological) distance. But he also foregrounds

the fact that he is writing from this perspective, and sets out, in his fiction, to explore the implications of this location. Rushdie, in this sense, does not claim to speak from the perspective of 'Indians' – a diverse body in itself, as Rushdie frequently points out, that it would be impossible to speak about from any singular perspective anyway. Rather, he claims to speak from the perspective of the privileged migrant Indian intellectual in a complex, even compromised, but not entirely unworkable position. This is a position that, by his own admission, has its drawbacks – it means that he writes as an 'outsider' from several cultures and an 'insider' of none, and it means that his writing emerges out of an experience of disjuncture and discontinuity. It has always been Rushdie's insistence, however, that this position may also have advantages, and that it is on the basis of these advantages that the value of his fiction should be judged.

The capacity of Rushdie's fiction to foreground the ambivalences of its own cultural location – his refusal, in his own terms, to simplify that which is not simple – may, for some readers, prove irritating or, even, ideologically disabling. As Aijaz Ahmad argues, 'There is a quality of linguistic quicksand' in his writing that makes it seem as if he is 'forever … taking back with one hand what he has given with the other'.[10] Tabish Khair argues in a similar vein that Rushdie's 'self-criticism' is a 'defensive manoeuvre' that 'seeks to pre-empt criticism without providing enough (let alone independent) space for the narration of the other whose criticism is being pre-empted'.[11] Other readers however find Rushdie's willingness to steal a march on potential critics by a 'rigorous questioning [his] own assumptions, of the ground that [he stands] on', refreshing and accurately reflective of the need for all statements to position themselves.[12] Graham Huggan, for instance, has argued that it is Rushdie's capacity to 'stage' his 'marginality' knowingly for a mainstream audience whilst simultaneously mounting a critique of 'the dominant culture's need for subaltern others' that constitutes the principal political force of his writing.[13] 'One of the ironies of [Rushdie's] career to date', in Huggan's estimation, 'is that it has been built on opposing, while also perpetuating, the commodified exoticisms that are endemic to [the] East–West literary encounter'.[14]

Whether the reader finds Rushdie's political location evasive or enabling, it is clear that his fiction – because of his complex cultural position and because of the readiness with which he analyses that position – intersects with many of the most pressing debates in contemporary cultural and political affairs, including issues of migrancy, cultural and religious affiliation, the values of political action and the nature of political writing in the twentieth and now twenty-first centuries. It is with debates such as this that the current book is primarily concerned.

Political and intellectual contexts

In a journalistic reflection on the *Granta Magazine* selection
of the 'Best of the Young British Novelists' for 1993, Salman
Rushdie rejects the idea, temporarily mooted in the early 1990s,
that the years of Margaret Thatcher's government (1979–90)
had produced a 'lost generation' of writers. Such a notion,
Rushdie suggests, is disproved by the most cursory survey of a
literary scene that includes such budding luminaries as Louis de
Bernières, Tibor Fischer, Lawrence Norfolk and A. L. Kennedy.
Nevertheless,, Rushdie goes on to imply, there remains an
element of truth in the common supposition that the dominance of Thatcherism throughout the 1980s had a significant
and deleterious impact on the British writers who had learned
their craft during that decade. '[I]t was easy to see, all over the
landscape of contemporary fiction, the devastating effect of the
Thatcher years', Rushdie observes:

> So many of these writers wrote without hope. They had
> lost all ambition … all desire to wrestle with the world.
> Their books dealt with tiny patches of the world, tiny
> pieces of human experience – a council estate, a mother, a
> father, a lost job. Very few writers had the courage or even
> the energy to bite off a big chunk of the universe and chew
> it over. Very few showed any linguistic or formal innova-
> tion. Many were dulled, and therefore dull. (SAL, 38)

Putting aside discussion of whether this assessment of British
fiction in the late 1980s is accurate, it is clear that Rushdie means
to contrast the perceived timidity of this later generation with

the political robustness and aesthetic intrepidity of his own. Emerging from the ideological proving ground of 1960s radical student consciousness, suckled at the teat of anti-Vietnam protests and defiant libertarian civil rights movements, the novelists who started their careers in the 1970s, according to Rushdie, were invested with greater belief that it was one of the functions of fiction to confront the world, its authorities, its pieties and its settled perceptions, with an unflinching stare, a coruscating pen, and a turn for anti-establishmentarianism, iconoclasm and mulish disrespect. The legacy of the 1960s, imprinted on the writers of the 1970s and early 1980s, for Rushdie, is a faith in the possibility of political change, and a belief that the arts can help to bring about that change. This view is echoed by Rushdie in a conversation with Angela Carter, another myth-debunking writer of Rushdie's generation, for *Vogue* magazine in 1985. 'One of the things that was always attractive about [Britain]', he reflects:

> was its tradition of dissent, of stepping outside the bounds of conformity and looking again – and of saying, it's not like that, it's like this … What does concern me now is the way in which social criticism has more or less stopped … in the sixties, people believed there were always alternatives. It was a creative way of thought. Now people accept loss of energy and loss of faith in their ability to change their lives. They call this realism.[1]

Carter is in agreement. '[S]omething happened during the seventies', she observes:

> It showed in literature, too. Culture lost its nerve. Everything became more insular. People started to want to read about the fluff in their navel. Rather than about the fluff in other people's navels. Or about the fluff in the cosmic navel … [2]

The resistance to such perceived political resignation is apparent in almost all of Rushdie's writing, from his early bile-spewing satires on South Asian political leaders in *Midnight's Children* and *Shame* through his serio-comic eructations of anger at institutionalised racism in the British police force in *The Satanic*

Verses to his interrogations of the global power of the US in *The Ground Beneath Her Feet, Fury* (2001) and *Shalimar the Clown* (2005). In all these cases, Rushdie assertively demonstrates that he *is* a writer who is prepared to bite off big chunks of the world and chew them over. Rushdie's political engagement, however, is not just registered in the subject matter he chooses to address; his political arguments are also inseparable from his conception of the nature and function of the arts. This much is apparent from the comments cited above, in which his demand for linguistic and formal innovation shares paragraph space with the demand that writers wrestle to see the world anew, and in which the hunt for political 'alternatives' in the 1960s is conceived of as a '*creative* way of thought'. For Rushdie, politics is central to his art, but his art is also central to his politics.

To further explore Rushdie's conception of the relationship between art and politics, which is the principal aim of this chapter, we must turn to three essays written by Rushdie in the early 1980s, at the juncture of his career when he was starting to define his public role as a novelist after the successes of *Midnight's Children* and *Shame*. These essays, which might, with a degree of critical licence, be seen to amount to a manifesto of his views on the political functions of art, are 'Imaginary Homelands', written in 1982, 'Outside the Whale', written in 1984, and 'The Location of Brazil', written in 1985. Arguably the most revealing of all these is 'Outside the Whale', written in partial response to George Orwell's 1940 essay, 'Inside the Whale', in which it is suggested that writers, rather than engaging directly in politics, should climb inside a metaphorical whale where, with 'yards of blubber between [themselves] and reality', they will be 'able to keep up an attitude of the completest indifference' to the world.[3] This argument is inspired by the realisation, on Orwell's part, that both 'Progress and reaction have ... turned out to be swindles', and that 'there is nothing left' for the writer 'but quietism – robbing reality of its terrors by simply submitting to it':

> Get inside the whale – or rather, admit you are inside the whale (for you *are*, of course). Give yourself over to the world-process, stop fighting against it or pretending that

you control it; simply accept it, endure it, record it. That
seems to be the formula that any sensitive novelist is now
likely to adopt.[4]

This, Rushdie argues, 'looks very like the plan of a man who has
given up the struggle': 'Even though he knows that 'there is no
such thing as keeping out of politics', he attempts the construction of a mechanism with just that purpose' (IHL, 96). Whilst
Rushdie does not 'presume to blame [Orwell] for adopting this
position', living as he did 'in the worst of times' (IHL, 96–7),
he does insist that it is important to dispute his conclusions,
because:

The quietist option, the exhortation to submit to events, is
an intrinsically conservative one. When intellectuals and
artists withdraw from the fray, politicians feel safer …
Passivity always serves the interests of the status quo, of
the people already at the top of the heap. (IHL, 97)

Works of art, in Rushdie's view, 'cannot be separated from politics, from history' because they 'do not come into being in a
social and political vacuum' (IHL, 92). This in turn means that
the writer who seeks to be apolitical in his or her writing is
not avoiding politics, as he or she might believe, but offering
an implicit vote for 'things as they are'. Artists, if they are to
contest 'things as they are' must not abdicate their responsibility, but must 'make the very devil of a racket':

Certainly, when we cry, we cry partly for the safety we
have lost; but we also cry to affirm ourselves, to say, here
I am, I matter, too, you're going to have to reckon with
me. So in place of Jonah's womb, I am recommending
the ancient tradition of making as big a fuss, as noisy a
complaint about the world as is humanly possible. Where
Orwell wished quietism, let there be rowdyism, in place of
the whale, the protesting wail. (IHL, 99)

Precisely how writers are to enter the fray of politics is made
clearer by Rushdie in the two remaining essays cited above,
'Imaginary Homelands' and 'The Location of Brazil'. In the
former, Rushdie offers a belated response to a question posed by

the left-wing playwright Howard Brenton to a panel of novelists that included Rushdie at an Oxford University conference.
Brenton, taking exception to the assertion made by a member
of the panel that it was one of the functions of writing to find
'new ways of describing the world', had asked whether writing
should not 'seek to do ... more than to describe' (IHL, 13).
Rushdie answers Brenton in the essay by arguing that 'description is itself a political act ... that redescribing the world is the
necessary first step towards changing it' (IHL, 13–14). The novel
becomes political, in other words, not by engaging directly in
political issues (necessarily) but by describing the world in a
way that contests or resists the interpretations of it offered by
the more official organs of power. This act of description, or re-
description, in turn, is assumed to have political value because
the ways in which we understand and interpret the world – our
knowledge of it and about it – have a vital shaping effect upon
the way we as individuals, and (the slightly more difficult point)
as collectivities, act in the world.

Rushdie elaborates on this argument in the third essay under
discussion – on Terry Gilliam's fantasy film about a future totalitarian state, *Brazil* (1985). Here he avers that it is specifically
the fiction maker's capacity to use unusual, fantastic, surrealistic
effects that gives a work its political power. At the start of the
twentieth century Viktor Shklovsky famously argued that the
defining feature of poetry, but also literature more generally, was
its capacity to make the familiar strange;[5] here Rushdie argues,
as others – most notably Brecht – have argued before him, that
the act of making the familiar strange gives art its most dynamic
oppositional, political strategy because it empowers readers or
viewers to doubt what political authorities with a vested interest
in keeping things as they are have presented as facts. 'To dream
is to have power', Rushdie contends in a sloganising vein:

> Techniques of comedy, metaphor, heightened imagery, fantasy
> ... are used to break down our conventional, habit-dulled
> certainties about what the world is and has to be. Unreality
> is the only weapon with which reality can be smashed, so
> that it may subsequently be reconstructed. (IHL, 122)

Magic realism, by implication – or at least the politically and historically grounded mode of magic realism employed by writers such as Rushdie (and we might add Günter Grass and Gabriel García Márquez) – is conceived of as an inherently radical form of writing, because it develops fictional strategies in which accepted ('realist') representations of the world are destabilised by their encounter with forms of representation which are less easily contained or controlled within 'normative', 'rationalist' discourses.

In all three essays Rushdie is presenting the artist as an oppositional figure, a figure by definition antagonistic to received authorities, a figure well placed to dispute the 'descriptions of the world' offered by politicians because he or she has the imaginative capacity to offer alternative descriptions in their place. If this seems to overstate the power of the novelist, however, it should also be remembered that Rushdie does not expect that 'speaking truth to power' in this way will necessarily cause power to change. Only bad books change the world, as Angela Carter pointed out to Rushdie, back in the days before *The Satanic Verses* proved otherwise.[6] The novelist's task, in Rushdie's conception, is far more modest:

> You can't set out to change the world with a book. What you *can* do is change something small inside the minds of a few people. Whatever book you read that makes a really profound impact upon you in some way changes you forever.[7]

For the critic Aijaz Ahmad such a claim would be typical of the confusion in Rushdie's political thinking. On the one hand Rushdie is strident and vocal about the need for political change, on the other hand he expresses a kind of modernist despair that prevents him from believing in the reality – or the achieveability – of collective social transformation.[8] In Ahmad's view Rushdie's inability to believe in the possibility of change is the result of his identification with post-structuralist modes of thinking that emphasise discourse analysis, rather than Marxist forms of political praxis that require collective action. Such modes of thinking, according to Ahmad, make power an effect

of 'knowledge' alone, and so locate responses to power in discursive rather than activist cultures; a process that has the effect of
valorising the activities of reading and writing (describing and
re-describing) enormously, but that diminishes faith in (indeed,
sows distrust for) systematic, pragmatic political ideologies.

A similar view seems to be implicit in the question Howard
Brenton posed to Rushdie and his colleagues at that 1982 conference. Howard Brenton, also a Marxist, presumably asked the
question because he believed that literature must do slightly
more than 'describe' in order to have political effect. Rushdie,
as we have seen, offers what Ahmad would term a 'post-structuralist' response to Brenton by suggesting that changes in our
discourses concerning the world will produce changes in the
material constitution of that world. It is a reasonable guess that
Brenton was dissatisfied with this response, since he himself
would argue that, whilst the ways in which we see the world will
be important in shaping our political attitudes, truly politically
committed art must be capable of motivating and mobilising its
audiences to seek change outside of the aesthetic realm. Evidence
for this may be found in Brenton's comments to Catherine Itzin
for her book *Stages of the Revolution*, in which he insists that
'Writers on the left' must 'be a vanguard' because:

> they have to provide survival kits for people who are
> active politically … Theatre doesn't actually argue politi-
> cally, that is done in meetings and parties and unions. But
> the theatre can illuminate what matters in those political
> meetings. So they go hand in hand. But theatre itself is not
> a political act – the political act is voting.[9]

Rushdie is definitively not of this view, since he does not believe
that writing should be at the service of party politics. That said, in
certain passages of his non-fictional work Rushdie does identify
himself with aspects of Marxist thought. In his lecture to staff
and students at the University of Aarhus on 7 October 1983, for
instance, he describes his politics as 'broadly speaking Marxist',
and argues that 'Marxist politics have much more relevance in
India than they have in some Western countries' (and this is in
response to objections from the left that his representation of

Marxists as 'conjurers and card-sharpers' in *Midnight's Children* was unsympathetic).[10] He has, however, repeatedly resisted association with Marxism as it is manifested in formal political movements. Hence, when the Communist Party telephoned him and, on the basis of his anti-racist community work, asked him to join, he refused, as he tells Angela Carter by way of an anecdote:

> I got a call from the Communist Party, by the way. They were inviting me to speak on some platform. They said, 'We understand you're not a brother.' I let that pass. They said, 'You would be speaking in your personal capacity' (as opposed to someone else's I suppose). I said no thank you. And they said, 'Well, you *are* associated with radical libertarian politics.' And I managed to say, 'Yes, but *you're* not.'[11]

In Rushdie's fiction this critical view of party politics – especially Marxist party politics – takes the form of a number of satirical portraits of Marxist figures. Prominent amongst these are the covert reactionary ('opposition man') P. S. Moonshy in *Grimus* (1975) and the defeated and cowardly Qasim the Red in *Midnight's Children*. By far the most effective comic passage at the expense of Marxism, however, occurs in *The Moor's Last Sigh* (1995), when Camoens da Gama, hearing that Moscow have organised a troupe of 'Counterfeit Lenins' (MLS, 29) for propaganda purposes, has the idea of assembling a body of performing Lenins suited to the Indian context. After much wheedling, he persuades the authorities in Moscow to send over one of their 'fake Ulyanovs' (MLS, 28) to inspect and approve his, but upon arrival the emissary remains unimpressed, remarking, as his interpreter expresses it:

> These persons have blackness of skin and their features are not his. Too tall, too short, too fat, too skinny, too lame, too bald, and that one has no teeth ... two beards at least are improperly affixed in spite of the admonishing presence of the proletariat. (MLS, 30)

Such caricatures of orthodox earnestness suggest that, whilst Rushdie shares with Marxist political philosophy a belief in

historical materialism, his suspicion of programmatic and potentially coercive organised movements has prevented him from
endorsing Marxism as a systematic political practice that might
be implemented in India or elsewhere.

Rushdie's emphasis on the political value of re-description
in the act of writing finds its theoretical analogue in Edward
Said's analysis of cultural representation and Homi Bhabha's
work on ambivalence, mimicry and hybridisation, to which we
shall turn in due course. The writings of both these theorists,
however, has an older mooring to which we need to revert if we
are to understand the historical provenance of Rushdie's view of
the political function of the writer: this is the work of the Italian
Marxist Antonio Gramsci, whose theory of 'hegemony' has (to
Ahmad's dissatisfaction) provided post-colonial criticism with a
means of analysing the role played by culture in reinforcing or
resisting imperialism.

Gramsci's argument, subsequently appropriated by 'radical
literary theory' and fused with a Foucauldian understanding of
power relations, is that dominant social classes establish their
political ascendancy most effectively and enduringly not by the
use of force alone but by employing culture – which includes
language and literature – to persuade 'subaltern' classes to
consent to their subordination. Hegemony is thus that form of
political dominion that is achieved when the dominated group
has accepted its dominion on ideological and cultural grounds.[12]
In formulating his ideas Gramsci was responding to the established Leninist form of Marxism in which it had been argued
that successful revolution depends upon the seizure of state
power alone.[13] This approach, in Gramsci's view, may have
proved viable in the initial phases of the Marxist revolution in
eastern Europe where, he believed, 'the state was everything'; it
had, however, failed in western Europe where the capitalist state
had been able to rely upon 'a sturdy structure of civil society'
to buttress and reinforce it.[14] In order for Marxism to be able
to secure a socialist revolution in the West, it was Gramsci's
principal innovation to argue, it would have to modify its 'philosophy of praxis' to such an extent that it was able to recognise

that the power exercised by a state is invested as much in civil society as it is in coercive bodies such as parliament or the army; and that, as a result, successful challenges to the power of the state needed to be mounted from within the sphere of culture as well as the spheres of politics and economics.

Edward Said's first major theoretical study, *Orientalism* (1978), may be seen as an application of Gramsci's theory of hegemony to an analysis of the functioning of colonialism, since it examines the process by which the coloniser establishes power in the colonies by dominating them ideologically through teaching practices, the dissemination of language and literature, bureaucratic policy and cultural representation. More specifically, Said's book seeks to show, in some detail, how European intellectuals, writers and policy makers of the eighteenth and nineteenth centuries were engaged in the mediation of a complex of discursive practices concerning the 'East' which constructed 'Eastern' civilisations as inferior so as to validate Europe's acts of imperialist expropriation. These discursive practices are what constitutes 'Orientalism' for Said, and under this designation he includes all representations of the 'East' that fashion it as irrational, tyrannical, sensual, sensationalist, mystical, exotic, unknowable and, in consequence, in need of civilising by the 'West'. The West, by a binary logic, is represented as the opposite of the East in all these respects, and so comes to stand for all that is rational, responsible, democratic, and normative. Such hierarchising knowledge of Orient and Occident is produced, as Said argues at his most Gramscian, in culture, which acts 'dynamically along with brute political, economic, and military rationales' to create a 'world made up of two unequal halves'.[15]

If we accept the Saidian contention that colonialism is a cultural process as well as a military and economic process, and if we accept Gramsci's view that cultural domination reinforces domination effected by force, then we must also accept the view that cultural responses to colonialism – through writing, re-writing, reading, re-reading, teaching, talking – may have a role to play in the political process of decolonisation. If culture is one of the means by which the coloniser imposes upon the colonised, then resistance to colonialism may also be effected by challenges on the cultural level. The question remains, of course, as to how such cultural challenges can be effected – and this is a problem that has confronted all anti-colonial and post-colonial artists who have sought to write against (paint against, perform against) colonial occupation. Some of these artists have advocated the revival of native cultural traditions that can be set in opposition to the 'alien' colonial cultural traditions, or have advocated the outright rejection of the culture of the coloniser (its languages and its aesthetic forms). Both Said and Homi Bhabha, however, have argued persuasively that, since there is no going back to a world before European colonialism, resistance literature must now work within the hybridised cultural contexts that colonialism has helped bring into being. As Said insists in his later work *Cultural Imperialism* (1993), in which he turns specifically to consider opposition to colonialist discourses in literature, it has become one of the preconditions of post-colonial resistance that it 'must to a certain degree work to recover forms already established, or at least influenced or infiltrated by the culture of empire'.[16]

Culture and Imperialism was conceived by Said as a continuation of the project begun in *Orientalism*, but also as an attempt to absorb some of the criticisms that had been made of the earlier work in the intervening years. Prominent amongst these criticisms was the argument that the Foucauldian conception of power employed by Said in *Orientalism* had prevented him from being able to conceive of a viable form of opposition to Western discourses concerning subject peoples. If Orientalism is represented as a hegemonic discourse so totalising that it is impossible to emerge from it 'into a beyond of true knowledge', as Dennis Porter argues in '*Orientalism* and its Problems', then it becomes unclear how Said means to assert that 'alternatives to Orientalism are possible' and that 'a knowledge as opposed to an ideology of the Orient can exist'.[17] Problems such as this in *Orientalism*, according to Porter, are the result of a methodological incompatibility between Gramsci's concept of hegemony, which allows for process and change, and Foucault's discourse theory 'which presupposes the impossibility of stepping outside of a given discursive formation by an act of will or consciousness'.[18] For Gramsci, as a Marxist, there must be a real (material) Orient that exists outside the hegemonic discourses concerning it, and that can be identified and used as a corrective to the Orientalist construction; but for Foucauldian post-structuralists there is no Orient outside the texts that constitute it, and so no concept of the 'East' that the anti-colonial writer can present as 'more true' than that fashioned by discourse.

Said's response to such critiques in *Culture and Imperialism* is to redefine discursive formations like Orientalism so that they are conceived of no longer as coherent or monolithic structures with unitary intent but as complex assemblages that may contain internal contradictions. This allows him to argue that Western texts of the colonial period (such as the novels of Conrad) do not straightforwardly embody an Orientalist discourse about the non-West, but articulate discrepancies internal to those discourses. It also allows him to argue that counter-hegemonic texts, though they are unable to achieve a critical relationship with dominant hegemonic discourses *from outside*, are able to disrupt those discourses from within. In this way, Said is able, without needing to locate a position of 'pure' knowledge outside of discourse, to offer a description of politicised fictions that

> rechart and then occupy the place in imperial cultural forms reserved for subordination ... self-consciously, fighting for [recognition] on the very same territory once ruled by a consciousness that assumed the subordination of a designated inferior. Hence *reinscription*.[19]

This process of recharting Said calls *the voyage in* – a 'variety of hybrid cultural work' in which the oppositional writer makes aesthetic and ideological incursions into the imperial centre so that the centre can be critically re-examined.[20] Such a process, for Said, is exemplified by the work of post-colonial writers such as Salman Rushdie, who *write back* 'to the metropolitan cultures' in order to disrupt 'the European narratives of the Orient' and '[replace] them with either a more playful or a more powerful new narrative style'.[21] At the heart of Rushdie's writing, for Said, is 'the conscious effort to enter into the discourse of Europe and the West, to mix with it, transform it, to make it acknowledge marginalized or suppressed or forgotten histories'; an effort that constitutes the primary political force of his work, and that has made him one of the English language's principal decolonising writers.[22]

These observations on anti-colonial political resistance by Said seem to be confirmed by Rushdie's own understanding of his political role, as described above. Like Said, he believes that it is impossible to *step out* of the determining structures that the history of colonialism has made him an inheritor of, so, like Said, he conceives of resistance (or at least the resistance that he is capable of offering from his cultural location) as a process that must involve *stepping into*, or *stepping across the lines of*, dominant social discourses and endeavouring to challenge them from within. The political nature of Rushdie's writing is thus responsive, in that it seeks to reply to descriptions of the world that are already in place and to disrupt (or identify ambivalences within) those discourses. This does not mean, however, that he views his work as purely reactive, because the terms of his narrativisation, the creative originality of the fictional process, for Rushdie, enable him to hybridise existing discourses to such an extent that they become capable of *saying something else*. In the dominant conceit of *The Satanic Verses* he can 'By using what is old, and adding to it some ... thing of [his] own ... make what is new' (SAL, 73). This process of creating newness out of existing discourses is, for Rushdie, something that is characteristic of all artistic creation – it is, however, an especially weighted aspect of artworks that are created out of the experience of colonialism, for in this scenario the interaction of cultural influences is a product of unequal power relations, and the aesthetic choices made will constitute a reflection upon those power relations.

This conception of newness as a form of cultural impurity is investigated in some detail by the critical theorist Homi Bhabha, who sees anti-colonial resistance as a product of the dissonance created when the colonised (or once colonised) culture begins to

incorporate but also to reformulate the discourses of the coloniser. In one of Bhabha's most important essays, 'Of Signs Taken
for Wonders', this process is described by reference to missionary
attempts to introduce Christian teaching into the sub-continent
in the nineteenth century. Here Bhabha contrasts the intentions
of the missionaries in introducing Christian teaching via the
Bible with the treatment of biblical narrative by the natives who
receive it. For the missionary workers, Bhabha argues, the introduction of the Bible is a dimension of the 'civilising mission', by
which the colonised natives come to accept the superiority of
the word of the coloniser. In this scenario the sign of the English
book derives its power from the idea that it is the 'original' sign,
the true sign, that the native must adopt as his or her own.
Paradoxically, however, the very act of accepting – or repeating
– the sign of English power fractures that sign because it reveals
that the meaning of the sign resides not in its originality but
in its capacity to be repeated and transformed. The repetition
of the idea of Englishness in the colonial context thus comes
not to affirm an idea of originary and authoritative Englishness
but to destabilise the discourse by revealing its ambivalence. In
Bhabha's terms:

> As a signifier of authority, the English book acquires its
> meaning *after* the traumatic scenario of colonial differ-
> ence, cultural or racial, returns the eye of power … Para-
> doxically, however, such an image can neither be 'original'
> – by virtue of the act of recognition that constructs it –
> nor 'identical' – by virtue of the difference that defines it.
> Consequently, the colonial presence is always ambivalent,
> split between its appearance as original and authoritative
> and its articulation as repetition and difference.[23]

In *The Moor's Last Sigh* Rushdie provides a near perfect analogue for this Bhabhalian process of repetition and alienation
(or 'flawed mimesis') when he has the Reverend Oliver D'Aeth
fall prey to a sudden realisation of the 'uncertainty' that has
been brought into being by the attempt to inscribe signs of
Englishness on to the Indian landscape. At Fort Cochin, D'Aeth
reflects,

> the English had striven mightily to construct a mirage of
> Englishness ... English bungalows clustered around an
> English green ... there were Rotarians and golfers and tea-
> dances and cricket and a Masonic lodge. (MLS, 95)

This 'conjuring trick', however, is one that D'Aeth easily sees
through:

> D'Aeth ... couldn't help ... seeing the bloodsucker lizards
> beneath the English hedges, the parrots flying over the
> rather un-Home-Counties jacaranda trees. And when he
> looked out to sea the illusion of England vanished entirely;
> for the harbour could not be disguised, no matter how
> Anglicised the land might be, it was contradicted by the
> water, as if England were being washed by an alien sea.
> Alien and encroaching; for Oliver D'Aeth knew enough
> to be sure that the frontier between the English enclaves
> and the surrounding foreignness had become permeable,
> was beginning to dissolve. India would reclaim it all. They,
> the British, would – as Aurora had prophesied – be driven
> into the Indian Ocean. (MLS, 95)

The colonial attempt to enforce likeness, to repeat the culture of
the coloniser in the colonies, Rushdie implies, has the effect of
destabilising Englishness; rendering it *not what it was*, and so
undermining the basis of its authority. It is this destabilisation
of the idea of England within the colonial context, as D'Aeth
intuits, that will ultimately provide the basis for the Indian
revolt against British colonialism; an argument also made by
Bhabha, who proposes that it is in the identification of ambivalence within discourses that resistance becomes actualised:

> In the doubly inscribed space of colonial representation
> where the presence of authority – the English book – is
> also a question of its repetition and displacement ... the
> immediate visibility of [the colonial] regime of recognition
> is resisted. Resistance is not necessarily an oppositional
> act of political intention, nor is it the simple negation or
> exclusion of the 'content' of another culture, as a difference
> once perceived. It is the effect of an ambivalence produced
> within the rules of recognition of dominating discourses as
> they articulate the signs of cultural difference.[24]

If this form of resistance seems fairly passive (since the ambivalence created is simply an effect of colonial processes) it is also
the case, in Bhabha's view, that the self-conscious foregrounding
of ambivalence within discourses may become a strategy of
subversion that turns 'the gaze of the discriminated back upon
the eye of power' in more determined ways.[25] The difference
between these forms of resistance is apparent in the difference
between the default ambivalence that Oliver D'Aeth recognises
in colonial presence and the intention of his creator, Rushdie,
to foreground that ambivalence as an anti-colonial strategy. In
the case of the former, the repetition of the idea of Englishness
in India during the colonial period simply creates an uncanny
sensation that may become 'the grounds of intervention'.[26] In
Rushdie's case, the wilful repetition of ideas of Englishness (its
language, its literary forms, its modes of expression, its assumptions about non-Englishness) is part of a politicised design to
assault the legacy of the English and make it his own. The first
of these forms of mimicry imitates with an intent to please
but almost accidentally causes 'other 'denied' knowledges [to]
enter upon the dominant discourse and estrange the basis of
its authority'; the second uses mimicry to create 'signs of spec-
tacular resistance' as 'a form of defensive warfare'.[27] It is this
form of mimicry, for Bhabha, that enables active and aggressive
political resistance to colonialism:

> Then the words of the master become the site of hybridity
> – the warlike, subaltern sign of the native – then we may
> not only read between the lines but even seek to change
> the often coercive reality that they so lucidly contain.[28]

Critics of Rushdie such as Ahmad or Brennan remain scep-
tical of these arguments. Writing within the discourses of the
coloniser, they insist, makes Rushdie's work complicit with, not
oppositional to, colonialism; they also cite Rushdie's class and
privileged social position as evidence that he is in league with
dominant European power structures, not in antagonism to them.
The most forceful rejection of Rushdie's formula for political
resistance staged by Ahmad resides in his perceptions of where
Said, Bhabha and Rushdie depart from Gramsci's strictly Marxist

conception of hegemony. Such intellectuals, for Ahmad, may have successfully appropriated the Gramscian argument that the contestation of power needs to take place at the level of culture, but they read Gramsci out of context, selectively rather than programmatically, because they do not, simultaneously, accept that cultural resistance is meaningless without a corresponding struggle, at the level of the nation ('particular collectivities of people'), for 'different kinds of national projects and … a revolutionary restructuring of one's own nation state'.[29] A writer of Rushdie's cultural location, he argues, may appear to challenge imperialistic formations at the level of ideas, but because he is not rooted in any identifiable national community (indeed, because he challenges the very idea of nation) it is impossible for him to offer a challenge to imperialistic and neo-imperialistic formations at the level of practical, collective action.

There is a sense in which Marxist attacks on the value of the kinds of political intervention practised by 'Third World cosmopolitans' and Foucaludian defences will never be reconciled. Between Ahmad's form of Marxism and post-structuralist discourse analysis there is such a world of difference that it is unlikely that the twain shall ever meet. The former believe that political struggle requires conformity to a programmatic political ideology and must be rooted in national and class based oppositional formations, the latter believe that discursive challenges to imperialistic modes of thought may be useful to an anti-imperialist struggle whether they are rooted in a specific national or class consciousness or not. The former, moreover, believe that political praxis needs to have faith in the ideal that imperialism in its totality can be contested and overthrown; the latter see the current imperialistic episteme as an inescapable power structure that may be modified and resisted locally and strategically but not overcome through a coherent and decisive process of revolutionary restructuring.

Whatever the reader's view of these respective oppositions, Rushdie's politics must be understood as a less grandiose project for transformation than the Marxist project. His aim is not revolution, or the attainment of the ideal state (these, indeed, he would present as political dangers). His aim, rather, is to assist in the process of decolonising the mind along the lines suggested by Said and Bhabha's analysis: by questioning – or identifying ambivalent spaces within – patterns of thought and modes of behaviour that reinforce the colonialist (Orientalist) hegemony. If there is an anti-imperialist element to this project, it is not a nation-based collective project of organised resistance but an intention to change his readers attitudes towards the idea of empire, and to the forms of discourse about identity that are used to support empire. Indeed, Rushdie's work is at its most forceful politically not when it is dealing with macro-challenges to imperialism but when it offers challenges pitched in the field of identity politics to preconceived ideas of race and ethnicity, and when it struggles to give voice and aesthetic form to expressions of identity that are not, conventionally, accommodated within the Western canon and the discourses it supports. Hence, when W. L. Webb in interview asks Rushdie to clarify his view (expressed fictionally in *The Satanic Verses*) that description can be a political act, it is precisely this aspect of his thought that Rushdie focuses on:

> *Salman Rushdie*: The point is that if you come from the black communities in [Britain], the power of other people to describe you is much greater than your power to describe back. And so, one can't see it as a fair struggle at the moment, because we are described, and we are described into corners, and then we have to describe our way out of corners, if we can. And it seems to me that that's one of the things I was trying to do: I was trying to contest descriptions.
> *W. L. Webb*: As a political act, it would be a description back.
> *Salman Rushdie*: Yeah, exactly. (CSR, 87)

Such a positioning of Rushdie's political intentions does, importantly, give Rushdie's writing a community of praxis (diasporic migrant communities in the West) and, in his earlier works at least (the unofficial trilogy of *Midnight's Children*, *Shame* and *The Satanic Verses*), his fiction seems to derive some

of its characteristic power from this sense of a political location. The accident of the *fatwa* has had the unfortunate effect
of severing Rushdie, violently, from this community, and, in the
long run, from Britain, making it impossible to continue along
the trajectory he was following in community-based anti-racist
campaigning. Whereas in the late 1980s he was able to insist
that he belonged to a community – even if it wasn't a community with a single cultural or geographical focus (a stereoscopical
community) – by 1999 he was arguing that he had

> come down on the side of those who by preference, nature
> or circumstance simply do not belong. This unbelonging
> – I think of it as *disorientation*, loss of the East – is my
> artistic country now. Wherever my books find themselves
> … that's my only home. (SAL, 294)

This removal of cultural and political grounding in Rushdie's
later years may help to explain the shift in his political focus,
from selective, specific engagements with relatively local (albeit
still quite broad) socio-cultural scenarios, towards ranging medi-
tations on the global, multi-national situation.

Having considered, in theoretical terms, the political aims of
Rushdie's writing – and having demonstrated that Rushdie's
main aesthetic and political strategy is to *write back* to cultural
forms associated with colonialism, it will now be useful to apply
this discussion more concretely, by considering how Rushdie's
interventions work in specific contexts. The following chapter
will, therefore, concentrate upon the inter-linked fields of
Rushdie's use of the English language and his use of the European novel form. The aim in both cases will be to consider how
Rushdie's aesthetic transformations in these fields may be seen
to have political intent, and to assess the value of such aesthetic
strategies as political interventions.

Writing in English

Towards the close of the eighteenth century, as the British parliament became yearly more concerned with the role played by its representatives in Indian administrative affairs, debates concerning the moral obligations of colonial rule intensified. For the East India Company, who had hitherto enjoyed an unquestioned dominance in the shaping of policy in India, the sub-continent was a resource to be mined, rather than a culture (or body of cultures) to be nurtured, so methods of governance that ensured minimal disruption of daily Indian life, and hence minimal disruption of trade, were favoured. Increasingly, however, a powerful consortium of interests in Britain, made up predominantly of utilitarian humanists and evangelical missionaries, was putting pressure on the British government to recognise a duty of care in India. If Britain were to enjoy the fruits of Indian soil, influential groups such as the Clapham Sect argued, they should also accept the moral burden which imperialism brought (Kipling was later to call it the 'white man's burden') and bring Christian civilisation and sound ethical education to India.

The argument of the Clapham Sect is cogently expressed by Charles Grant in an article of 1797: *Observations on the state of society among the Asiatic subjects of Great Britain, particularly with respect to morals, and on the means of improving it.* 'The Hindoos err, because they are ignorant, and their errors have never fairly been laid before them', Grant observes:

> The communication of our light and knowledge to them, would prove the best remedy for their disorders, and this

remedy is proposed, from a full conviction that if judi-
ciously and patiently applied, it would have great and
happy effects upon them, effects honourable and advanta-
geous for us.[1]

The communication of 'light' to 'darkness', Grant concedes,
might easily be made in 'the medium of the languages of [India]'.
The principal thrust of his argument, however, is that a moral
and religious education in English would be more desirable in
the colonies because English will, in his view, provide the Indian
with access to a 'world of new ideas' more effectively than any
vernacular. 'With our language', Grant goes on:

much of our useful literature might, and would, in time
be communicated … the Hindus would see the great use
we make of reason on all subjects, and in all affairs; they
would also learn to reason, they would become acquainted
with the history of their own species, the past and present
state of the world; their affections would gradually become
interested by various engaging works, composed to recom-
mend virtue; the general mass of their opinions would be
rectified; and above all, they would see a better system of
principles and morals.[2]

The effective victory of arguments such as Grant's over those
favoured by the East India Company was signalled by two acts:
the 1813 Charter Act, which relaxed controls on missionary
activity in India and committed the British to greater (and more
programmatic) intervention in native education, and the 1835
English Education Act, which made English the medium of
instruction in Indian higher education.[3] The latter was produced
under the influence of one of the scions of the Clapham Sect,
Thomas Babington Macaulay, whose now infamous 'Minute on
Indian Education' issued in the same year spells out some of the
intentions implicit in the act. Continuing where Grant had left
off, Macaulay argues for the primacy of English literature over
all other literatures, and also recommends that, since it is prag-
matically impossible to teach English to Indians of all classes,
it will be expedient to 'form a class who may be interpreters
between us and the millions we govern; a class of persons, Indian

in blood and colour, but English in taste, in opinions, in morals, and in intellect'.[4]

As both Gauri Vishwanathan and Alastair Pennycook have demonstrated in their respective studies, arguments such as those made by Grant and Macaulay, though couched in terms that emphasised moral obligation and duty, are energised by a practical concern with how best to secure power. Hence Grant is concerned with both the honour and the *advantage* of imposing English beliefs and principles upon Indians, and Macaulay – far more explicitly – wishes to create an intermediate class of 'brown Englishmen' as a buttress for imperial power. '[T]he question of how England can serve the people of India', as Vishwanathan observes, 'blends indistinguishably with the question of how power can best be consolidated', and 'Duty towards the people is seen … as the end point of a process of consolidation of territorial control'.[5] The introduction of English as an institutional language in India, in this regard, is not a process unconnected with the establishment of British colonial power, but is rather, part and parcel of an ambitious act of hegemonic fortification.

The fact that English education in India may be seen as a tool for the cultural domination of Indians, designed to cement and extend the dominion already effected through military and economic means, makes explicit a central problem confronting an anti-colonial and post-colonial writer such as Rushdie, whose literary language of choice is English. Briefly stated: by using English Rushdie lays himself open to the charge that he is not only accepting the legacy of British imperial rule but legitimising the culturally imperialistic act that brought English into being as a sub-continental language. Some of Rushdie's more aggressive critics have made this argument against him with force. Aparna Mahanta, for instance, using a purposeful echo of Macaulay's fantasy of brown-skinned Englishmen, argues that writers like Rushdie are nothing but the apotheosis of an imperial dream. '[His] importance', she writes

> is that he is symptomatic of a new breed of Indians – an elite nurtured and brought up in English, reluctant, shame-faced inheritors of the colonial traditions, cut off from

the living, throbbing reality of deprivation and struggle. Like grandfather Aziz of 'Midnight's Children' these new Indians have a hole where the [heart] should have been, they are frozen and atrophied, creatively impotent like Sinai ... playthings of history. With no traditions except those sneeringly thrown at them by the departing Sahibs ... they are cut off from their roots, aerobic plants, exotics with aerial roots.[6]

Our attitude to such arguments will depend upon our view of how language works, and of the extent to which a language is capable of being recouped from its use in adversarial hegemonic circumstances. At one extreme of this debate, as Alastair Pennycook has observed, is the view expressed by George Steiner in a 1959 essay concerning a very different (some would suggest incomparably different) political scenario: that of the use of the German language after the Holocaust. For Steiner the complicity of the German language in Nazi crimes – its historical availability to authoritarian modes of address and the distortions it underwent during Nazi rule – meant that it had become a language closed to further uses in literature. 'Use a language to conceive, organise, and justify Belsen', Steiner argued;

use it to make out specifications for gas ovens; use it to dehumanise man during twelve years of calculated bestiality. Something will happen to it. Make of words what Hitler and Goebbels and the hundred thousand *Untersturmführer* made: conveyors of terror and falsehood. Something will happen to the words. Something of the lies and sadism will settle in the marrow of the language. Imperceptibly at first, like the poisons of radiation sifting silently into the bone. But the cancer will begin, and the deep set destruction. The language will no longer grow and freshen.[7]

Though Steiner is suggesting that the situation of German after the Holocaust was exceptional, due to the ferocity of Nazi racist ideology, his argument nevertheless serves to identify a problem inherent in all attempts to use languages that have been implicated in systems of oppression or occupation. Languages, for Steiner, are not innocent of, or incidental to, the kinds of discourse they are used to express, but facilitate such discourses by making certain kinds of expression possible. In some instances, moreover, the violent uses made of a language are so programmatic and so extreme that, flexible though languages are, that language may die and become unavailable to subsequent recuperation. Revealingly, the Bengali writer Jyotirmoy Datta, writing in 1966, applied Steiner's arguments concerning the German language directly to English, announcing that English in post-colonial India should be regarded as a dead medium, capable of carrying information but not feeling.[8]

Ranged against Steiner or Datta's arguments are a number of alternative possibilities. Languages, it might be objected, are never homogeneous no matter how systematically they have been used to mediate discourses of hatred, especially if we accept Mikhail Bakhtin's view of language as inherently dialogical. German may have been the language of Goebbels and Himmler, but it was also the language of resistance, of (as Steiner concedes) Brecht and Mann. Languages, in addition, are not static systems but dynamic and historically transformatory ones that are in a state of constant flux. Hence German, though it may have become deadened to feeling by certain kinds of usage in the period of Nazi ascendancy, could be (and, indeed, was if we consider writers such as Günter Grass) recuperated in the postwar period.

Various commentators have offered defences of the Indian use of English along these or similar lines. English, it is often observed, has remained a current language in India for over two centuries, and for at least fifty years of those two centuries it has been used as an Indian language independently of the presence of British rulers. In that time, as Gurcharan Das avers in his essay 'A Novelist's Faith', originally delivered at a seminar held by the University of Bombay in March 1991, the English language in India has not only become part of the environment but has also been made into one of India's many languages. It is, he writes, 'a nice sounding idiom that has emerged … under the bright Indian sun – virile and self-confident. It is no longer imitative – nostalgic of 'London fogs' or 'Surrey dews' or Oxbridge or the BBC. It is an Indian voice.'[9] Given English's widespread and transformatory uses, he goes on, 'to seek to *remove* English today from India is just as intrusive ... as it was to *introduce* it during the time of ... Macaulay'.[10]

Perhaps the most eloquent of Indian defences of English comes from Sujata Bhatt, who, in her 1988 poem 'A Different History', offers the apparently pragmatic argument that, if we were to regard violence as inhering in language, then all languages would become untenable, and we would resort to silence. 'Which language', she asks, 'has not been the oppressor's tongue?'[11] Since the answer is clearly none, so far as Bhatt is concerned, we must allow that language is recuperable, that:

> ... after the torture,
> after the soul has been cropped
> with a long scythe swooping out
> of the conqueror's face -
> the unborn grandchildren
> grow to love that strange language.[12]

Even in Bhatt's affirmative approach to uses of English, however, is a grudging note that should warn readers against an unqualified celebration of global uses of the language. In the first place, Bhatt's reasons for using English hardly represent an unqualified commendation – more a bending to necessity. In the second place, Bhatt's English is a language that remains 'strange' even after it has become 'loved'. This sense of the strangeness of English in India dominates other poems by Bhatt in the same collection, notably 'Search For My Tongue', in which she has to resort periodically to her native Gujerati because there are aspects of herself and her experience that she cannot express in English.[13] Bhatt's poetry, in these regards, even whilst it reflects the dynamic presence of the English language in Indian literature, registers the difficulties involved in using English, and the problematic weight of its historical freight of colonialist imposition.

Revealingly, an equivalent argument is made by George Steiner in an article on the fiction of Günter Grass, written in 1964 – five years after his article on the obsolescence of the

German language for literature. The work of Grass, Steiner concedes, may, to some extent, be regarded as having confounded his earlier arguments because it demonstrates that German has once more become a 'verbal instrument of uncanny virtuosity'.[14] Steiner, however, resists the conclusion that Grass has rescued German from fascistic usage, urging instead that Grass has of necessity created a partly failed literature in German because the language remains irrecoverable:

> Grass has understood that no German writer after the holocaust could take the language at face value. It had been the parlance of hell. So he began tearing and melting; he poured words, dialects, phrases, clichés, slogans, puns, quotations, into the crucible. … it is as if Grass had taken the German dictionary by the throat and was trying to throttle the falsehood and cant out of the old words, trying to cleanse them with laughter and impropriety so as to make them new. Often, therefore, his uncontrolled prolixity, his leviathan sentences and word inventories, do not convey confidence in the medium; they speak of anger and disgust, of a mason hewing stone that is treacherous or veined with grit. In the end, moreover, his obsessed exuberance undermines the shape and reality of the work. Grass is nearly always too long; nearly always too loud. The raucous brutalities which he satirizes infect his own art.[15]

There are a number of parallels that can be drawn between the fiction of Grass and the fiction of Rushdie – many of which are suggested by Steiner's description of Grass's work. Both writers stretch their respective languages to breaking point by incorporating into them a range of materials drawn from different social or cultural bases and different fictional or aesthetic forms; both employ carnivalesque techniques to create an atmosphere of hilarious (and sometimes riotous) renewal; and both are using these techniques with the more or less explicit aim of contesting previous uses of the languages. Most commentators who consider the parallels between German literature in the wake of the Second World War and literature in English in the aftermath of empire, including Rushdie himself, present these strategies as methods of overcoming and rejuvenation.[16] Steiner's perspective on Grass's postwar treatment of German, however, gives us a new perspective on Rushdie's post-colonial use of English; for Steiner's argument about Grass, applied to the fiction of Rushdie, yields the conclusion that Rushdie's fiction does not reflect the successful appropriation of English but is a fiction of the *failure* of English. Post-colonial writing in English, on this view, is a form of writing that grows out of a recognition that English literature is not recuperable but must be re-written in order to be destroyed.

Steiner's assertion that writers who work in the languages of oppression can only ever fight against those languages is echoed in the critical argument advanced by Alastair Pennycook in his study of English usage, conducted from the perspective of an EFL teacher in Hong Kong. The post-colonial critical consensus, Pennycook complains, seems to be that the reclamation of English for counter-hegemonic purposes should now be easy or conflict-free, that English has become suddenly and magically detached from its colonial past and neo-colonial present, and that 'turning English into a tool for one's own use is simply a matter of writing about the local context and sprinkling a few local words here and there'.[17] On the contrary, he argues that:

> such resistance and change is hard work, that the adherence of [colonialist] discourses to English, and their constant reinvocation in many contexts from travel writing to English language teaching, make attempts to change this relationship between language and discourse an uphill task.[18]

Pennycook's warning is a necessary one, and one that is clearly developed from substantial and current observations concerning how English is taught around the world. To recognise the difficulty of reappropriating English, however, is not to suggest that all attempts to reappropriate it are flawed or doomed to failure. On the contrary, it is to recognise the value of those attempts at reclamation that embrace the difficulty of the task – that invent new literary languages and new literary forms in order to be able to meet the considerable challenge of forcing a language into new shapes. Much of the best post-colonial fiction in English has been engaged in precisely this project – and if it is the case, as Pennycook argues, that these fictions have, in recent years, been brought back into the orbit of 'the mainstream white academy' by the post-colonial studies industry, this should not detract from the achievements of the fiction itself, which has, by mutilating, maiming, and cursing, cleared a space in English for contestatory voices that wish to *speak back* to the colonial heritage of the language.[19]

Whilst the colonial heritage of English is one of the problematics faced by writers who choose to use the language for counter-hegemonic literature, however, there are, as Pennycook's argument makes clear, additional problems involved in the use of English that stem not from the colonial past but from the role played by English in the neo-colonial present. English remains the global *lingua franca* of power, and access to English plays a major determining role in access to resources, wealth and public station. Given this, the choice made by writers such as Rushdie to write in English may be seen as problematic not simply because English was once the language of colonialism but because English is *still* the language of a neo-colonial elite. Indeed, the vast majority of hostile responses to Rushdie's use of English coming out of India today are focused not upon the problems of its British imperial heritage but upon the privileges accrued, and the compromises made, by the Indian writer who abandons the 'vernacular' in order to write in the language of global power. Some of these criticisms are summarised by Rushdie himself in his introduction to the volume of writing he co-edited with his then partner Elizabeth West, *The Vintage Book of Indian Writing in English* (also published in a slightly different form in the *New Yorker*). In this introduction Rushdie identifies several distinct accusations that are levelled at Indian English writers: first, they are 'too upper-middle-class', second, they lack 'diversity in their choice of themes', third, they possess 'inflated reputations on account of the international power of the English language, and of the ability of Western critics and publishers to impose their cultural standards on the East', fourth, they live 'in many cases, outside India' and so are 'deracinated to the point that their work lacks the spiritual dimension essential for a 'true' understanding of the soul of India', and, finally, fifth, they suffer from what Pankaj Mishra has called 'Rushdie-itis' – a condition, according to Mishra, that has 'claimed Rushdie himself in his later works' (SAL, 164). Few of these criticisms, as Rushdie observes, 'are literary in the pure sense of the word ... Rather, they are about class power and belief' (SAL, 164) – issues not irrelevant to the discussion of culture and literature, but not ultimately relevant to judgements about the *quality* of literature.[20] He nevertheless goes on to offer a range of arguments in response to the criticisms, which, on the whole, seem to start by conceding the truth of the allegation, only to contest the deductions made on its basis. For instance, he concedes that 'The point about the power of the English language ... contains some truth' (SAL, 165), but contends that anglophone Indian writing should not be seen as evidence that the West is foisting a canon upon the East, but, on the contrary, that the 'East [is] ... imposing itself on the West' (SAL, 165). English is, Rushdie acknowledges, 'the most powerful medium of communication in the world', but the fact that Indian writers show a growing mastery of this medium of communication should be a matter of celebration, rather than critique:

> One important dimension of literature is that it is a means of holding a conversation with the world. These writers are ensuring that India, or rather, Indian voices ... will henceforth be confident, indispensable participants in that literary conversation. (SAL, 165)

Whilst many of Rushdie's points seem fairly made, if open to further debate, there is one argument surrounding English-language writing in India that Rushdie's essay does little to temper. This is the argument that the access writers in English have to a global market has had the effect of elevating their importance disproportionately in relation to writing being done in vernacular languages. Indian writers in English, a number of Indian commentators have complained, are seen by the rest of the world as *the* Indian writers, whilst writers in the rest of

India's languages are neglected, both in terms of exposure and in terms of the size of their advances. Rushdie, as a younger and apparently more humble writer, himself drew attention to this problem. '[M]ajor work is being done in India in many languages other than English,' he reminds readers of his essay 'Commonwealth Literature Does Not Exist', 'yet outside India there is just about no interest in any of this work. The Indo-Anglians seize all the limelight. Very little is translated; very few of the best writers ... or the best novels are known, even by name' (IHL, 69).

In the later piece of writing we have been discussing, however, Rushdie turns coat and argues something very different: 'the prose writing – both fiction and non-fiction – created in [the post-liberation] period by Indian writers working in English', he suggests, 'is proving to be a more interesting body of work than most of what has been produced in the sixteen 'official languages' of India, the so-called 'vernacular languages', during the same time' (SAL, 160).

This assertion, together with its unfortunate redeployment of Macaulay's arrogant lucubrations about writing in Indian languages (that one shelf of European literature is worth the entire output of Indian and Arabic literature put together), predictably infuriated his critics, and has served to further polarise supporters of Indian writing in English and supporters of Indian writing in languages other than English. Both parties are, in a sense, defending their own territory: the supporters of vernacular literature attack the privilege of English-language writers, the English-language writers defend themselves by trumpeting their own achievements. More amicable middle ground would no doubt be found if champions of the vernacular recognised that the solution to the problem was not to condemn writers in English but to promote greater knowledge, appreciation, distribution and translation of non-English writers, and if the writers in English took greater heed of the work of the younger Rushdie, who – as Bishnupriya Ghosh has ably shown – sought to undermine rather than confirm the over-simplistic binary opposition that pits vernacular languages against English. English in India, as Ghosh's own argument runs, is not a language disconnected from Indian realities, but has itself become a vernacular, subject to significant variations as a result of differential class and regional use. Rushdie's 'localised or regionalised urban (Bombayite) use of English', in particular, 'far from being the antithesis to the vernacular lives in memory of it'.[21]

This argument requires Ghosh to reject the 'received' view of Rushdie's representation of India, which holds that Rushdie writes India for the West and so 'translates most of the 'Eastern' cultural signs for his Western audience'.[22] On the contrary Ghosh insists, there is, in Rushdie's fiction, a wealth of local referencing, and *situated* language use the significance of which Western readers will not always understand, and the importance of which Rushdie does not necessarily 'flag' for his Western audience. The presence of this situated contextual knowledge ('historical, popular cultural, linguistic and so forth'), for Ghosh, means that Rushdie's work is (once more, contrary to received wisdom) 'inextricably harnessed to its space of enunciation', and therefore constitutes 'an act of vernacular resistance that prevents his work being sold merely as a global commodity disengaged from the milieu of which it speaks'.[23]

Ghosh laments, however, that in recent years – particularly in the *Vintage/New Yorker* article – the amount of criticism levelled at Rushdie has led him to adopt a more 'reactionary' position, in opposition to the vernacular. Ghosh concludes, therefore, with the hope that Rushdie, 'a writer whose energetic and vibrant use of English galvanised a new beginning for Indian writing in English', will take heart from an affirmative and assertive new generation of Indian writers in English such as Arundhati Roy, and 'will move away from defensive stances and critical aporias to claim his place in an emergent tradition of Indian vernaculars'.[24]

The tradition of Indian fictive prose writing in English may be said to begin with the first anglophone Indian novel, *Rajmohan's Wife*, written in 1864 by Bankimchandra Chatterjee and serialised in the short-lived Calcutta journal *Indian Field*.

Commentators, including Rushdie himself, have tended to dismiss this novel as the first tentative efforts of a writer who went on to produce far better things in his native Bangla (in Rushdie's brief assessment it is 'a poor melodramatic thing' (SAL, 167)). Meenakshi Mukherjee, in her 'Introduction' and 'Afterword' to the 1996 edition of *Rajmohan's Wife*, has more affirmative things to say about the novel, but concedes that it has had no great impact upon Indian English literature either on its publication or in later years.[25] A more comprehensive flourishing of the Indian novel in English occurred seventy or so years later, with the publications of Mulk Raj Anand's fictions of social critique *The Untouchable* (1935) and *Coolie* (1936), R. K. Narayan's first Malgudi novel *Swami and Friends* (1935) and Raja Rao's Gandhian-Marxist-inspired novel of rural Indian life *Kanthapura* (1938). The 'foreword' to this latter work is of particular interest to students of Rushdie's fiction since it includes one of the first prominent formulations of the demand for Indian writers to develop an Indian English 'dialect' that will 'some day prove to be as distinctive and colourful as the Irish or the American'.[26] 'The tempo of Indian life must be infused into our English expression, even as the tempo of American or Irish life has gone into the making of theirs,' Rao writes:

> We, in India, think quickly, we talk quickly, and when we move we move quickly. There must be something in the sun of India that makes us rush and tumble and run on. And our paths are interminable ... we tell one interminable tale. Episode follows episode, and when our thoughts stop our breath stops, and we move on to another thought. This was and still is the ordinary style of our storytelling.[27]

Rao's commitment to the transformation of English, as well as his desire to revolutionise the novel in English by importing into it the rhythms of the Indian storyteller, clearly anticipate Rushdie's later experiments with the form. On the publication of *Midnight's Children*, however, Rushdie located his novel not in the tradition of anglophone writing initiated by writers such as Rao, but in distinction to it. Asked in 1982 by Jean-Pierre Durix how he 'situated [himself] in relation to other English-speaking

Indian writers ... like Mulk Raj Anand, Narayan or Raja Rao', Rushdie replied, to Durix's surprise, that he did not at all:

> This idea that there is a school of Indian-British fiction is a sort of mistake. Writers like Mulk Raj Anand and Narayan have many more affinities to Indian writers in the Indian languages than they do to a writer like me who just happens to be writing in English. Apart from the accident that we all use English, I don't think there's a great deal in common. (CSR, 9)

Other commentators have begged to differ. Uma Parameswaran, in *The Perforated Sheet*, enumerates several significant continuities between Rao's work and Rushdie's, and concludes that whilst 'Rushdie may not believe there exists an Indo-English stream of literature or that he is part of it ... literary historians would have to disagree'.[28] Likewise, Wimal Dissanayake has placed Rushdie in direct succession to Rao, because they are 'in their diverse ways ... seeking to decolonise English with the common purpose of creating a richer, more vibrant and complex literature'.[29] Rushdie, however, has repeatedly maintained that his attempts to 'break away from the manner in which India had been written about in English' have only one Indian precedent, and that is G. V. Desani's extraordinary comic novel of 1948 *All About H. Hatterr*, a book which the youthful Rushdie alighted on by chance, and which had an electrifying effect upon him:

> The way in which the English language is used in that book is very striking; it showed me that it was possible to break up the language and put it back together in a different way ... one [other] thing it showed me was the importance of punctuating badly. In order to allow different kinds of speech rhythms or different kinds of linguistic rhythms to occur in [*Midnight's Children*], I found I had to punctuate it in a very peculiar way, to destroy the natural rhythms of the English language; I had to use dashes too much, keep exclaiming, putting in three dots, sometimes three dots followed by semi-colons followed by three dashes ... That sort of thing just seemed to help to dislocate the English and let other things into it. Desani does that all the time in *Hatterr*. (CSR, 10)

James Joyce's novels *Ulysses* and *Finnegans Wake* might have suggested these fictional tactics to Rushdie in a different context, but Desani, in Rushdie's estimation, was the first writer to give modernism an Indian dimension and, in so doing, was one of the first Indian writers to make the aesthetic and formal challenge to the novel in English a 'more global' phenomenon than European modernism had done.[30]

The need for a decolonised novel, like the need for a decolonised English, is a result of the form's implication in colonial history. The novel was, as Anita Desai has pointed out, an alien import from the West brought to India as part of the baggage of colonialism.[31] It was also a literary form saturated, since its inception, with Orientalist assumptions about the 'East', and a component in an Indian educational programme that Gauri Vishwanathan has demonstrated in *Masks of Conquest* was designed to reinforce British ideological domination in India.[32] Whilst some Indian writers of novels sought to contest – or side-step – this compromised literary tradition by writing novels in languages other than the European languages in which the form originally took shape, Rushdie, as we have seen, seeks to rework the language of the English novel in the belief that 'the instrument of subservience' can become 'a weapon of liberation'.[33] The challenge to the English language, however, is one that could have been staged in diverse literary and theatrical forms, including poetry, drama and philosophy. It is an aspect of Rushdie's vital contribution to the field of novel writing expressly that, in addition to his linguistic interventions, he also engages in a specific challenge to the novel form by interrogating the structures that are unique to this genre of writing. For instance, Rushdie, as will be apparent to many readers, seeks to hybridise the (already hybrid) novel form by forcing it to absorb non-novelistic narrative machineries that it has not, in its dominant manifestations at least, characteristically incorporated. Most prominently, Rushdie adds a distinctly Indian strain to the novel's already multi-vocal register by drawing extensively upon Indian (Hindu) epic narratives such as the *Ramayana* and the *Mahabharata*, and upon popular tale cycles which assimilate elements of Indian, Persian and Arabian storytelling traditions such as *The Arabian Nights* or its less Orientalised cousin Bhatta Somdeva's ninth century Sanskrit story compendium *Kathasaritsagara* (*The Ocean of Streams of Story*). Behind Rushdie's interest in both sets of sources (roughly divisible into mythic-epic and folkloric) is a further interest in un-named Indian storytellers who may be presumed to have disseminated these tales over centuries and who can still be heard plying their trade today. The nature of this influence is most effectively illustrated by Rushdie's account of a trip he made to hear an Indian storyteller spinning fictions in Baroda in 1983 – an event that led him to recall the extent to which 'the shape of the oral narrative' had influenced the writing of both *Midnight's Children* and *Shame*. This shape, as Rushdie notes, is 'not linear', it 'does not go from the beginning to the middle to the end' like the classical Aristotelian narrative, but is 'pyrotechnical': it

> goes in great swoops, it goes in spirals or in loops, it every so often reiterates something that has happened earlier to remind you, and then takes you off again, sometimes summarises itself, it frequently digresses off into some- thing that the story-teller appears just to have thought of, then it comes back to the main thrust of the narrative.[34]

Rushdie was sufficiently impressed with this oleaginous and recursive form to 'attempt the creation' in *Midnight's Children*

> of a literary form which corresponds to the form of the oral narrative and which, with any luck, [would] succeed in holding readers, for reasons of its shape, in the same way that the oral narrative holds audiences for reasons of its shape, as well as its narrative.[35]

The result is a novel that has a number of features more commonly associated with spoken storytelling conventions than with written ones: it is highly digressive but always returns to the main point; it employs 'formulaic repetition' of the kind that Milman Parry and Albert Lord identified as characteristic of literature with oral origins;[36] it offsets the linearity of its central plot (a young man's maturation narrative) with an anti-linear tendency to return repeatedly to an established constellation of narrative motifs or '*Leitsätze*'; and finally, it is self-conscious, both in its recognition of the importance of the storyteller and in its awareness of the role played by an attendant audience. The functions of this quality of orality in *Midnight's Children* are manifold. Nancy E. Batty has argued persuasively that narrative patterns derived from collections such as the *Arabian Nights* enable Rushdie to build suspense into his narrative – a function of oral narrative that Rushdie himself clearly advances in his account of the Baroda yarn spinner.[37] Robert Irwin, alternatively, has suggested that the relative informality and exuberance to be found in carnivalistic, folkloristic texts like the *Nights* is used by Rushdie as a means of challenging orthodoxy and officialdom in religious and political spheres. 'Rushdie's *Nights*', for Irwin, 'represents an alternative tradition in Islamic literature, something to set against the dour decrees of the mullahs of the Middle East and the dictators of the Indian sub-continent'.[38] More critically, some commentators have seen Rushdie's deployment of Indian (or 'Eastern') narrative sources within the European, anglophone novel as an effort to package Indian culture in a form that allows it to be readily appropriated and consumed on the global (Westernised) market. In his potent assessment of representations of Africa in world art in *In My Father's House*, Kwame Anthony Appiah, in 1992, accused postmodern 'Western-style, Western trained' African writers in 'Western languages' of being a '*comprador* intelligentsia ... who mediate the trade in cultural commodities of world capitalism at the periphery'.[39] Similar assertions are often made about Rushdie as a mediator of Indian culture. Aijaz Ahmad, for instance, has argued that, though Rushdie may promote the view in his writing that his borrowings from the *Mahabharata* and the *Ramayana* give his fiction a 'quintessential Indianness [of] form', his fiction's clear lines of descent from European modernism and postmodernism demonstrate that such a view is deceptive, and that Rushdie is, in fact, a writer of Western fictions who uses the veneer of Indian storytelling to reinforce the appeal of his fictions to Western readers.[40]

Such observations about Rushdie's fictions are criticisms of his work only if we assume that Rushdie wishes to conceal the fact that he is transforming the traditions of Indian oral storytelling when he makes use of them in the context of the modernist or postmodernist novel. At no point, however, does Rushdie suggest that he is using Indian folk materials in the hope of giving his fiction the appearance that it is 'returning' to an originary and authentic mode of Indian/Eastern narration; neither has he ever suggested that he is seeking to avoid the fact that his fictions are heavily dependent, at one and the same time, upon both Indian *and* Euro-American intellectual traditions. On the contrary, Rushdie is seeking, wilfully and self-consciously, to place elements of the Euro-American novelistic tradition in new conjunctions with elements of the Indian (or Arabic) story-telling tradition in order, firstly, to see how one tradition might productively transform the other and, secondly, to show how fictions have been brought into new hybrid relations in his own experience, as a migrant intellectual working in increasingly globalised, post-colonial arenas.

Some of the most effective analyses of Rushdie's intentions in borrowing vernacular cultural material from the Indian tradition are those that have assimilated the concerns of critics such as Ahmad and Appiah, whilst also recognising, in the work of cosmopolitan writers such as Rushdie, a complex and self-conscious relationship with the commodification process. Graham Huggan in *The Postcolonial Exotic*, for instance, argues that, whilst metropolitan writers such as Rushdie have benefited from the post-colonialism industry's play to exoticism, they have also 'succeeded in sustaining a critique of exoticism in their work'.[41] 'This critique', for Huggan, 'is located ... in forms of cultivated exhibitionism: the deliberately exaggerated hawking of Oriental(ist) wares by a narcissistic narrator'.[42] In a similar vein, Bishnupriya Ghosh, extending her arguments concerning English language use to cosmopolitanism more generally in her monograph *When Borne Across*, argues that it has become necessary to recognise a significant difference between privileged economic globalists, who seek unproblematic global exchanges

of commodities, and politicised literary cosmopolitans, who seek
to interrupt 'their own global circulation'.[43] Too often, Ghosh
argues,

> there is a metonymic slide where all cosmopolitans come
> to be either purveyors of the global market or nostalgia
> nomads. Hence the commercial success of South Asian
> writing in English is too quickly understood as a canny
> play to global demand: a scene where bourgeois cosmo-
> politan writers market India for an increasingly mobile
> and dispersed Indian bourgeoisie.[44]

There is, Ghosh concedes, some 'overlap in lifestyles and location' between economic globalists and cosmopolitan writers, but
it does not follow that the two groups 'necessarily share ... ideological frameworks'.[45] The former may shore up their economic
appeal to the world by making India and its economic produce
marketable in all cultural contexts, but there is a category of the
latter – *literary cosmopoliticals* – who create works (fictions, in
this instance) that have social and linguistic specificity, and that
cannot, therefore, be marketed to the world without requiring
something back from the world: an imaginative migration,
perhaps, and an awareness that 'other' cultures cannot be 'translated' into English without supplementary spaces of ambivalence
and ambiguity being opened up. These writers, Ghosh suggests,
emphasise 'historical contingency and performance over any
reified production of the local', with the result that entry into
their representational worlds

> demands constant linguistic motility, and resists replication
> for the purposes of commodity fetishism. Thus,, Rushdie's,
> [Upamanyu] Chatterjee's and [Arundhati] Roy's projects
> both render India communicable (the local fetishized as
> national) and undercut full communicative access.[46]

Rushdie's use of pseudo-oral Indian storytelling registers, on this
reading, functions *in part* to signify ideas of Indianness to non-
Western readers, but, because non-Western readers are simultaneously made aware that they cannot have full comprehension
of the storytelling cultures to which Rushdie alludes, they also

function to demonstrate the impossibility of any immediate consumption of Indian vernacular material.

There are also more particular ramifications of Rushdie's use of an oral register that it is worth noting here. Firstly, Rushdie uses the oral voice (a technique defined by the Russian formalists as *skaz*)[47] because it enables him to emphasise the *placement* of the literary utterance and, in so doing, to reveal that literature is not an ahistorical event, that occurs independent of community and culture, but, rather, one that grows out of a cultural exchange that has social, and political, significance. Rushdie thus has a defined narrator, Saleem, relay the text of *Midnight's Children* to a specified auditor, Padma, at a specified place and time, in order to emphasise the fact that this story does not transcend the conditions of its telling, but is rather, shaped by those conditions. Secondly, and connectedly, Rushdie uses *skaz* because it removes the authority of the disembodied voice from the fiction, and replaces it with an uncertain author figure, whose words, like the words of the speaking individual, are fallible, and whose perceptions have to compete with the perceptions of others in a multi-vocal and dialogue-bound environment. In both these cases the vocal registers employed by Rushdie are designed to assault any pretence at objectivity in the novel by demonstrating that all speech and writing comes from somewhere and is, therefore, shaped by the subjective concerns of an unreliable individual, performing to meet the demands of a fickle audience, and informed by the historical and ideological agendas of a unique cultural location.

Rushdie's use of an oral register, in this sense, coincides with a distinctly modernist and postmodernist agenda for the novel since it serves to undermine the assumptions concerning storytelling and authority implicit in the conventional realist text. Thus, whilst, as Rushdie's Baroda anecdote persuades us, his use of techniques such as circularity, repetition, digression and improvisation connects his work to a very old, pre-enlightenment, pre-literate mode of narrative structuring, he is able, at one and the same time, to exploit the fact that these ancient narrative methods merge seamlessly with the 'circulating codes' that Roland Barthes identifies as the means by which the modern writerly text works against the conventional readerly text. The difference between the two aleatory styles remains, of course, that where traditional storytelling was not reacting – on an overt level at least – to an established narrative orthodoxy, postmodern literature pits itself explicitly, even militantly, against that orthodoxy. Nevertheless, both modes meet, and are made complicitous in the fiction of Rushdie, because they share – one innocently, *avant la lettre*, one knowingly, *après la déluge* – a resistance to the kinds of narrative form favoured in European Enlightenment aesthetics, and to the kinds of philosophic world view implied in such aesthetics.

Rushdie also seeks to resist linearity in narrative form by borrowing formal strategies from technologically developed media such as film – a medium that, Rushdie told Sara Rance in 1992, has been 'a much bigger influence on [him] than books' (SRI, 106). The advent of film as a mass medium in the twentieth century, Rushdie explains to Rance, has had the effect of changing audience expectations of narrative to such an extent that techniques that would once have seemed experimental in literature have become a staple part of an audience's – and a readership's – narrative expectation:

> There are generations of people for whom [the language of film] has become effortless. We know what a jump cut is, we know what a flashback is. People are used to a whole range of techniques that are not just linear narrative … We've got a readership which understands about sophisticated and strange ways of putting information together and doesn't find it difficult. (SRI, 106)

To neglect to use this language in the novel, Rushdie argues, is to fail to remain true to the idea of the novel – as a perennially rejuvenated genre capable of absorbing innovative stylistics into its capacious form. Rushdie's own novels have, consequently, endeavoured to incorporate filmic stylistics in various ways. For instance the extended sequence in *Midnight's Children* in which Ahmed Sinai's abortive attempts to pay ransom money to the Ravana Gang are juxtaposed, in the form of interspersed 'clips', with Amina Sinai's visit to the fortune teller (MC, 80–8) takes a formal cue from the techniques of cinematic montage developed by filmmakers from Sergei Eisenstein onwards. Likewise the format in which Saleem's childhood is presented – with foregrounded moments, fade outs and fast forwards – draws as much upon the methods filmmakers use for screening past-life as it does upon the techniques of the classic literary *Bildungsroman*.

The specific films that have influenced Rushdie, like all his influences, range across the medium. Prominent amongst these influences are the 'art-house' films of Fellini, from whom Rushdie 'learned how one might transmute the highly charged material of childhood and private life into the stuff of showmanship and myth' (SAL, 76). Also significant for Rushdie are Bombay Talkies, or 'Bollywood' films, the pleasures of which Rushdie has described as the cinematic equivalent of 'eating junk food' (SAL, 6). Two filmmakers in particular have had a discernible and lasting impact on Rushdie's writing. The first is the surrealist auteur Luis Buñuel, whose *Chien Andalou* (with Salvador Dalí)[48] and *Cet obscur objet de désir* provide Rushdie with filmic precedents for the aesthetic attempt to disrupt settled perceptions using striking, fantastical and dreamlike imagery. Rushdie cites *Cet obscur objet de désir* at the start of an essay on Rudyard Kipling, claiming that he had once intended to 'borrow' Buñuel's device of having two actresses playing the same woman for a documentary on Kipling in order to dramatise the idea that Kipling's was 'a personality in conflict with itself' (IHL, 74). The documentary was never made, but it might be argued that the surrealist obsession with the threat to coherent identity brought about by doubling, splitting and twinning is one that Buñuel has bequeathed many of Rushdie's works, from the grotesque Flapping Eagle/Grimus synthesis of his first novel to the shadowy twin selves of *The Ground Beneath Her Feet* and *Fury*. Such images, of course, have sources other than film – in the doppelgängers of Gothic literature for instance – but the peculiar ease with which film, notably surrealist film, allows for an assault on the coherence of the individual body and the transformation of one self into diverse selves, seems to have had a particular impact upon the development of the slippery, migrating, and transmigrating entities that populate Rushdie's fictional universe. The highly disorientating depiction in *The Satanic Verses* of Gibreel Farishta as he attempts to negotiate London's streets, unable to distinguish dream from reality and unable to piece together his shattered perceptions, for instance, seems to owe a particular debt to the effects used by Buñuel, and may go some way towards explaining Rushdie's extraordinary statement to Rance, that 'Buñuel is more important to [him] than Joyce' (SRI, 106).

The second major filmmaker to have influenced Rushdie's work is the Bengali writer-director Satyajit Ray, creator of *Pather Panchali* (*The Song of the Little Road*) and the subsequent two films of the 'Apu' trilogy. In Rushdie's essay on Ray in *Imaginary Homelands*, written originally as an extended review of Andrew Robinson's biography *Satyajit Ray: The Inner Eye*, he suggests that Ray's importance, for him, is less to do with the style of his filmmaking, than with his cultural significance. Ray, Rushdie argues, provided a vital early impetus to his career, because he was the figure who demonstrated that there was an 'Indian dimension' to the 'explosion of creative genius' that was 'New Wave' cinema (IHL, 108). Ray's stylistic and aesthetic influence on Rushdie, however, should not be underestimated – although the Ray films that are most obviously referenced in Rushdie's work are not his better known domestic realist films but, more appropriate to Rushdie's fabular tastes, his fantasies *Goopy Gyne Bagha Byne* (*The Adventures of Goopy and Bagha*), *Hirak Rajar Dese* (*The Kingdom of Diamonds*), *Joi Baba Felunath* (*The Elephant God*) and, Rushdie's personal favourite, *Sonar Kella* (*The Golden Fortress*). This influence is at its strongest in Rushdie's own children's fantasy *Haroun and the Sea of Stories* (1990) in which a number of allusions to these films work alongside parallel allusions to Western fantasies to help create Rushdie's vision of a hybrid story sea. Specifically, Rushdie's *Haroun* borrows from Ray's *Goopy Gyne Bagha Byne* the names of the Plentimaw fishes (Goopy and Bagha), the comic device of a character who loves singing in spite of an execrable voice (a misfortune that Ray gives to Goopy Gyne before a magic wish grants him the voice of Anup Kumar Ghosal), the central plot of a peaceable and music-loving kingdom at war with a violent militaristic regime, and the striking image of dancing ghosts – the cinematic presentation of which (in 'negative') has clearly informed Rushdie's literary visualisation of the 'shadow warrior' Mudra.[49] Rushdie also references Ray's works substantially in *The Moor's Last Sigh*, in which 'The great Bengali film director' is transmuted into 'Sukumar Sen' who makes a 'series of haunting, humane films' that bring to Indian cinema 'a fusion of heart and mind' (MLS, 173). Here too, the films that receive most attention are the 'films for children in which Sen let his fantasy rip, in which fish talked, carpets flew and young boys dreamed of previous incarnations in fortresses of gold' (MLS, 173).

Film is not the only visual medium to have influenced Rushdie's style. *The Moor's Last Sigh* explores the interconnections between the fine arts (notably modern Indian painting) and literature, and *The Satanic Verses* – as well as being a 'movie novel' – draws freely from the slough of the junk television show, emphasising, in particular, the ways in which channel hopping can bring surprising new conjunctions into being. Rushdie also makes regular ekphrastic use of the photographic image. For instance the photographic imagination can be seen at work in *Midnight's Children* in the extended sequence in which an old photograph of various characters operates as a mnemonic device in Saleem's efforts to recapture the past. Photography is, in addition, one of the dominant thematic devices in Rushdie's sixth novel *The Ground Beneath Her Feet* – in part because the narrator is a photographer who uses his medium as a 'way of understanding the world' (GBF, 210), and in part because the novel's subjects, celebrities, live their lives under the gaze of the camera. Rushdie himself, of course, had, by the time of writing *The Ground*, ample experience of being photographed: a subject he considers at length in an article for *Egoïste* concerning a 'portrait photograph' that was taken of him by Richard Avedon in 1997 (SAL, 113–17). The photographer whose work has the most in common with Rushdie's writing, however, and who no doubt figures substantially in the 'heaps of photography books' that Rushdie tells Peter Kadzis he owns, is neither a celebrity portraitist nor media paparazzi, but Sebastião Salgado, whose catalogue of images of late twentieth-century migrations offers a visual parallel for Rushdie's literary explorations of the same subject (CSR, 226). 'For Salgado as for myself,' Rushdie writes, 'the migrant, the man without frontiers, is the archetypal figure of our age' (SAL, 415).

Movies, photographs and television programmes have a relatively high profile in Rushdie's fiction in part because they are products of the contemporaneity that Rushdie seeks to explore in his fictions, but also because they assist him in the task of disrupting the conventional form of the novel which, in its 'realist' guise, has practised a linearity of narrative that the visual image may be seen as formally resistant to. The photograph, rather than operating diachronically in narrative sequence, functions synchronically as a static 'snapshot' of the past that can be used (as Rushdie certainly uses it) as a means of capturing moments taken out of time. Film, likewise, has from its inception taken advantage of the medium's technological capacity to suggest that reality doesn't always function in a naturalistic way but, like oral storytelling, more often than not happens pyrotechnically – in swoops and whirls, in flashbacks and fast forwards. The techniques of film and photography in these senses combine with the structurally comparable techniques of oral narrative to assist Rushdie in his continuation of the modernist project of making the novel 'new' – of trying to extend what the novel is capable of doing, and, therefore, what it is capable of saying.

Intertextuality, influence
and the postmodern

Attention to the epic, oral, filmic, televisual and photographic models employed in Rushdie's novels give some indication of the referential range of his fiction – but the above account has by no means exhausted the potential list of Rushdie's influences. Treated comprehensively, such a list would run to many pages, and would, no doubt, become very boring.[1] Rushdie's reasons for practising such a referential artform may be explained in various ways; but certainly one of the central explanations must be that Rushdie writes in this way because he believes, and because he wishes to assert that he believes, that the act of authorial creation does not happen in a vacuum, is not the product of an inspired moment of original genius, but depends upon, indeed springs from, innumerable preceding acts of authorial (and artistic) creation effected by other writers, storytellers, artists and intellectuals. This is an idea expressed eloquently by Rushdie in a lecture given at the University of Toronto in 1999, in which he juggles with the poetic notion, suggested by the etymology of the word 'influence', that the act of authorial creation is imaginatively associated with liquid and fluidity. 'I have always envisaged the world of the imagination not so much as a continent as an ocean', Rushdie reflects:

> Afloat and terrifyingly free upon these boundless seas, the writer attempts, with his bare hands, the magical task of metamorphosis. Like the figure in the fairy-tale who must spin straw into gold, the writer must find the trick of weaving the waters together until they become land:

until, all of a sudden, there is solidity where once there was only flow, shape where there was formlessness; there is ground beneath his feet ... The young writer, perhaps uncertain, perhaps ambitious, probably both at once, casts around for help; and sees, within the flow of the ocean, certain sinuous thicknesses, like ropes, the work of earlier weavers, of sorcerers who swam this way before him. Yes, he can use these 'in-flowings', he can grasp them and wind his own work around them. (SAL, 69–70)

This image, which is also given fictional treatment in Rushdie's novella for children *Haroun and the Sea of Stories*, recalls, in some tangential respects, the description of textuality and intertextuality provided by Roland Barthes in his much quoted account of 'The Death of the Author'.[2] For Barthes too, 'a text is ... a multi-dimensional space in which a variety of writings, none of them original, blend and clash. The text is a tissue of quotations drawn from the innumerable centres of culture'.[3]

There are, however, several crucial differences between Rushdie's conception of the sea of stories and Barthes's vision of intertextual flux. For Barthes, in the first place, the fact that the author forms fictions from a tissue of pre-existent texts means that his or her agency is significantly diminished; as a guarantor of meaning the author is obsolete, or has, at least, become a mere channel through which the whisperings of the pre-existing texts, 'the already read', communicate directly with the reader. Rushdie, however, as an author himself, and as an author whose forceful personality is imprinted firmly upon his writings, offers us a much more potent and dynamic image of the author as agent; as a kind of magician or wielder of primal matter who is able to create new out of old. This more favourable view of the author as creator (if not determinant) of meaning is clarified by Rushdie later in the lecture with an unambiguous assertion of the priority of the author-figure over his or her intertextual antecedents: 'If influence is omnipresent in litera-ture', he writes:

it is also, one should emphasize, always secondary in any work of quality ... By using what is old , and adding to it

> some new thing of our own, we make what is new. In *The Satanic Verses* I tried to answer the question, how does newness enter the world? Influence, the flowing of the old into the new, is one part of the answer. (SAL, 72–3)

Rushdie here insists upon an idea that is absent in Barthes: the idea that the author, though he or she receives language from pre-existent cultural uses, also welds languages and discourses into new forms of saying or – particularly relevant to Rushdie – new forms of cultural expression. According to Barthes 'the writer can only imitate a gesture that is always anterior, never original'; but for Rushdie the writer fuses anterior forms of saying with his or her own culturally, historically, politically distinctive outlook to create a third thing that, though it comes from somewhere, is not identical to the point of departure.[4] Such a conception of the author as a figure capable of forging new ways of seeing the world is crucial to anti-colonial writing in which it is essential to the author of resistance that he or she is able to speak and think differently to the ways in which he or she has been spoken and thought in the past. Hence Rushdie can write in English and adopt the European book as a vehicle for his fictions, but still maintain that he is not restricted by these superficially alien media to purely European modes of perception.

Barthes too, of course, was interested in finding a politically distinct voice to the dominant voice of the traditional author, and he does this by giving the power to make meaning into the hands of the reader rather than the hands of the paternalistic 'author-god'.[5] It remains the case, however, that Barthes's theory of intertextuality as expressed in 'The Death of the Author' seems to leave no room for newness in the act of writing. His bold rhetorical act allows him to assassinate the traditional author who seeks to fix meaning but it also, almost accidentally, removes the power of resistance from the author who seeks to create different ways of perceiving the world.

This leads us to a second major difference between Barthes's theory of intertextuality and Rushdie's theory of influence.[6] Barthes's view of textual interaction, whilst it has cultural and ideological significance, depends on a relatively abstract theory of language and linguistic structure. Rushdie's view of textual interaction, by contrast, is more overtly tailored to illustrate something about the ways in which cultures interact. Rushdie's metaphorising of the process of in-flowing and in-fluence, accordingly, is ultimately, the product of a concern not with the ways in which language constitutes a text but with the ways in which the cultural products of one community interpenetrate and cross-pollinate another. More particularly, as Rushdie swiftly makes clear in his lecture, his vision of the story sea is designed to provide evidence for the idea, central to his aesthetic practice, that 'streams of other people's consciosuness ... can flow towards the writer from almost anywhere': that the work of some Latin American writers may be inspired by the work of the Bengali poet Rabindranath Tagore, that the novels of the English writer Jane Austen may, in 'metropolitan mid-twentieth century Bombay', meet the fictions of Anita Desai or Vikram Seth (SAL, 70). From the 'transcultural, translinguistic capacity of influence', as Rushdie notes,

> we can deduce something about the nature of literature: that ... books can grow as easily from spores borne on the air as from their makers' particular and local roots. That there are international families of words as well as the more familiar clans of earth and blood. (SAL, 70)

Rushdie's concept of intertextuality in this regard is intimately bound up with the concept of hybridity. The mixing of texts and textualities within the novel is a paradigm for (or a product of) the mixing of cultures in society. Or, to phrase the argument slightly differently, the inherent plurality of the text – as it is understood in intertextual theory – becomes an extension of Rushdie's insistence, staged in thematic and aesthetic terms, that all cultures are inherently plural, inherently intertextual, and that any ideological insistence upon purity, separation and singularity is a falsification of culture, just as it would be a falsification of language. Whilst the post-structuralist intertextual theories of Julia Kristeva and Barthes would not exactly exclude this more culturally orientated understanding of the concept – whilst, indeed, they would wholeheartedly endorse such a use of the theories they have developed – their own focus upon linguistic structures rather than linguistic locations tends to elide the cultural and historical specificities of speech acts. As Graham Allen argues in his lucid study of the subject, Barthes's theorisation of the concept of intertextuality may depend upon the idea that the text is constituted out of a collision of diverse discourses, but his 'conception of these forces remains unattached to the specific social and institutional sites within which such utterances occur'.[7] Likewise, Kristeva's analysis of interdependent semiotic systems, though it is founded on an insistence that all acts of writing and speaking 'contain within them the ideological structures and struggles contained in society through discourse', is none the less expressed in language that 'seems to evade human subjects in favour of the more abstract terms, text and textuality'.[8] A more culturally orientated understanding of intertextuality, Allen argues, which emphasises the connections between dialogism in language and dialogism in society, comes in the work of the theorist from whose work Kristeva originally developed the concept of the intertextual: Mikhail Bakhtin, whose writings, as a result, may offer critics more effective tools in the study of Rushdie's novels.

Like Barthes, Bakhtin provides a vision of complex linguistic intertextuality that anticipates Rushdie's characterisation of narrative as a sea-like multiplicity of vocalities. 'The word, directed towards its object', as Bakhtin writes:

> enters a dialogically agitated and tension-filled environment of alien words, value judgements and accents, weaves in and out of complex interrelationships, merges with some, recoils from others, intersects with yet a third group: and all this may crucially shape discourse.[9]

In contrast to Barthes, and in greater affinity with Rushdie, Bakhtin is interested in this vision of linguistic flux not because of what it tells us about the nature of writing but because of what it tells us about the social and cultural arrangements that give form to the flux. If 'Discourse lives', for Bakhtin as for Rushdie, it lives because it only ever has meaning 'beyond itself, in a living impulse'.[10] '[I]f we detach ourselves completely from this impulse,' Bakhtin warns, 'all we have left is the naked corpse of the word, from which we can learn nothing at all about the social situation or the fate of a given word in life'.[11]

This emphasis on the cultural importance of language in Bakhtin's writings is far more useful to an understanding of the problematics and potentialities of language use in a post-colonial context than the less materially located theories of the later post-structuralists because it places a marked emphasis on the extent to which language is already owned by another speaker, made to serve established power structures, and must be wrested – with considerable creative effort – away from its antecedent contexts. In Bakhtin's terms:

> the word does not exist in a neutral and impersonal language ... but rather it exists in other people's mouths, in other people's contexts, serving other people's intentions: it is from there that one must take the word, and make it one's own.[12]

This insight into the ways in which the word is *possessed* and carries the history of its possession with it can help us to understand how, and why, post-colonial writers must contest the linguistic and literary forms that history makes them inheritors of. Equally importantly, it can help us understand how complex (dialogic, multi-vocal, heteroglossic) a text remains even after it has been appropriated by the post-colonial author. This is because language, for Bakhtin, whilst it is spoken in one social context, always has the power to summon up the many other social contexts in which words have meaning. 'Language is not a neutral medium that passes freely and easily into the private property of the speaker's intentions,' for Bakhtin, 'it is populated – overpopulated – with the intentions of others. Expropriating it, forcing it to submit to one's own intentions and accents, is a difficult and complicated process.'[13]

A clearer exposition could hardly be given of the 'complicated process' in which Rushdie is engaged: the process of recognising the power structures implicit in language, of negotiating and modifying those power structures, and of foregrounding the ways in which those power structures can still speak through language, even in spite of the desires of the speaker.

This culturally situated understanding of textual relations serves to distinguish Rushdie's writing from the more banal forms of mainstream 'postmodernism' which have found themselves subject to critique for their lack of historical awareness. Rushdie's fiction may draw upon the postmodern for a number of its narrative strategies, but his postmodernism is a product not of textuality or of language alone but of cultural hybridisation, in which the 'free play of signifiers' within the literary text takes place because it has been *historically validated*. Alternatively put, whereas signifiers in the forms of the postmodern that Marxist theorists such as Fredric Jameson would seek to criticise are in free play because they are not connected to a stable set of significances, signifiers in Rushdie's work are in free play because history and colonialism have put them into free play. Rather than being a modernist solely by intellectual choice, in this sense, Rushdie, and writers like him, have been made into modernists by history and by colonisation. In Rushdie's own words, 'those of us who have been forced by cultural displacement to accept the provisional nature of all truths, all certainties, have perhaps had modernism forced upon us' (IHL, 12–13).

The need to subordinate postmodern aesthetics to cultural relevance is concisely expressed by Rushdie in response to Kumkum Sangari's suggestion in interview that his writing may be seen as postmodern because of the readiness with which it examines its own assumptions. Rushdie readily accepts Sangari's description of his work, but argues that the explanation for his textual self-questioning has more to do with 'physical and cultural displacement' than with postmodern aesthetics. Being a migrant from one culture to another, Rushdie explains, 'makes you self-conscious about your position', and this in turn 'obliges you to establish the ground you stand on' (SRI, 70). If such self-consciousness coincides with the aesthetic self-consciousness of postmodernism, Rushdie implies, he is only too happy to exploit the coincidence. The reflexive postures of his fiction, however, are struck *in the first instance*, because of his overriding concern to locate himself as a speaker, and to explore the grounds of diasporic identity – both of which are desires that spring from cultural and political experiences, rather than from a desire to conform with literary trends.

Rushdie's magpie approach to the postmodern has some similarities to the uses of the postmodern made by a number of feminist writers. These writers, as Patricia Waugh argues, have found postmodernist aesthetic strategies useful to the extent that they enabled them to engage in the 'narrative disruption of traditional stories', but have avoided an absolute affirmation of postmodernist conclusions, because these conclusions proved limiting in the context of feminism's wider political aims.[14] Many women writers, Waugh suggests, including Angela Carter, Jeanette Winterson, Margaret Atwood, Maggie Gee and Fay Weldon, 'are using postmodern aesthetic strategies of disruption to re-imagine the world in which we live' while rejecting the 'nihilistic implications' of a theory that, she believes, undermines political practice by questioning 'the notion of effective human agency, the necessity for historical continuity in formulating identity and a belief in historical progress'.[15] In so doing, these contemporary feminist writers are engaged in a long-established countercultural practice defined by Hélène Cixous in her rousing and polemical 'Laugh of the Medusa' as 'stealing and flying', whereby women (in Morag Shiach's description of the process) 'must steal what they need from the dominant culture, but then fly away with their cultural booty to the 'in between', where new images, new narratives, and new subjectivities can be created'.[16]

Clearly a similar flight is undertaken by anti-colonial writers like Rushdie who employ an equivalent strategic eclecticism: feathering their nest with those elements of a given discourse that are tactically useful, but abandoning those elements that lack sufficient lustre or that prove politically disabling.

The reasons Waugh gives for feminists' suspicion of postmodernism, however, are not identical to Rushdie's. For Waugh, politicised feminists must be suspicious of postmodernism because 'Feminism needs coherent subjects'.[17] For Rushdie, by contrast, the principal political thrust of his fiction is to locate and identify

a form of political agency that doesn't need coherent subjects
– that works through a migrant, hybridised form of subjectivity
that is discontinuous, conflictual, that doesn't add up to a whole
self. This dimension of Rushdie's thought is usefully echoed by
Homi Bhabha in *The Location of Culture* when he warns that
the reaction against postmodernist thought by post-colonial
theorists should not lead to a return to the idea that politics can
or should be grounded in a 'consensual and collusive 'liberal'
sense of cultural community'.[18] Agency and political resistance,
for Bhabha, are effected not independently of discourse in the
realm of abstractable or totalisable knowledge (epistemology)
but in the midst of the 'displacements and realignments that are
the effects of … antagonisms and articulations' in the domain
of living culture. Thus:

> agency requires a grounding, but it does not require a
> totalization of those grounds; it requires movement and
> manoeuvre, but it does not require a temporality of conti-
> nuity or accumulation; it requires direction and contingent
> closure but no teleology and holism … . The individua-
> tion of the agent occurs in a moment of displacement. It
> is a pulsational incident, the split-second movement when
> the process of the subject's designation – its fixity – opens
> up beside it, uncannily, *abseits*, a supplementary space of
> contingency.[19]

Bhabha therefore locates the agency available to post-colonial
counter politics not in the places that postmodernism cannot
reach but in the very places that postmodernism has helped to
theorise.

Postmodernism, we might conclude, is useful to Rushdie
to the extent that it enables an assault on the totalising forms
of knowledge and assimilative ideas of identity upon which
discourses of colonialism and racism have previously depended;
it becomes a burdensome theoretic for Rushdie only if it severs
its analysis of discontinuous identities and fragmented selves
from their roots in contemporary multicultural arrangements
and post-colonial social realities. Some theorisations of the
postmodern will, for this reason, be more useful to Rushdie

than others. Lyotard's critique of all explaining metanarratives, for instance, and Foucault's explorations of the ways in which systems of knowledge are shaped by structures of power, both help us to better comprehend Rushdie's materially located engagement with imperial authority. By contrast Jean Baudrillard's arguments that reality is an 'esthetic hallucination', and that world events such as the 1991 Gulf War were media-constructed *simulacra* (or simulated copies without any independently existing 'original') are less enabling for the politicised post-colonial writer.[20] Indeed, many of Rushdie's dismissive comments about postmodernism in interviews and essays seem to be directly primarily at Baudrillardian forms of the discourse that would seek to deny the referential link between the work of the writer and the world beyond the writer. This becomes most explicit in his non-fictional analyses of world events such as the conflict between Sandinistas and contras in Nicaragua, where he recognises the degree to which media construction has helped shape the war, but rejects the more extreme view that the war has become a purely televisual event. 'To visit Nicaragua was to be shown that the world was not television, or history, or fiction', Rushdie writes, 'The world was real, and this was its actual, unmediated reality' (JS, 135).[21]

The kinship between Bakhtin's theoretical writing about the novel and Rushdie's practice suggests an alternative means of understanding Rushdie's place in the history of the genre. I have previously argued that Rushdie is seeking to challenge the conventional novel as a form bequeathed to India by British colonialism. This is certainly one aspect of his engagement with the form; there is another sense, however, in which Rushdie's fiction does not work *against* the novel but is the very manifestation of something that the novel has always done, that, indeed, defines the novel as a genre. This argument is made possible by Bakhtin's assertion that the novel form comes into being *as an effect* of cultural hybridisation; that it: 'begins by presuming fundamentally differentiated social groups, which exist in an intense and vital interaction with other social groups'.[22] 'A sealed-off interest group, caste or class, existing within an internally unitary and unchanging core of its own', Bakhtin argues, 'cannot serve as socially productive soil for the development of the novel'. Rather, the novel, in order to emerge as a vital literary form, 'must have the sense that it is surrounded by an ocean of heteroglossia'; an effect that 'will occur only when a national culture loses its sealed-off and self-sufficient character, when it becomes conscious of itself as only one among *other* cultures and languages'.[23] According to this reading of the development of the novel, Rushdie's work, with its energising collision of cultural accents, need not be seen as a radical break in the history of the novel but as a stage in its unfolding, the meeting of cultures in the colonial act of expropriation having created further contexts within which the novel can find 'ever newer *ways to mean*'.[24]

In the late 1960s George Steiner, having announced the death of the German language, announced the death of the novel on the basis that 'The novel embodies the linguistic conventions, the psychology, the habits of sensibility, the code of erotic and economic power relations, of precisely that middle-class civilisation which is now passing'.[25] The novel flourished, Steiner records, from 1830 to 1930, between the age of Balzac and the age of Proust and Joyce, but was, by the 1960s, 'obviously over, gutted by two world wars and the decline of Europe from economic preponderance'.[26] This argument, Rushdie points out, could be made only by a man whose literary map remains an imperial one: 'Only a Western European intellectual', Rushdie writes in his 'Defence of the Novel':

> would compose a lament for an entire art-form on the basis that the literatures of, say, England, France, Germany, Spain and Italy were no longer the most interesting on earth … The half-century whose literary output proves, for Steiner … the novel's decline is also the first half-century of the post-colonial period. Might it not simply be that a new novel is emerging, a post-colonial novel, a de-centred, transitional, inter-lingual, cross-cultural novel, and that in this new world order, or disorder, we find a

better explanation of the contemporary novel's health.
(SAL, 56–7)

The radical differences between George Steiner's view of the novel and Bakhtin's will be starkly apparent. Whilst Steiner's theory of the novel locates the form in a singular moment of consciousness – that of the European bourgeoisie – and sees it as dying when that consciousness comes under threat, Bakhtin presents the novel as a product of interanimating (linguistic) consciousnesses that comes into being through the threat that is posed to a dominant ideological authority by different ways of speaking about, and conceptualising, the world. Whilst Steiner's theory of the novel thus fails to anticipate its post-colonial futures, Bakhtin's theory is *already* proleptically post-colonial because it defines the novel as hybrid in its very formal constitution. If Rushdie is *writing back* to the novel, therefore, he is not *writing back* to the novel *per se*, but only to that form of the novel that has become a falsification of the matrix of social relations that have produced him as a writer. This form of the novel, broadly, is the form against which he defines his own aesthetic: the realist text that seeks to present the illusion that there is a singular way of seeing the world that is normative and that we all share.

Biographical contexts

If the reservoir of Rushdie's imaginative resources is substantially fed by stories drawn from the complex intertextual sea of world narrative, it is also generously topped up by events taken from his own biography and family history. *Midnight's Children*, for instance, borrows extensively from Salman's early life to supply the details of Saleem's childhood; it also tells the 'family secret' that his mother had been married before and offers a fictionalised and comedic version of his father's addiction to alcohol. Likewise, *Fury*, written twenty years later, harvests Rushdie's experience of his separation from his wife Elizabeth West and young son Milan to provide the emotional intensity of the account of Malik Solanka's separation from Eleanor and Asmaan. The habit of utilising family yarns for storytelling seems to be one that Rushdie had learned from his mother, who, as he tells Ian Hamilton, was 'the keeper of the family stories' because of her 'incredible genealogical gifts'.[1] Rushdie and his sisters, he recalls, only had to ask her about an obscure and distant family member and she would, as Hamilton puts it, 'be ready with the low-down': 'She would tell you who their mother had married or who their fourth cousin was or the terrible scandal that had happened to the grandparents.'[2]

If Rushdie has taken an interest in the mundane (but never banal) details of everyday life from his mother, however, he has also taken a leaf from the storytelling books of his father, who, as he tells Hamilton, was a peddler of yarns of a different sort:

One story fell into another story. Some of them were

rooted in the 'Arabian Nights,' but he would embellish them and some he would tell straight, probably depending upon how imaginative or tired he was feeling. That they never ended is what I remember.[3]

Rushdie, we might speculate, has borrowed a little from each parent in order to create an imaginative register that draws upon experience for its raw material, but that transforms this raw material into something altogether more fantastical and bizarre. Thus, though the details of Saleem's life resemble Rushdie's in some superficial respects there are also significant differences: unlike Salman, Saleem becomes telepathically receptive to the voices of other children, lurches from dramatic crisis to dramatic crisis and, ultimately, falls victim to events that Rushdie himself (having left India for England in 1961) never experienced directly. Likewise, though Salman's grandfather like Saleem's grandfather came from Kashmir and was a doctor who trained in Germany, he, in contrast to Aadam Aziz, never married his wife after seeing her through a hole in a sheet, never lost his religion after being struck by a tussock and shedding three fairy tale drops of blood and never became involved in nationalist politics. In all cases, the autobiographical elements have been freely adapted to suit the demands of a fiction that is more concerned to use elements of fantasy to dramatise the experience of pre- and post-colonial India than it is to offer a veracious account of Rushdie's childhood.

The process Rushdie undergoes in his transformation of 'real' people into fictional characters is effectively illustrated by his use of a close friend of one of his aunts, the Urdu poet Faiz Ahmed Faiz (1911–84), as a model for the character Nadir Khan in *Midnight's Children*. The parallels between the experiences of Faiz and those attributed to Khan are fairly explicit: Khan, like Faiz, has to go into hiding because his political affiliations have made him a target of attack; Khan, like Faiz, is a Communist when this is a dangerous thing to be; and Khan, like Faiz, needs to be hidden in a cellar, the trapdoor to which is concealed under a carpet (in Faiz's case the carpet was in Rushdie's aunt's house). There are, however, two crucial and revealing differences between Faiz's experiences and those Rushdie gives to Nadir Khan. The first is a matter of timing: Faiz was forced into hiding in Pakistan because of his outspoken resistance to the idea of the separately constituted religious state *once that state had already come into being*; Khan, by contrast, is forced into hiding in India for opposing the idea of Pakistan prior to partition and its official creation. The reason Rushdie makes this change is, presumably, to do with the political focus of the novel: Rushdie in *Midnight's Children* wishes to mount a critique of the political compromises that led to the partition of India, so he pitches Faiz's political resistance to the idea of Pakistan backwards into the 1940s.

The second major difference between the Faiz that Rushdie knew as a young man and the personification of him as Nadir Khan in *Midnight's Children* is one of attitude; for where Rushdie, in his non-fictional account of Faiz, presents him as a man to be greatly admired, the fictional character of Nadir Khan in *Midnight's Children* is, in stark contrast, a ridiculous figure: a coward whose political impotence is translated into sexual impotence. Faiz, Rushdie writes, 'was the first great writer I ever met': a 'political figure and a very public writer' whose 'double-sided conception of the writer's role, part private and part public ... would ... become mine as well' (SAL, 431–2). Khan is a 'fat poet'; 'lank-haired, over-weight, [and] embarrassed' (MC, 57–8). The reasons for this transformation must, once more, be sought in Rushdie's political intentions in the novel. Faiz was a Communist who praised the Soviet Union in the era of Stalinism, and who was awarded the Lenin Peace Prize in 1963. Rushdie admired him as a writer for 'taking on the central issues of his time both inside and outside his poetry', but he did not admire him for his political allegiances. When Faiz enters *Midnight's Children*, accordingly, he enters it not as the poet who was Rushdie's friend and mentor but as a vehicle for Rushdie's potent satirical denunciation of Communism in mid-twentieth-century India. The 'true character' of Rushdie's source, we might deduce, becomes irrelevant, because in his fictional universe the political, symbolical and aesthetic functions of that character override all 'personal' considerations.

A comparable tendency seems to be at work in Rushdie's transformations of historical figures. In *Shame*, which includes Rushdie's most explicit political caricatures, the rulers of Pakistan between 1971 and 1983 – Zulfikar Ali Bhutto and Zia ul-Haq – are converted into their cartoon equivalents Iskander Harappa and Raza Hyder.[4] In making this conversion, Rushdie argues, he had no interest in presenting faithful representations of the men themselves. 'I have no way of knowing whether the personalities of Iskander and Raza are actually like those actual personalities', he told John Haffenden, 'It really wasn't my purpose to invent portraits of them' (CSR, 39). His purpose, rather, like his purpose in the case of Faiz, was to use them as figures through which the political activities that they represented could be lambasted.

The fictional procedure of converting political figures into cartoonish vehicles for satirical agendas is not, perhaps, guaranteed to make Rushdie friends in high places. Indeed, Rushdie's habit of caricaturing political figures has, to date, earned him a law suit, exclusion orders from several countries and a death sentence (if we regard the *fatwa* as, in part, a by-product of his portrait of Khomeini in *The Satanic Verses*). Controversial as Rushdie's political attacks have been, however, many would recognise that such representations are licensed (if not made unproblematic) by the conventions of satire. Applying the technique to members of your own family, by contrast, seems a more intimately exposing procedure, and much was made in the press – particularly upon the publication of *Midnight's Children* – of the adverse reactions of Rushdie's family to the novel. Rushdie initially insisted that his family understood that the characters in the books were not themselves, and told Haffenden that his mother 'could never see what the fuss was about' (CSR, 32). Fifteen years later, however, Rushdie was prepared to admit to Ian Hamilton that the family were indeed 'shocked', and that his father Anis had more or less 'disowned' him.[5] Rushdie also later admitted to upsetting his sister Sameen by telling a journalist that the incident in which a girl is subjected to a racist assault on the London Underground in *Shame* was based upon something that happened to her. '[I]t was exaggerated when it came out in the papers,' Rushdie recalls, 'and she was furious with me. I mention it in the book in the context of saying that the girl is not one girl but many, so that the instance in the book is not just my sister' (CSR, 52). Materials from reality, Rushdie implies by way of self-exculpation, achieve a different kind of representative weight when they enter into the world of fiction because they cease to be records of personal memories and become symbolic of shared social and cultural experiences.

Though his fictions often seem more autobiographically revelatory than he himself is prepared to admit, this defence does seem, in Rushdie's case, to be broadly valid. He is not a writer who uses autobiography as a means of self-exploration and personal revelation – 'confessional' writers, as they are sometimes called – but a writer who finds in autobiography points of departure for narratives with different kinds of significance. 'When I began [*Midnight's Children*]', as he told Haffenden, 'it was more autobiographical, and it only began to work when I started making it fictional. The characters came alive when they stopped being like people in my own family' (CSR, 35). The mining of Rushdie's fiction for personal references, therefore, though it has curiosity value, is not, ultimately, the most informative use that can be made of his autobiography. 'His books have a spirit of connection with real life', as Hamilton writes: 'But the spirit is mischievous. Readers who try to tease out links between Rushdie's life and Rushdie's fiction are likely to end up feeling teased.'[6] Far more useful is the understanding Rushdie's biography gives us of the cultural, social and political locations of a writer for whom such locations are crucially important. It is in this spirit that the following account is written.

On the eve of partition Salman Rushdie's parents, Anis Ahmed Rushdie and Negin Rushdie (née Butt), elected to leave Anis's home city of Delhi and move south-west to Bombay. They had decided against the journey to Pakistan being made by many other Muslims in 1947 because they, like Ahmed Sinai in *Midnight's Children*, felt 'more like Indians than Muslims' (CSR: 217–18). Anis had recognised, however, that to remain in

Delhi in 1947 would be to invite trouble since it was likely to be the front line in any potential partition disturbances. Bombay, with its 'multiplicity of commingled faiths and cultures' (IHL, 16), seemed more likely to guarantee relative safety for Muslims who chose to remain in India after the separation. Their eldest child, Ahmed Salman Rushdie, was, accordingly, born on 19 June 1947 in the city that was to become for him what London was to Dickens: a recurrent location or a nostalgic absence in all his fictions and the urban inspiration for his thematic and aesthetic celebration of 'highly spiced nonconformity' (MC, 299).

Prior to her marriage to Anis, Negin had been a school-teacher in Aligarh. She had also, as mentioned, been married before and, at some point, had changed both her names – though the details remain obscure. Anis was a businessman who had inherited much of his wealth from his father – Salman's grandfa-ther – who was a minor poet and a flourishing leather-and-cloth entrepreneur. Both Rushdie's parents were practising Muslims, but neither, as Rushdie later noted with approval, 'was insistent or doctrinaire' (IHL, 376):

> Two or three times a year, at the big Eid festivals, I would wake up to find new clothes at the foot of my bed, dress and go with my father to the great prayer-*maidan* outside the Friday Mosque in Bombay, and rise and fall with the multitude … The rest of the year religion took a back seat. I had a Christian ayah (nanny) [Mary Manezes], for whom at Christmas we would put up a tree and sing carols about baby Jesus without feeling in the least ill-at-ease. My friends were Hindus, Sikhs, Parsis, and none of this struck me as being particularly important. (IHL, 376–7)

In this liberal atmosphere Rushdie was able to familiarise himself with the tenets of the religion whilst never feeling the pull of faith too deeply. He abruptly lost all belief in God at the age of fifteen, however, and, in a scene later fictionalised in *The Satanic Verses*, ate a ham sandwich to mark the occasion. When no thunderbolt arrived to strike him down, he concluded, like many atheists before him, that God, if he had ever existed, was now dead, and that all faith in transcendental solutions should be abandoned.

> From that day to this, I have thought of myself as a wholly
> secular person, and have been drawn towards the great
> traditions of secular radicalism – in politics, socialism; in
> the arts, modernism and its offspring – that have been the
> driving forces behind much of the history of the twentieth
> century. But perhaps I write, in part, to fill up that emptied
> God-chamber with other dreams. (IHL, 377)

As this last observation might suggest, Rushdie's loss of faith in
God, does not mean that God has remained absent from his writings. On the contrary, Rushdie, despite his lack of belief, regards
Islam as his birthright, and returns repeatedly in his writing
to the narratives of Islam that have had a significant shaping
effect upon his identity. As he tells *The Far Eastern Economic
Review*:

> I have a great interest in the stories of religion, which seem
> to me to be the codes with which human beings have tried
> to understand their presence on the planet and discuss their
> moral behaviour. Obviously these are of colossal impor-
> tance as texts. But I don't subscribe to the literal truth of
> the Bible story or the Koran story or the Talmud story. My
> perspective is that of someone who takes a serious interest
> in religion without being a devout believer. (SRI, 100)

Religion, in this sense, has remained one of the constant sub-
texts of Rushdie's fiction, though his approach to matters of religion is always that of a secular thinker, seeking to understand
and interrogate, rather than affirm.

Rushdie enjoyed a privileged childhood, living in one of the
grand mansions off Warden Road ('Windsor Villa') and attending
the elite Cathedral and John Connon School – a period of his
life transmuted into fiction in the middle sections of *Midnight's
Children*. From these years date Rushdie's early, but by no
means insignificant, fictional and cultural influences. He and his
school friends went to see 'Bollywood' movies, read comic books
and pulp fiction, and bought records from the 'Rhythm House'
record store in Bombay – later a model for the 'Rhythm Centre'
in his rock 'n' roll novel *The Ground Beneath Her Feet*.

Two fictions in particular had a deep and lasting impact upon Rushdie's youthful imagination. The first was the Hollywood film *The Wizard of Oz*, which was the inspiration for his creative writing debut, aged ten, entitled 'Over the Rainbow'; the second was *The Arabian Nights*, a collection of tales that he would claim years later on the radio programme *Desert Island Discs* would be the one he would most like to have with him were he to be marooned because it 'contains all other stories'.[7]

When Salman reached thirteen his father, fondly recalling his own years in England as a student at Cambridge, decided to send him to the British public school Rugby. Already familiar with the English language and aspects of English culture as a result of his early education and early reading, Rushdie went willingly to Rugby, not quite knowing what to expect, but anticipating that England would be 'as wonderful a prospect as Oz' (SAL, 4). He was however shocked to find that many of the English considered him to be a 'wog' and, as such 'below even working-class English status'.[8] On one occasion Rushdie returned to his study to find one of the students with whom he shared a room writing 'Wogs go home' on the wall above his chair. Rushdie also recalls taking issue with a candidate in a mock school General Election who was speaking in favour of stronger immigration laws. Rushdie asked the candidate whether or not he, as a black man, would be excluded from Britain under the new controls. 'You're not black,' the student replied, 'you're a peculiar brownish colour. But yes, you too would be denied entry to this country.'[9]

These experiences at Rugby inspired Rushdie to write an autobiographical novel entitled *Terminal Report* about a schoolboy who is radicalised by his confrontation with prejudice. The novel was an immature work, but as his first substantial attempt at fiction it led him to seriously entertain the possibility of becoming a writer. Over twenty years later Rushdie would return to his Rugby days as a source of fiction in *The Satanic Verses*, which also features a protagonist who, if not-quite radicalised by his experiences, is none the less steeled for a confrontation with England and Englishness. In a memorable and much cited scene that Rushdie later argued was 'one of the few stories I've used in fiction which needed no embellishment at all',[10] his hero, Saladin Chamcha, is presented with a kipper at a school breakfast, and finds in it a metaphor for his current situation:

> He sat there staring at it, not knowing where to begin. Then he cut into it, and got a mouthful of tiny bones. And after extracting them all, another mouthful, more bones. His fellow-pupils watched him suffer in silence; not one of them said, here, let me show you, you eat it in this way. It took him ninety minutes to eat the fish and he was not permitted to rise from the table until it was done. By that time he was shaking, and if he had been able to cry he would have done so. Then the thought occurred to him that he had been taught an important lesson. England was a peculiar-tasting smoked fish full of spikes and bones, and nobody would ever tell him how to eat it. He discovered that he was a bloody-minded person. 'I'll show them all,' he swore. 'You see if I don't.' The eaten kipper was his first victory, the first step in his conquest of England. (SV, 44)

Whilst Rushdie was still at Rugby his parents, having spent two years living in London to be nearer their son (an episode fictionalised in the short story 'The Courter'), finally made the decision to move from India to Pakistan. There were a number of reasons for the move, Rushdie later explained, but prominent amongst these was the fact that the family in Bombay were beginning to suffer from anti-Muslim prejudice. 'There were questions about my family's loyalty to India: as Muslims who hadn't left', Rushdie recalls. 'There were court cases. The government took over my father's properties, as being evacué properties.'[11] In *Midnight's Children* the seizure of Rushdie's father's properties is translated into fiction when the 'freezing' of Ahmed Sinai's 'assets' results in his testicles being turned into 'little cubes of ice' – a fine example of Rushdie's habit of literalising metaphors to produce fantastical scenarios.

The young Rushdie was fiercely antagonistic to his parents' move to Pakistan. Already feeling cut off in England, he now no longer had the consolation of returning to the city of Bombay that he thought of as his home. When he heard that his father had sold Windsor Villa, he later noted, he 'felt an abyss open beneath [his] feet' (SAL, 195). This was not the last time that the ground would be removed from under Rushdie's feet, nor indeed would it be the greatest displacement that he would suffer; it was however a key stage in the process of what he would later call his 'dis-orientation': loss of the 'east'.

Rushdie's family's move from India to Pakistan is fictionalised in *Midnight's Children*, though Saleem, in the novel, is not at school in England but with the family in India. The subsequent intermittent trips that Rushdie made to visit his family in Pakistan become, in his third novel, *Shame*, the basis for the Rushdie-like narrator's experience of Pakistan as a country he has had to learn 'in slices' (S, 69). Perhaps reflecting his personal distress at his family's move (though there are also broader political motives) Pakistan, as it appears in both *Shame* and *Midnight's Children*, is a bleak and unforgiving place in contrast to the wonderfully various and endlessly recreated India. '[T]his was the difference between my Indian childhood and Pakistani adolescence', Saleem muses in *Midnight's Children*: 'in the first I was beset by an infinity of alternative realities, while in the second I was adrift, disorientated, amid an equally infinite number of falsenesses, unrealities, lies' (MC, 315).

Because of the excellence of his academic achievements at school Rushdie won a scholarship to Cambridge University. After his experiences at Rugby he was inclined to turn the scholarship down and return home (perhaps to Bombay) to write, but his father, mortified at the prospect of his son becoming a writer, insisted that he accept the scholarship; so in 1965 (assisted by the fact that Pakistan was now at war with India) Rushdie was, in his own words 'bullied' back to England (CSR, 32). Cambridge, however, turned out to be a very different experience to Rugby. Rushdie found the student body far more diverse and accepting, and quickly became assimilated into university life – most prominently by involving himself in theatre through the Cambridge Footlights Club, in which he trod the boards alongside Germaine Greer and David Hare.

At Cambridge Rushdie read history; a subject that seems to

have influenced the philosophical speculations concerning the 'objectivity' of the historical record that appear in his later fiction. On the first page of his first published fiction the character Virgil Jones is described as 'something of a historian', on the brink of making 'his rendezvous with a small historical event':

> If he had known, he would have philosophised at length about the parade of history, about the historian's inability to stand apart and watch; it was erroneous, he would have said, to look upon oneself as an Olympian chronicler; one was a member of a parade. An historian is affected by the present events that eternally recreate the past. (G, 13)

Such approaches to history appear to echo the philosophies of history that were becoming popular in academic circles during Rushdie's time at Cambridge. In 1965 Arthur Danto had published his influential *Analytic Philosophy of History* in which he had argued that our explanations of historical events depend upon the kinds of stories we are attempting to tell about those events. In 1964, similarly, W. B. Gallie, in his *Philosophy and the Historical Understanding*, had contended that 'whatever understanding and whatever explanations a work of history contains must be assessed in relation to the narrative from which they arise and whose development they subserve'.[12] These narratological constructions of history, later to be developed much more ambitiously by Hayden White in his prodigiously influential *Metahistory* (1973), seem to have informed much of Rushdie's writing, particularly his conflations of historical and fictional accounts of events, and his demonstrations of the ways in which historical processes are given meaning (and indeed change their meaning) according to the narrative structures that are used to mediate them.

Also influential for Rushdie's later career was an elective he chose for part two of his History Tripos (final honours examination) on 'Muhammad, Islam and the Rise of the Caliph'. Since only five people registered to do the course, the lecture series was cancelled, but Rushdie was eager enough to persuade his Director of Studies, Arthur Hibbert, to supervise him independently. The research Rushdie conducted for this paper was to form the basis, twenty years later, for his highly controversial fictional examination of the life of the prophet in his fourth novel *The Satanic Verses*. '[T]hat's interesting', Rushdie remembers thinking when he came across an account of the incident of the Satanic Verses: 'there's something there, you know ... [I'll] put it away in my head'.[13]

After finishing his degree at Cambridge Rushdie returned to Pakistan and started working for Pakistan's television service in Karachi. He did not feel at ease in Karachi, however, primarily because of its censorious atmosphere. A screening of Edward Albee's *Zoo Story* that he produced and acted in had to be cut because it mentioned 'pork' and referred to god as a 'coloured queen', and an article he wrote for a small magazine was suppressed, without explanation, by the press council. He soon returned to London, took British citizenship, and started to work in fringe theatre, performing in improvisatory shows such as the musical *Viet Rock* (a protest against the Vietnam war written by Megan Terry) and the multimedia rock 'n' roll extravaganza, *Rain Day Woman*, both staged at the Oval House Theatre, Kennington. Like the semi-autobiographical narrator of Rushdie's later short story 'The Harmony of the Spheres', also an Indian from Bombay who has studied at Cambridge, Rushdie, at this time of his life, sported 'a Zapata moustache and shoulder length hair' (captured in Faye Godwin's photographic portrait of him of 1975). Perhaps also like that narrator, it was at this point that Rushdie came into contact with the occult forms of knowledge that were 'part of the *zeitgeist*' in the 1960s and early 1970s and that run, like an ongoing refrain, through his subsequent novels (EW, 137).

Rushdie's career as an actor was short-lived, since he believed that he only 'had a limited future' in the profession (SAL, 108). In the early 1970s he took work as a part-time advertising copywriter for Sharp MacManus (and later Ogilvy and Mather) in order to support himself whilst he worked on a novel, 'The Book of the Pir'. This novel, a satire about a Muslim holy man (who later reappears as Maulana Dawood in *Shame*), was finished by 1973, but Rushdie decided that it was too experimental ('sub-Joyce' he called it) and put it aside to work on a book for a science fiction writing competition that Liz Calder, a friend of Rushdie and his partner, Clarissa Luard, had drawn his attention to. The resultant novel, *Grimus*, did not win the competition – one of the judges, Brian Aldiss, had liked it, but the remaining two, Kingsley Amis and Arthur C. Clark, had not. Despite this setback, however, Calder, who was working as an editor for Gollancz, persuaded the company to publish the book anyway.

Readers familiar with Rushdie's later works will not be surprised by some of the fictive preoccupations of *Grimus*. As in much of Rushdie's subsequent writing, the novel is concerned to explore themes of wandering (or migration), diasporic community, the quest for a homeland (or the fictiveness of homeland), the problem of hybridised identity and the status of the outsider in society. It is also recognisably a work by Rushdie in terms of form: the mythic coexists with the mundane, paragraphs strive to outdo one another in their capacity to accommodate a crowd of allusions and narrative effects, and many voices – none of them reliable – speak to the reader in divergent styles and manifold accents. Unlike Rushdie's later novels, however, *Grimus* also lacks many of the features that are now seen as constitutive of his writing: the unflinching (and often libellous) location in easily identifiable cultural, historical and political milieux; the persistent concern with cultural and national identity in the aftermath of empire; and – most strikingly – the interest in the forms that South Asian identity has taken in the age of mass-migration and globalisation. Partly because these elements were not present to root Rushdie's fictive playfulness in more solid contemporary concerns, *Grimus* was published in 1975 to what Liz Calder called 'unusually vitriolic' reviews.[14] David Wilson in *The Times Literary Supplement*, whilst conceding, in a kind of backhanded compliment, that it was an 'ambitious, strikingly confident' novel, condemned it, punningly, as 'fable-minded' and as 'an elaborate statement of the obvious decked out in the mannerisms of Oxford philosophy'.[15] Peter Tinniswood in *The Times* was even more scathing:

> What has he achieved? A modern Pilgrim's Progress? A knockabout odyssey? A Sci Fi bumper fun book? I do not know. I am baffled. Brian Aldiss says the author uses prose as plumage. It is hateful to be unkind to a first novel, but I suspect that under the gaudy feathers there lies a rather sickly, skinny chicken.[16]

Rushdie was understandably devastated by this reception, but such was his ambition as a writer that he determined to continue, and so started work on a new novel about the movie industry called *Madame Rama*. This was never published (Calder, to Rushdie's chagrin, turnined it down on behalf of Gollancz), though material from it has ended up in both *Midnight's Children* and *The Satanic Verses*.

On the small advance that Rushdie earned for *Grimus*, he and Clarissa Luard decided to travel to India and Pakistan. It was on this trip, according to Rushdie, that the novel *Midnight's Children* 'was … born'. 'I realised', he notes in 'Imaginary Homelands', 'how much I wanted to restore the past to myself, not in the faded greys of old family-album snapshots, but whole, in CinemaScope and glorious Technicolor' (IHL, 9–10). Rushdie worked on the novel for five years, still supporting himself through advertising. In April 1976 he married Clarissa, and in 1979 their son Zafar was born.

Midnight's Children was published in 1981 by Jonathan Cape, the publishing house to which Liz Calder had moved. As a five-hundred-page epic of twentieth-century Indian history *Midnight's Children* was not expected to do well by publishers, who tended to believe, according to Calder, 'that books on India didn't sell, and that big books on India sold worst of all' (SRI, 181). Contrary to expectations, however, *Midnight's Children* sold forty thousand copies in hardback, and received tremendous reviews. For Robert Towers in the *New York Review of Books* it was 'one of the most important [novels] to come out of the English speaking world in this generation', and V. S. Pritchett in *The New Yorker* dubbed Rushdie 'a master of perpetual storytelling'.[17] *Midnight's Children* went on to win the Booker Prize for 1981, and has since become one of the more widely read pieces of literary fiction in the world. The novel also attracted less welcome attention however. Some Muslims, in a foreshadowing of later events, were offended by satirical comments made in the novel about the Prophet Muhammad, and Indira Gandhi, India's Prime Minister, successfully sued Rushdie and his publishers because of a libellous comment it made about her. The suit was not, as might be expected, brought for Rushdie's grotesque portrayal of her as 'The Widow', nor for his accusations of election malpractice, state-organised violence and mass murder, but for a single sentence in which her son, Sanjay Gandhi ('labia lips'), accuses his mother of causing his father's death by neglecting him.[18] The Old Bailey in 1984 found in favour of Gandhi, and Rushdie and his publisher, Jonathan Cape, had to pay court costs, print an apology in *The Guardian* and remove the offending passage from subsequent editions of the novel. According to Katherine Frank in her account of the episode, 'Mr. Rushdie and Mrs. Gandhi', the fact that this accusation of libel was successful undermined the distinction between non-fiction and fiction that Rushdie was later to insist upon in the *Satanic Verses* controversy. Novels that use real names and make a clear attempt to portray real people, according to the court judgement, should be subject to the same kinds of legal restraints that govern other forms of writing such as biography and journalism.[19]

After the success of *Midnight's Children*, Rushdie started immediately on his next novel *Shame*. The book may be seen as a companion piece to *Midnight's Children* since it fiction-alises events from recent Pakistani history. Where *Midnight's Children* is diffuse in its treatment of history, however, *Shame* is telescopic, the presidencies of Zia ul-Haq and Zulfikar Ali Bhutto forming its sole subject matter. Events, moreover, are not described directly, as they are in *Midnight's Children*, but are 'translated' into fantastic allegory: Pakistan becomes not-quite-Pakistan (or Peccavistan), Bhutto becomes Iskander Harappa and General Zia becomes Raza Hyder. The reviews for *Shame* were good, and, like *Midnight's Children*, it was short-listed for the Booker Prize. This time, however, it was beaten to the prize by J. M. Coetzee's *Life and Times of Michael K*, upon which Rushdie indulged in a highly publicised sulk and accused the judges of bias. The widespread coverage of this event in the British press helped to establish the familiar characterisation of Rushdie that persists in the media to the present day: that of Rushdie the egotist, Rushdie the (in the words culled by Rushdie himself from Mary Kenny's singularly vicious attack upon him in the *Daily Mail* in 1993) 'bad-mannered, sullen, graceless, silly, curmudgeonly, unattractive, small-minded, arrogant' writer (SAL, 267). The determination with which this characterisation has been pursued in certain sections of the media makes it difficult to separate sensationalist reportage from 'reality' in representations of Rushdie. Certainly it is apparent that Rushdie is an ambitious and driven novelist who is fiercely defensive of his work and who has, as a result, alienated members of the writing community. There is little evidence, however, that the more grotesque caricatures of him have any basis in truth. Rushdie's public appearance, and accounts of him by serious journalists, reveal him to be generous-spirited, funny and engaging. The 'modish derogation' of Rushdie and his work, as John Sutherland has argued, is motivated more by journalistic cynicism than any desire to report with fidelity.[20] More provocatively, Roger Woddis adopts the voice of an imaginary detractor to imply that media antagonism towards Rushdie smacks of racism: 'I mean, they come over here and appropriate the English novel, win our literary prizes, take our women and our publisher's money. Why can't they stick to their own language?'[21]

In 1984 Rushdie visited Australia for the Adelaide literary festival and travelled across the country by car with the writer Bruce Chatwin, who was researching his novel *The Songlines*

(1987). According to Chatwin, the character Arkady in the novel was based upon Rushdie, though Rushdie, in his essay 'Travelling With Chatwin', suggests otherwise, claiming that they met 'an Australian of Russian descent' in Alice Springs 'who is a much more obvious model' (IHL, 233). Whilst in Australia Rushdie began a tumultuous affair with the travel writer Robyn Davidson, who later fictionalised him as Zac Appelfield in her novel *Ancestors* (1989). Rushdie returned the favour by transforming her into Alleluia Cone in *The Satanic Verses*. Both representations contain an admixture of affection and irritation.

Upon returning to England, Rushdie told Clarissa that he had, as she put it, met someone he liked as much as her.[22] Within a year they had sold the house they owned together in Highbury and bought separate residences. Rushdie set up home in St Peter's Street, Islington, and Davidson agreed to come to London to be with him. The relationship was not an easy one, however, and, after a further year of what Liz Calder called 'volcanic' disagreements, Davidson returned to Australia.[23] Shortly afterwards, in November 1986, Rushdie met and began a relationship with the American novelist Marianne Wiggins.

On completing *Shame* Rushdie had started work on his fourth novel, *The Satanic Verses*. But in July 1986 he interrupted the writing process to visit Nicaragua as a guest of the Sandinista Association of Cultural Workers (ASTC) – 'the umbrella organisation that brought writers, artists, musicians, craftspeople, dancers and so on, together under the same roof' (JS, 4). The occasion of his visit, Rushdie tells his readers, was the seventh anniversary of the 'triumph' of the Frente Sandinista de Liberación Nacional (Sandinista National Liberation Front) over the Somoza dictatorship.

Whilst in Nicaragua Rushdie met most of the prominent members in Daniel Ortega's left-wing government that, having been declared 'pro-Soviet' by the Reagan administration, was having to defend itself against a US-backed rebel army, the contras. Rushdie's first full-length work of non-fiction, *The*

Jaguar Smile, is the product of these meetings: 'a portrait of a moment, no more, in the life of that beautiful, volcanic country' (JS, 5). This travelogue-cum-political-treatise, as Rushdie later explained in interview, has three distinct agendas organised into an organic whole by the 'convention of a person … travelling around' (SRI, 79). Firstly, it is an 'imagistic attempt to evoke the place through a series of almost metaphorical images' (Rushdie cites, as an example, the device of Sandina turning into his hat); secondly, it is 'a more conventional kind of travel writing … with … straight-forward description of places and people'; and thirdly, it involves 'a series of set piece political encounters – interviews with leaders and opposition figures and so forth' (SRI, 79).

Rushdie's assessment of the political situation in Nicaragua is unashamedly partisan. He arrived shortly after the International Court of Justice in the Hague had ruled that US aid to the contras was in violation of international law (a judgement that the US House of Representatives had blithely ignored by granting a further $100 million worth of funds for the counter-revolution) and his analysis of the war is coloured by this event. 'The Reagan administration', he writes:

> wasn't interested in international law, at least not when its custodians found against the US. The situation was surreal: the country that was in fact acting illegally, that was the outlaw, was hurling such epithets as *totalitarian*, *tyrannous* and *Stalinist* at the elected government of a country that hadn't broken any laws at all; the bandit was posing as the sheriff. (JS, 26)

The United States, Rushdie later adds, ought to have had more sympathy with the revolutionary nationalist agenda of the Sandinistas given that it too was 'born of a revolution, and not so very long ago, at that' (JS, 52).

Rushdie's sense of the injustice of a powerful imperialist force bullying a lesser power is, he tells us, informed by his own cultural background. 'I was myself', he reflects early in the book:

the child of a successful revolt against a great power, my consciousness the product of the triumph of the Indian revolution. It was perhaps also true that those of us who did not have our origins in the countries of the mighty West, or North, had something in common – not, certainly, anything as simplistic as a unified 'third world' outlook, but at least some knowledge of what weakness was like, some awareness of the view from underneath, and of how it felt to be there, on the bottom, looking up at the descending heel. (JS, 4)

In this respect *The Jaguar Smile*, like all Rushdie's fictions, sets out to analyse (and demystify) the mechanisms of power and imperialistic control, and to investigate the processes by which individuals and communities achieve (or fail to achieve) a sense of cultural independence.

As might be anticipated, *The Jaguar Smile* inspired widely divergent responses (divided, as Ian Hamilton points out, 'along party lines').[24] Bono of U2 admired it so much that it formed the groundwork for the later friendship between Rushdie and himself. Likewise, Edward Said judged it 'a masterpiece of sympathetic yet critical reporting'. The *New Republic*, conversely, in a review that Rushdie later observed had been written by a leading member of the contras (Xavier Arguello), condemned it as 'a bad book … because of its remarkable superficiality'.[25] Arguello has some pertinent things to say about *The Jaguar Smile*. He questions, for instance, whether it is possible for an author 'to write objectively about a country one knows almost nothing about' after only a few days' visit – 'particularly when the visit has been organised by its government'.[26] He also makes some superficial assertions of his own, however, when he castigates the Sandinistas for their lack of 'progress' in Nicaragua without any mention of the role played by the contras and the US in ensuring this lack of progress, or when he describes the contras as 'fighting for democracy' whilst wilfully ignoring the fact that they were waging an undemocratic war against a constitutionally elected government.[27] More alarmingly, he offers the following bizarre half-justification for dictatorship:

Before the revolution there was a dictatorship, yes: but there was also a vital, ebullient people, replete with an inexhaustible variety of types, rogues and virtuosos, thieves and pillars of rectitude, all jostled together.[28]

Perhaps the most striking and revealing contrast in media responses to Rushdie's book is to be found between Michael Massing's article on 'Snap Books' published in *New Republic* on 4 May 1987, and Said's substantial article on 'Irangate' published in *The London Review of Books* three days later. According to Massing, Rushdie's *The Jaguar Smile* is one of a rash of publications – which also includes Joan Didion's *Salvador* – featuring big-name celebrity authors who 'parachute into a country, take a quick look around, then write an entire book about their experience'.[29] Such books, Massing adjudges, can tell readers little about the affairs of the country in question because they are primarily 'about the writer himself': 'In snap books, war and revolution serve primarily as backdrops against which star writers can shine'.[30] Said – taking, like Massing, the brevity of Rushdie's visit as premise – reaches a radically different conclusion. For Said, books like *The Jaguar Smile* represent a fledgling form of counter-politics that can provide readers with alternatives to the dominant media stereotypes peddled in the West by officially sanctioned career 'experts'. 'What we have', in books like *The Jaguar Smile*, Said argues, is:

a critical, a counter-archival, literature employing reading methods, investigative skills, and a kind of relentless erudition, unavailable to mainstream specialists – the so called area experts whose real concern is going along with the imperial idea.[31]

Two years after this lively exchange of views, in his book on *The Satanic Verses* 'affair', Daniel Pipes, director of the Foreign Policy Research Institute in Philadelphia that advises the American government's Security Council, provided a summary of all the bad reviews the book had received (in effect, those published in *New Republic*) and declared his agreement with them. *The Jaguar Smile*, he asserts, is a naive broadside against American influence in the world that proves Rushdie's 'profound polit-ical irresponsibility'.³² This observation is designed to provide further evidence for Pipe's thesis that Rushdie is 'an immature and spoiled intellectual' (by which he means left-winger) who 'despises the entire West, which for him is a place 'stuffed with money, power and things''.³³ It is worth pointing out that Pipes misquotes Rushdie here in order to overly simplify his posi-tion. In fact, Rushdie is not writing about 'hatred of the West' but about his own problematic relationship with Nicaragua as a migrant living in the West. The passage occurs at the end of *The Jaguar Smile* (not, as Pipes implies, in *The Satanic Verses*) when Rushdie bids farewell to a fellow traveller returning, like him, to Europe from South America: 'We parted in Madrid', he writes:

> and returned to our separate lives, two migrants making our way in this West stuffed with money, power and things, this North that taught us how to see from its privileged point of view. But maybe we were the lucky ones; we knew that other perspectives existed. We had seen the view from elsewhere. (JS, 137)

It is also worth bearing in mind, when reading Pipes's account of *The Jaguar Smile* (and of Rushdie's work more generally), Said's forceful critique of Pipes in 'Orientalism Reconsidered' as a neo-Orientalist commentator 'whose expertise … is wholly at the service not of knowledge but of an aggressive and inter-ventionary state – the US – whose interests Pipes helps to define'.³⁴

Rushdie himself, in his 1997 Preface to the second edition of *The Jaguar Smile*, has expressed reservations about aspects of the book:

> The whole truth would involve a clearer account of the Sandinista leadership's strange susceptibility to the lure of international celebrity; more detail about the incompe-tence of much of their bureaucracy; more criticism of their treatment of the Miskito Indians. (JS, xvi)

However, he insists that 'These are the failings of any book written quickly, and in the heat of a passion'. '[E]ven with ten years hindsight', he adds:

> I stand by the fundamental judgements and attitudes of
> *The Jaguar Smile*, and feel, if I may say so, proud of my
> younger self for taking these 'snapshots' of that beautiful,
> benighted land; for getting more things half-right than
> half-wrong. (JS, xvi)

Shortly after his return from South America, Rushdie was on
the road again, this time in India to make a documentary entitled
'The Riddle of Midnight'. The documentary, designed to mark
the fortieth anniversary of Indian Independence and his own
fortieth Birthday, was conceived as a non-fictional companion
piece to *Midnight's Children*. Forty years after Independence,
Rushdie wanted to know what the 'real-life counterparts' of the
magical Midnight's Children (those born in 1947) were doing
and what they thought Independent India had become as it
entered its fifth decade (IHL, 26). Rushdie could hardly have
chosen a more difficult time for this retrospective, since it came
less than a year after a high court judgement had seemed to
permit extremist Hindus to occupy the Babri Masjid mosque at
Ayodha. The occupation of the mosque had sparked widespread
communal violence across India, with the result that what
Rushdie found when he returned to the country of his birth
was 'The politics of religious hatred' (IHL, 27). After this trip
Rushdie was not to return to India for thirteen years, so when he
came to fictionalise his home city of Bombay in his 1995 novel
The Moor's Last Sigh it was to this darker, more fractured, more
pessimistic vision that he reverted.

Back in London, in January 1988, Rushdie and Marianne
Wiggins married. The couple settled down in his Islington home
– Rushdie returning to *The Satanic Verses*, Marianne Wiggins
writing *John Dollar*. Both novels were completed in the same
week, Rushdie dedicating *The Satanic Verses* 'For Marianne' (a
dedication removed in later editions for her safety), Wiggins
dedicating *John Dollar* 'for beloved Salman'.[35]

Between his completing the first draft of *The Satanic Verses*
and the final version, Rushdie's father, Anis, died of cancer. This
event prompted Rushdie to change the ending of the novel so
that the character Saladin Chamcha, who had originally returned

to India too late for a reconciliation with his dying parent, now managed to return in time for a death-bed scene (SRI, 105). The result of this last-minute change is one of the most emotionally charged sequences in Rushdie's writing, which more commonly maintains a satirical distance from its material.

The impact of the death of Rushdie's father also seems to have carried over into his following two fictions. *Haroun and the Sea of Stories*, Rushdie's novel for children, was written for his son Zafar from whom events had separated him, but the central relationship between a storyteller and his son also recalls the relationship between Rushdie and his own father. When Rushdie began his next 'big grown up novel', *The Moor's Last Sigh*, moreover, he told Suzie Mackenzie that he 'found himself going back to where he had ended years ago, to the death scene between father and son' (SRI, 184). 'Something had happened there', he reflects, 'Some impulse 'to let more emotion in'' (SRI, 184). Between the publication of *The Satanic Verses* and the publication of *The Moor's Last Sigh*, however, many other things had occurred to change the shape of Rushdie's life.

The Satanic Verses went on sale in Britain on 26 September 1988, having been auctioned to Viking-Penguin for $850,000 by Rushdie's new agent Andrew Wylie (Calder had been unceremoniously sacked). The novel is predominantly about the experiences of Indian and Afro-Caribbean migrants living in London, but it also includes several dream sequences concerning the life of the Prophet Muhammad and the nature of religious revelation. These scenes – particularly a scene in which a group of prostitutes in a brothel impersonate the wives of Muhammad to titillate customers – led to protests by some Muslim readers and reviewers, which were noted by the Indian government, who promptly banned the book (Rajiv Gandhi's Congress-I Party was facing an election and did not wish to risk losing the Muslim vote). Other nations with significant Muslim populations also made moves to ban the book – including Pakistan, Saudi Arabia, Egypt, Indonesia and South Africa. Several Indian publishers and booksellers protested against these acts of censorship, as did PEN international and the Index on Censorship. Rushdie himself wrote a letter of protest to the Indian Prime Minister in which he argued that freedom of expression ought to be at the foundation of any democracy, and pointed out that the 'offensive' sequence concerning Muhammad 'happened in a dream, the fictional dream of a fictional character, an Indian movie star, who is losing his mind'.[36] The ban was not revoked, however, and by now, some Muslim groups in Britain had started mobilising against the book. Dr Syed Pasha, as Secretary of the Union of Muslim Organisations in Britain, initiated a campaign to have the novel banned in the UK and demanded that the British government prosecute Rushdie. Mrs Thatcher's government declined on the basis that 'people who act within the law should be able to express their opinions freely' and (more problematically) that the British laws on blasphemy applied only to Christianity.[37] Several demonstrations were then staged by outraged Muslims and in Bradford, Bolton and then Hyde Park copies of *The Satanic Verses* were publicly burned – an act of spectacular, and highly evocative, protest that promptly made what was becoming known as the Rushdie 'Affair' headline news across the globe. Rushdie declared himself to be deeply distressed by these demonstrations, not only because of their challenge to basic freedoms but also because they were made by the very immigrant groups about whose experiences he felt himself to be writing: 'to be rejected and reviled by, so to speak, one's own characters', as Rushdie later wrote, 'is a shocking and painful experience' (IHL, 395). There was perhaps some limited consolation to be found in the fact that *The Satanic Verses* was now selling so well that Penguin were planning to print more copies to keep up with demand. The book had also become an international talking point in the way that no other book has before or since, precipitating arguments concerning the nature and bounds of free speech in sensitive, multicultural environments. Had such arguments remained academic or intellectual, such a debate might have proved constructive, no matter how vocal and fraught. Unfortunately, however, Rushdie, his family, his publishers and bookshops that stocked his books had all been threatened with violence, and, early in 1989, Rushdie received the distressing news that five demonstrators against his novel had been killed in clashes with the police in Pakistan. 'I feel completely horrified' Rushdie told a reporter, 'the worst thing of all is that what they say about the book has nothing to do with what I wrote'.[38] The worst was yet to come, however, when the Ayatollah Khomeini of Iran issued a *fatwa* (a decree) that demanded the execution of Rushdie and his publishers. The *fatwa* was read on Radio Tehran on Valentine's Day 1989. 'In the name of God Almighty', Khomeini declared:

> I would like to inform all the intrepid Muslims in the world that the author of the book entitled *The Satanic Verses*, which has been compiled, printed and published in opposition to Islam, the Prophet and the Koran, as well as those publishers who were aware of its contents, have been sentenced to death. I call on all zealous Muslims to execute them quickly, wherever they find them, so that no one will dare to insult the Islamic sanctions. Whoever is killed on this path will be regarded as a martyr, God willing.[39]

The following day, an Iranian cleric, Hassan Sanei of the 15-Khordad Foundation, seconded the Ayatollah's demand by placing a bounty on Rushdie's head: $2.6 million for an Iranian to kill Rushdie, $1 million for anyone else. That day Rushdie was due to attend a memorial service for his friend Bruce Chatwin, who had died of an AIDS-related illness. After some consideration Rushdie decided to keep his appointment, pursued by the world's media, but this was to be the last public appearance Rushdie was to be able to make for several years. The service completed, (and with Paul Theroux's black joke – 'you're next Salman' – to ease him on his way) Rushdie went into hiding, protected by British Special Branch Police. A few days later, after encouragement by the British government who were anxious about the safety of British hostages held in the Lebanon, Rushdie assented to the Iranian President Ali Khameini's request for an apology, and agreed to a cautiously worded statement, largely scripted by John Lyttle, the Archbishop of Canterbury's adviser on the hostage case. The statement read:

> As author of *The Satanic Verses* I recognise that Muslims
> in many parts of the world are genuinely distressed by the
> publication of my novel. I profoundly regret the distress
> that publication has occasioned to sincere followers of
> Islam. Living as we do in a world of many faiths this
> experience has served to remind us that we must all be
> conscious of the sensibilities of others.[40]

The Ayatollah's response was less cautious: 'Even if Salman
Rushdie repents and becomes the most pious man of time, it is
incumbent on every Muslim to employ everything he has got,
his life and his wealth, to send him to hell.'[41]

The diplomatic situation, meanwhile, was worsening. Twelve
European nations withdrew their ambassadors from Tehran on 20
February in protest against the *fatwa*, and, in subsequent days,
the United States, Canada, Australia and Brazil all demonstrated
their support for the move. The violence continued: twelve further
people were killed in rioting in Bombay, Rushdie's birthplace; two
bookstores in Berkeley, California (Cody's and Waldenbooks),
were firebombed; and two liberal Muslim clerics were murdered
in Brussels for protesting against the *fatwa*. In the following
years, amongst many more acts of injury, the Italian translator
of *The Satanic Verses*, Ettoro Capriolo, would be subjected to a
knife attack (3 July 1991), Professor Hitoshi Igarashi, the Japa-
nese translator of *The Satanic Verses*, would be stabbed to death
(11 July 1991), and Rushdie's Norwegian publisher William
Nygaard would be shot twice in the back (11 October 1993).
Nygaard, who survived against the odds, later observed, with
admirable stoicism, that being shot had been uncomfortable, but
that he was proud to be the publisher of *The Satanic Verses*. In
his book *The Price of Free Speech*, which collects together his
various statements about the 'affair' he adds that:

> My own attitude and that of others are not founded on
> courage, heroism or valour. Any Norwegian publisher
> would have done the same in the Rushdie affair. There
> is no alternative. Any alternative would undermine our
> whole tradition as guarantors of freedom of expression, a
> principle which Norwegian publishers have stood by for
> decades.[42]

The response from the literary and creative community was generally favourable to Rushdie – concerned as it was to defend the freedoms of writers and artists. Frances d'Souza and Carmel Bedford founded the International Committee for the Defence of Salman Rushdie and his Publishers (ICDSR), Tariq Ali and Howard Brenton rapidly wrote a one-act play, *Iranian Nights*, expressing their 'solidarity' with a 'brother author',[43] Harold Pinter organised a delegation of writers to march to Downing Street, and other writers – including Anthony Burgess, Wole Soyinka, Susan Sontag, Thomas Pynchon, Chinua Achebe, Anita Desai, Hanif Kureishi, Derek Walcott and Naguib Mahfouz (who himself received death threats) – publicly wrote and spoke out in support of Rushdie and his work. So many writers, indeed, were prepared to speak out in defence of Rushdie that in 1992 the German newspaper *Die Tageszeitung* 'was able to lead a consortium of newspapers in publishing a series of letters from eminent writers' – subsequently collected by the ICDSR as *The Rushdie Letters*.[44]

There were some dissenting voices from the creative community, however. At one extreme, the singer-turned-Islamic-convert Yusuf Islam (Cat Stevens) appeared to make the suggestion in a television interview that Rushdie should be burned to death. More moderately, Roald Dahl dismissed Rushdie as 'a dangerous opportunist', and both John le Carré and John Berger (the latter to Rushdie's great surprise) suggested that Rushdie should agree to the withdrawal of the book in order to protect publishers, booksellers and members of the general public who were now under increased threat from terrorism. The majority of booksellers, it seems, were not in agreement with them – a survey of American Booksellers showed that most were 'anxious to have a paperback version to sell ... for the principle as for the potential profit',[45] and a *Sunday Times* survey of a hundred bookshops in Britain showed that 57 believed that a paperback version of *The Satanic Verses* should be published whilst only 27 did not.[46]

Rushdie himself, in the early days of the *fatwa* remained relatively quiet – arguing later that he had done so, against his own nature, because he felt that his voice was 'simply not loud enough to be heard above the clamour of voices raised against [him]' (IHL, 393). His first substantial comment came in the extended essay published in the *Independent on Sunday* on 4 February 1990, 'In Good Faith', in which he defended *The Satanic Verses* as 'a love-song to our mongrel selves' and rejected the responses of 'the apostles of purity' who claim 'to possess a total explanation' (IHL, 394). He also posed, and answered for himself, the question that discussions of *The Satanic Verses* were increasingly turning upon

> What is freedom of expression? Without the freedom to offend it ceases to exist. Without the freedom to challenge, even to satirise, all orthodoxies, even religious orthodoxies, it ceases to exist. Language and the imagination cannot be imprisoned, or art will die, and with it, a little of what makes us human. *The Satanic Verses* is, in part, a secular man's reckoning with the religious spirit. It is by no means always hostile to the faith … the novel does contain doubts, uncertainties, even shocks that may well not be to the liking of the devout. Such methods have, however, long been a legitimate part even of Islamic literature. (IHL, 396)

Rushdie's second substantial comment on the *Satanic Verses* affair came a couple of days later, on 6 February 1990, when Harold Pinter delivered, on his behalf, the Herbert Read Memorial Lecture at London's Institute of Contemporary Arts. This lecture, entitled 'Is Nothing Sacred?', continues Rushdie's contemplation of the importance of free speech by considering whether or not 'the idea of the absolute freedom of the imagination' should be the one idea that is held to be 'sacred', 'holy' – beyond interrogation (IHL, 418). Tempting though this prospect is, however, Rushdie concludes that he cannot bear the idea of even the writer 'as secular prophet':

> Literature is an interim report from the consciousness of the artist, and so it can never be 'finished' or 'perfect' … The only privilege literature deserves – and this privilege it requires in order to exist – is the privilege of being the arena of discourse, the place where the struggle of languages can be acted out. (IHL, 427)

In later commentary on the affair Rushdie has elaborated these ideas, insisting repeatedly upon the need for the freedom to offend. *'The point,'* he writes in a 1999 newspaper column, *'is to defend people but not their ideas'*:

> It is absolutely right that Muslims – that everyone – should enjoy freedom of religious belief in any free society. It is absolutely right that they should protest against discrimination whenever and wherever they experience it. It is also absolutely wrong of them to demand that their belief-system – that any system of belief or thought – should be immunised against criticism, irreverence, satire, even scornful disparagement. (SAL, 324, Rushdie's italics).

The freedom to offend, Rushdie goes on to suggest, is an essential aspect of a free society. He even goes so far as to imply that causing offence itself produces freedom: 'Democracy can only advance through the clash of ideas, can only flourish in the rough-and-tumble bazaar of disagreement' (SAL, 325). This is an idea formulated for an earlier period by the French writer and satirist Voltaire, and Rushdie, accordingly, sees himself as an intellectual descendent of Voltaire. Blasphemy, he explains to Satoshi Yanai in interview:

> is a way of talking about a religious subject that is not approved of by religious orthodoxy … throughout human history that has been the way philosophy and philosophical thought have progressed. The European enlightenment was full of blasphemers; Voltaire was a blasphemer; it would have been impossible to think a new thought if one only accepted the view of religious orthodoxy. (SRI, 111)

The result of such thinking, as Rushdie had found to his cost, is a form of literature that is in danger of bringing down upon the head of its author the wrath of those forms of official thinking that it sets out to oppose. Voltaire was imprisoned in the Bastille then driven into exile, and Rushdie was forced into hiding. But such dire consequences for the author are worthwhile, Rushdie suggests, if we regard literature as a politicised form of expression the function of which is 'to try to increase the sum of what it is possible to say and what it is possible to think' (SRI, 160).

'Who wants safe books?' as Rushdie asks Jeremy Isaacs in a mulish temper: 'I wouldn't read one – wouldn't want to write one' (SRI, 160).

Perhaps the lowest point, for Rushdie in his time of hiding, came at the end of 1990 and the start of 1991 as the world started to forget about his plight, even though the threats were very much current. Britain, he felt, was prepared to renew relations with Iran because armament deals were being weighed in the balance against him, and his marriage to Marianne Wiggins, never especially secure, had broken up. '[D]ispirited and demoralised, feeling abandoned … I faced my deepest grief', Rushdie wrote in his essay 'One Thousand Days in a Balloon' (IHL, 434). It was in this state of mind that he decided to attempt to 'make [his] peace with Islam, even at the cost of [his] pride' by speaking the Muslim creed before witnesses (IHL, 435–6). His intention in so doing, he claimed, was to re-identify himself with – and enable himself to speak to – 'the broad community of British Asians, and the broader community of Indian Muslims' (IHL, 434–5) – but inevitably the gesture was seen as conciliation and cowardice by some of his supporters, and as insincere by his detractors (the Iranian newspaper *Jomhuri Eslamias* conceded that Rushdie's return to Islam might be a sign of bravery, but recommended that 'he show greater bravery and prepare himself for death').[47] '[M]y fantasy of joining the fight for the modernisation of Muslim thought, for freedom from the shackles of the Thought Police,' Rushdie concluded, 'was stillborn. It never really had a chance. Too many people had spent too long demonizing or totemizing me to listen seriously to what I had to say' (IHL, 436). Instead he determined to strive to keep a firm hold on the worldview which all his writing to that date had served to define:

> I must cling with all my might to that chameleon, that chimera, that shape-shifter, my own soul; must hold on to its mischievous, iconoclastic, out-of-step clown-instincts, no matter how great the storm. And if that plunges me into contradiction and paradox, so be it; I've lived in that messy ocean all my life. I've fished in it for my art. This turbulent sea was the sea outside my bedroom window

in Bombay. It is the sea by which I was born, and which I
carry within me wherever I go. (IHL, 438–9)

Rushdie's characterisation of his artistic inspiration as a 'messy
ocean' brings to mind the symbolism of his children's fiction
Haroun and the Sea of Stories, and emphasises the extent to
which this novella also operates as a kind of fictional defence of
his own writing. *Haroun and the Sea of Stories* was based upon
narratives that Rushdie had invented for his son during bathtime
storytelling sessions several years earlier, but it was written down
and formalised during the time that Rushdie spent being shuttled
from safe house to safe house by Special Branch police. Inevitably
these experiences have left their imprint upon the text. On a
practical level, *Haroun* became a means for Rushdie to connect
to his son at a time when they had been forcibly separated from
one another ('Read, and bring me home to you', is the last line of
the dedicatory acrostic). On a more allegorical level, Rushdie also
uses the fantasy of *Haroun* as a way of responding to his detractors by indirect means – celebrating storytelling and its freedoms,
and condemning censorious persecutors (Khattam Shud) who
unleash the forces of oppression against the creative artist.

Alongside this fictional examination of his current position,
Rushdie also, in his early years of hiding, made non-fictional
records of his experiences. In 1991 he published his first collection of essays, *Imaginary Homelands*, which included the
important defences of *The Satanic Verses* 'In Good Faith', 'Is
Nothing Sacred?' and 'One Thousand Days in a Balloon'. He
also kept a daily journal of events, which he told a number of
interviewers would one day form the basis of a non-fictional
work about the affair. No such work has yet appeared, though
Rushdie has included a substantial selection of his non-fictional
writings from these years – 'The Plague Years' – in his second
collection of essays, *Step Across This Line* (2002).

The year 1993 brought some consolations for Rushdie.
Midnight's Children won the 'Booker of Bookers' – the book
judged to be the best of all the winners in the prize's twenty-
five year history. Equally importantly, so far as Rushdie was
concerned, a book appeared in France entitled *Pour Rushdie*

(For Rushdie), which contained a hundred essays by Arab and Muslim writers defending free speech and his right to publish *The Satanic Verses*. In the 'Publisher's Statement' to the English translation of this book issued the following year, George Braziller argues that the writers of the volume aim to contest the *fatwa* of Khomeini by asserting that 'to condemn any writer to death for his ideas is intolerable and constitutes a disgrace both to the nation that they love and to the tolerant religion that has collectively nourished them for centuries'.[48] Braziller also lists the names of other Muslim and Arab writers who have been murdered or are under threat of death and torture for their writings, and suggests that the book is for them as well as Rushdie. *For Rushdie* is an important reminder that throughout the affair many Muslims opposed the *fatwa*. On 19 February 1989, six days after the declaration of the *fatwa*, a hundred intellectuals from Arabic and Islamic countries assembled in Human Rights Square in Paris to demonstrate against it; on 23 February eighty prominent British Asians, including some Muslims, signed a statement defending Rushdie and deploring the book burnings; in May 1989 the Muslim 'Women Against Fundamentalism' group was founded in Britain and declared its opposition to the suppression of *The Satanic Verses*; and on 2 June 1993, 127 Iranian artists and intellectuals, at great risk to themselves, signed an appeal in which they:

> unanimously raise[d their] voices in order to support Salman Rushdie, and … remind everyone that writers, artists, journalists and thinkers in Iran are daily undergoing censorship and that the number of Iranians who have already been imprisoned, or even executed, on the charge of 'blasphemy' is far from negligible.[49]

On the international scene, the situation also seemed to be improving for Rushdie. He had visited, and received promises of support (ranging from the lukewarm to the enthusiastic) from political figures in Spain, Norway, Germany and Sweden. In December 1992 the premier of Ontario, Bob Rae, had become 'the first head of any government to stand with [Rushdie] in public' (SAL, 247), and the following January President

Clinton's administration in the United States issued a 'very strong statement' in Rushdie's support that prepared the way for a meeting between Rushdie and Clinton in the White House on 24 November 1993. This Rushdie regarded as 'the most important moment of the campaign' since it was the first time that the American government had been explicit in his defence (SRI, 141–2).

For the following five years, however, Rushdie was to remain under substantial police protection, making only sporadic and highly managed public appearances. During this time he started to use his new-found public profile to defend other persecuted writers, and to condemn acts of violence committed by terrorist groups or tyrannical regimes around the world. He also returned to fiction-writing on a more consistent basis. In 1994 a collection of short stories appeared entitled *East, West* that gathered together material, some of which was as old as *Midnight's Children* (the first three narratives), some of which was new (the last three narratives). The collection contains some less successful work, such as the Shandyesque 'experimental' narrative 'Yorick' (Rushdie's own description of his first fictional attempts as 'sub-Joyce' springs to mind). But it also contains some of Rushdie's warmest and most engaging writings. The semi-autobiographical pieces 'The Harmony of the Spheres' and 'The Courter' both exhibit plenty of what *The Bookseller* refers to as 'human sympathy ... wit and lightness of touch' (qualities Rushdie's work is not automatically associated with) (CSR, 163).

East, West is organised into three parts: narratives about the 'East', narratives about the 'West', and hybridised fictions that explore the meeting of the two. The tripartite nature of this collection, as Rushdie points out, is reflected in the title, which contains 'East' and 'West' but also links them with a comma. '[T]he most important part of the title was the comma,' Rushdie explains, 'Because it seems to me that I am that comma – or at least that I live in the comma' (CSR, 163).

East, West was received well by a literary world eager for insights into how Rushdie's writing had been affected by the *fatwa*. 'The publication of *East, West*', Claire Messud wrote in

The Guardian, 'surely heralds the time for the public to step back and start reading again, and to remember that this man is an eminent artist rather than merely a political pawn'.[50] Rushdie regarded these short stories, however, like his journalism and like his children's fiction, as 'chamber music ... not the full orchestra' (SRI, 195). The full-orchestra would tune up again for Rushdie with the publication of his next major novel, *The Moor's Last Sigh,* in 1995.

The political breakthrough, for Rushdie, came in the summer of 1997 when Muhammed Khatami, a moderate cleric, was elected to the presidency of Iran, and set about trying to improve relations with Europe and America in the hope that Iran would be able to benefit from the lucrative trade agreements from which its pariah status had excluded it. This desire, combined with the West's eagerness to share in the profits from the new oil and gas reserves found in Iran, led to a renewed impetus, from both sides, to find a solution to the Rushdie affair. On 14 February 1998, on the ninth anniversary of the *fatwa,* the British Prime Minister Tony Blair met with Rushdie officially and made a public declaration of his government's support for his cause. The following week Rushdie met with the Foreign Secretary, Robin Cook, who urged Iran, on behalf of the European Union, to respect international law and abandon the death sentence. Seven months later, on 24 September, after extended negotiations, Iran's Foreign Minister, Kamal Kharrazi, met with Robin Cook, announced publicly that Iran did not intend to pursue the death sentence imposed by Khomeini, and disassociated his government from 'any reward which has been offered in this regard'.[51]

Whilst the assurance that the Iranian government did not intend to pursue the assassination of Rushdie was not new (the Iran government had, apparently, been assuring British diplomats for years that it did not intend to fulfil the *fatwa*), the publicity with which this assurance was made and the additional dissociation of the Iranian government from the bounty money were original developments. The Iranian government, it was understood, had no power to annul the *fatwa,* since it had been made by a religious figure whose word could not be gainsaid. The fact that a moderate government was prepared to distance itself from the religious hard liners in this way, however, was enough to satisfy the British government and Rushdie's supporters, who saw that to insist upon any more forceful and absolute rejection of the *fatwa* would compromise the efforts being made by Iran's new moderate government to resolve the affair without inflaming radical opinion. Radical opinion, inevitably, was inflamed. Two weeks after the Iranian government's statement on the *fatwa*, an extremist group of Iranian militants (the Association of Hizbullah Students at Tehran University) rejected the declaration, and announced a fresh bounty of £200,000 for Rushdie's murder. A *fatwa*, according to these hard-liners, was not revocable, and could not, in the words of one senior Iranian cleric, Ayatollah Muhammad Fazel-Lankarami, be 'subjected to the mundane demands of foreign policy'. 'All Muslims', he added, 'are duty-bound to execute the sentence against the apostate Rushdie, even if the government is not inclined to do so'.[52] Despite such declarations however, which are still in force, and despite the continuing risk to Rushdie from 'freelance' terrorists, Tehran's official disavowal of the *fatwa* was deemed sufficient for Rushdie to come out of hiding, and for the ICDSR to be disbanded on 19 October 1998. Since 1998 Rushdie has been able to conduct a more high-profile public life – and in April 2000 he was finally able to make his first trip to India since 1987, described movingly in his essay 'A Dream of Glorious Return' (SAL, 195–227).

Unsurprisingly, the concerns of Rushdie's post-*fatwa* fiction have been partially shaped by his experiences. This is most explicit in his first major novel written after the *fatwa*, *The Moor's Last Sigh*, which opens with its central character and narrator, Moraes Zogoiby, 'On the run', fleeing 'death under the cover of darkness' having endured extreme, life-threatening events (MLS, 3). When Moraes is cast out by his family, arrested for murder and consigned without hope to the grimly depicted Bombay Central jail it is not difficult to hear an echo, in his reflections, of Rushdie's own state of mind:

had I slipped accidentally from one page, one book of life
on to another – in my wretched disorientated state, had
my reading finger perhaps slipped from the sentence of
my own story on to this other, outlandish, incomprehen-
sible text that had been lying, by chance, just beneath? ...
A door – a whole life, a whole way of understanding life
– closed behind me. I stood in darkness, lost ... Something
– a defilement – had begun. (MLS, 285–6)

Likewise, when the artistic reputation of Moraes's mother the
painter, Aurora Zogoiby, is damaged as a result of sustained ideologically driven criticism, it is apparent that Rushdie is, on one
level, venting his anger at those who have similarly 'distracted
attention from the body of [his] real work' (MLS, 234). 'How
easily', Aurora laments, 'a self, a lifetime of work and action and
affinity and opposition, could be washed away under such an
attack!' (MLS, 234).

The novel is not simply reflective of Rushdie's disrupted
life experience, however, but also operates, like *Haroun and the
Sea of Stories*, as an assertive and self-empowering response to
persecution. This assertiveness is apparent in Rushdie's refusal
to shy away from controversy – vividly embodied in the novel's
unafraid and forceful critique of Hindu fundamentalist politics
in India – and in his stubborn refusal to be intimidated. 'By
embracing the inescapable', as Moraes tells us, 'I lost my fear
of it':

I'll tell you a secret about fear: it's an absolutist. With fear,
it's all or nothing. Either, like any bullying tyrant, it rules
your life with a stupid blinding omnipotence, or else you
overthrow it, and its power vanishes in a puff of smoke.
(MLS, 164)

'And another secret', he adds, in what appears to be a response
to accusations made by Marianne Wiggins in the press that
Rushdie had not behaved like 'the bravest man in the world'
(and whose inexplicable betrayal is mediated throughout via the
character of Uma):

the revolution against fear, the engendering of that tawdry
despot's fall, has more or less nothing to do with 'courage'.

It is driven by something much more straightforward: the simple need to get on with your life. I stopped being afraid because, if my time on earth was limited, I didn't have seconds to spare for funk. (MLS, 164)

Rushdie's seventh novel, *The Ground Beneath Her Feet*, further explores the effects of the *fatwa*, not least because it begins with a life-changing, world-reshaping earthquake on Valentine's Day 1989: the day the Ayatollah's decree was issued. *The Ground Beneath Her Feet* also registers the impact of the *fatwa* upon Rushdie's life in more indirect ways since it concentrates not on persecution and political violence but upon the experience of new-found (and not entirely desired) global celebrity. One of the consequences of the *fatwa*, as Martin Amis famously quipped, was that the Rushdie he knew 'had vanished into the front page'.[53] In the longer aftermath of the *fatwa*, D. T. Max observed in *The New York Times*, Rushdie executed another disappearing act, this time into the gossip columns.[54] Evidence for this development is not hard to find: the break-up of Rushdie's marriage to Elizabeth West, his partner since 1989 and his wife since 1997, and his elopement with and subsequent marriage to Padma Lakshmi, an actress and model half his age, received substantial press coverage, often in papers that do not customarily show an interest in literary fiction.

Typically for Rushdie, these developments are not ignored in his writing, but are subjected to sustained analysis. *The Ground Beneath Her Feet* engages in an analysis of the experience of media celebrity by following the fortunes of two Indian-born rock stars as they scale heights of fame that recall those reached by Madonna, Lady Diana and U2. Rushdie's subsequent novel, *Fury*, likewise engages in an examination of the consequences of global celebrity, although in this case Rushdie turns his attention away from mega-stardom towards the more idiosyncratic brand of cult celebrity achieved by its protagonist, Malik Solanka, who is clearly analogous to Rushdie himself.

Another much publicised development in Rushdie's affairs of the late 1990s was his move from Britain to the United States. During the writing of *The Ground Beneath Her Feet* Rushdie had been staying in London but 'Summering' in the Hamptons, Long Island. In 1999, however, Rushdie made the decision to move to America on a permanent basis. His reasons for the move had to do, in part, with his lingering resentment over the treatment he received from the British media during and after the 'Affair', but it was also the result of a developing love of New York, which appealed to Rushdie, because it, like the first city with which he fell in love, Bombay, was bustling, noisy and gave him 'the sense of being in a place where a lot of people had a lot of stories not unlike mine':

> Everybody comes from somewhere else. Everyone's got a Polish grandmother, some kind of metamorphosis in their family circumstances. That's a very big thing – the experience of not living where you started. It changes you in all kinds of ways.[55]

This shift to America is paralleled by a shift in the locations of Rushdie's fiction. *The Ground Beneath Her Feet* – written in both America and England – is a transitional novel in this respect, since it charts Rushdie's long journey from Bombay to London to New York: a triangle of cities that Rushdie regards as central to the structure of the novel, as well as to the structure of his own life (SRI, 283). This transition achieved, *Fury*, Rushdie's eighth novel, moves wholesale to Manhattan.

Reviews for *Fury* have been amongst the most lukewarm Rushdie has received since the publication of his first novel *Grimus*. At one extreme, and in a series of breathtaking generalisations, Matt Thorne in *The Independent* saw *Fury* as an opportunity to dismiss Rushdie's entire oeuvre. 'Rushdie has always been a sloppy writer', he 'argues', and *Fury* provides only 'pages and pages of the sort of gibberish that has been a part of Rushdie's writing since his novel, the execrable *Grimus*'. '[A]fter three major duds in a row,' the article concludes, 'it must be time for his relegation from the premier league'.[56] Justly incensed by the banality of such critical judgements, John Sutherland in *The Guardian*, having lamented Thorne's resort to football metaphors, condemns the 'concerted malice' of British reviewers and asserts that

Rushdie's ability honestly to pursue his trade has been damaged. Unfairly damaged. He deserves better from us. Supposing he had been abducted by fanatics after *The Satanic Verses*, and publicly beheaded in Tehran. What would the judgement have been? Adonais is gone – our greatest novelist, cut off in his prime. Now, apparently, he's a second division dud. But let's behead him just the same. It makes such wonderful copy. Shame on you, British book trade, shame on you British reviewers.[57]

Whilst Sutherland's reminder of Rushdie's importance as a novelist is welcome, however, his assumption that poor reviews of *Fury* are an exclusively British phenomenon is flawed. Charles Foran in the *Far Eastern Economic Review* calls it a 'slapdash attempt at the Great American Novel' and David Gates in *Newsweek* takes Rushdie to task for his 'terminally stinky prose'.[58] Perhaps the most balanced and clear-sighted reception of *Fury* comes from Boyd Tonkin in *The Independent*, who argues that, though the novel may not be Rushdie's best, he 'would rather read one page of flawed Rushdie than 1,000 of the soporific pap that often passes for 'literary fiction' in Britain today'. 'Even at his worst,' Tonkin adds, 'Rushdie will wake you up; even at their best, many of his politer peers will send you fast into a dreamless, idea-free sleep'.[59] *Fury*, to second Tonkin's view, has its weak moments, notably its depiction of Neela and its unpersuasive representation of a Pacific island revolution. But it also contains some of the best passages of writing that Rushdie has yet produced – notably, his Apuleian satire on contemporary America.

Given Rushdie's long history of transposing people of his acquaintance into his fiction, it is surprising that a number of critics found it worthy of remark that his current wife, Padma Lakshmi, is used as a model for Neela in *Fury*. Clarissa Luard, wife number one, appears, as Pamela Lovelace in *The Satanic Verses*. Marianne Wiggins, wife number two, appears as Uma in *The Moor's Last Sigh*, and her early life in America (as the daughter of a fundamentalist preacher who committed suicide) provides the basis for the childhood of Vina in *The Ground*

Beneath Her Feet. Likewise, *Fury* contains a representation of wife number three, Elizabeth West, (and child number two) in the personas of Eleanor and Aasman. What was new about the depiction of Padma in *Fury* – some of these reviewers argued – was that it was overly worshipful, and that the portrait of her was undigested: 'Neela seems so obviously based on the author's girlfriend, even down to a scar on her arm, [that] it is tempting to think of *Fury* as another accident caused by her astounding beauty', quipped Toby Clements in *The Times*.[60] A useful corrective to these arguments, however, is, once more, provided by Tonkin in *The Independent*, who reminds us that Rushdie is simply doing what he has always done. 'The critics who accuse Rushdie of penning a thinly veiled memoir and flaunting the traffic-stopping loveliness of his heroine', he writes, 'don't appear to have read the end. In the finale of *Fury*, Neela becomes a fanatical guerrilla leader in a South Pacific ethnic war, plainly based on Fiji's.' 'So far as I can tell', Tonkin adds:

> Ms Lakshmi has no immediate plans to quit the catwalk for the barracks. The truth is that for Rushdie, as for many other modern writers, chunks and fragments of autobiography join the rich mix of sources that ferment behind this or any novel.[61]

The United States publication of *Fury* coincided with the September 11 2001 terrorist attacks on the World Trade Center. This led Rushdie to claim that it was the only novel in the history of writing that had become 'out of date' at the same moment it was published, since that event had changed the world about which he was writing.[62] 'Like every writer in the world', Rushdie claimed, he is now 'trying to find a way of writing after 11 September 2001, a day that has become something like a borderline' (SAL, 436). Rushdie's ninth novel, *Shalimar the Clown* (2005), is the first to have been published after that 'borderline'. The novel does not address the events of '9/11' substantially, though it does offer a portrait of the evolution of an Islamic terrorist, and so can be said to offer a fictional exploration of the conditions that brought about the terrorist attacks of the early 2000s. However, whilst the novel includes depictions of radicalised 'Islamofascists', and whilst Rushdie used the occasion of publication to plead for a modernising 'Islamic Reformation', *Shalimar* does not lay the blame for contemporary violence solely at the door of Islam but locates it in a global postwar context that has been created as much by the West as the East.[63]

Barring some gripes concerning Rushdie's hyperbolic prose style, *Shalimar* was well received by reviewers.[64] Justine Hardy in *The Times* celebrated the fact that 'The puppet master is back' having been 'absent for a while, busy with re-invention, polemic and courtship'; likewise, Suhayl Saadi in *The Independent* argued that it is 'one of Rushdie's best novels yet'.[65] Certainly, *Shalimar* is less hectic, more grounded and more carefully structured than Rushdie's two previous, ranging, globally ragged fictions, *The Ground Beneath Her Feet* and *Fury*. It still exhibits Rushdie's trademark exuberance of style but, as John Updike points out in one of the most effective reviews of the novel, its plot 'beneath the tinsel and the outrage, the Hindu and Bollywood myth-making, the jittery verbal razzmatazz, is as simple as a legend'.[66] This refreshing element of simplicity in Rushdie's 2005 novel hints at the emergence of a mature style in his work.

PART II

Novels and criticism

From science fiction to history:
Grimus and *Midnight's Children*

> Any intellect which confines itself to mere structuralism
> is bound to rest trapped in its own webs. (Salman Rushdie,
> *Grimus*, 1975, G, 91)

> Back then I was partial to science fiction novels. (Salman
> Rushdie, *The Ground Beneath Her Feet*, 1999, GBF, 205)

Scenarios borrowed from science fiction fantasy appear in several
of Rushdie's novels. *Haroun and the Sea of Stories* features a
journey to a magical moon on an automaton bird, *The Satanic
Verses* alludes to the genre self-consciously by making several of
its characters voice-over actors in a popular science fiction television show, and *Fury* traces its protagonist's fascination with
the form back to his youth in the 1960s when he, like Rushdie,
was a devourer of 'science fiction novels of ... the form's golden
age' (F, 169). The science fictional imagination is at its strongest, however, in Rushdie's first published fiction, *Grimus* – a
novel that originated in a sci-fi writing competition organised
by Gollancz, and that, accordingly, has a number of elements
familiar from the pages of well-thumbed futuristic paperbacks,
including elixirs of immortality, a preoccupation with what Jorge
Luis Borges would call alternative 'causal relations' and a desire
to postulate and explore the existence of parallel dimensions.[1]
Because Rushdie sees science fiction not as an end in itself,
however, but as a springboard for the exploration of philosophical and political concepts, the novel may also be described
as a specific form of science fiction – a 'speculative fiction' – in
which the alien qualities of 'new worlds' are used as a means

of investigating and destabilising settled certainties concerning our own world.[2] (Hence, as Uma Parameswaran points out, the 'alien' world in *Grimus* – Thera, which orbits the star Nus in the Yawy Klim galaxy of the Nirveesu – is only an anagrammatised version of 'Earth, which moves around the Sun in the Milky Way galaxy of our Universe'.)[3]

Appropriately, the term 'speculative fiction' achieved particular currency in critical descriptions of the semi-science-fictional works of Rushdie's contemporaries Doris Lessing and Angela Carter, to whose novels of the 1970s and 1980s *Grimus* bears a passing resemblance.[4] In the works of these authors, as both Gerardine Meaney and Natalie Rosinsky have argued, the techniques of speculative fiction fulfil distinctive political aims. Geraldine Meaney, for instance, suggests that the alien qualities of the other-worldly possibilities of sci-fi 'operate as an exotic or unfamiliar element which allows the familiar (cognitive) to be presented in a new light and so made available to questioning'.[5] Natalie Rosinsky, in a similar vein, argues that the 'cognitive estrangement' of the audience from 'conventional reality' in speculative science fiction by Lessing and Carter 'prepares readers to question biases inherent in any dominant world-view' and so facilitates feminism's challenge to 'patriarchal realities'.[6]

In Rushdie's works this speculative method fulfils a comparable politicised function, assisting Rushdie in his stated aim of employing 'unreality' as a 'weapon with which reality can be smashed, so that it may subsequently be reconstructed' (IHL, 122). However, whilst it is relatively easy to detect the political and cultural intent of Rushdie's speculative scenarios in later novels such as *Midnight's Children* and *Shame*, in *Grimus* it is less immediately apparent what the reality is that Rushdie is seeking to smash, and why it is that he wishes to smash it. Reading *Grimus* retrospectively, and with a socio-political awareness that the text itself does not encourage the reader to adopt, it is possible to see in the novel a foreshadowing of the historical and cultural interrogations that are characteristic of Rushdie's later fictions. The novel's protagonist Flapping Eagle, for instance, similar to many of Rushdie's later protagonists, is a migrant who leaves his place of origin, travels through the world in search of a new (but elusive) homeland, and, in the process, becomes a hybridised (at least an *even more* hybridised) entity, unsure of the ground beneath his feet. The cultural disorientation experienced by Flapping Eagle, moreover, his inability to fit into the existing socio-cultural orders, the difficulties he experiences in finding an appropriate voice in which to speak, may also be seen to reflect the feelings of cultural alienation that Rushdie, as a young Indian living in London, may be presumed to have felt (a subject treated more directly and more analytically in *The Satanic Verses*). *Grimus*, however, not only fails to alert the reader to the possibility of such interpretations, it also seems to want to disguise them by burying them under an ever more elaborate mantle of allegories, metaphors, allusions, puns and mock-philosophical absurdisms. In this novel, unlike later novels, we might say, Rushdie seems to use allegory and fantasy, not as a means of facilitating his socio-political argument but as a means of camouflaging it.

The continuities and disparities between Rushdie's first novel and his later fictions are starkly apparent in the distinction between the imaginary homeland of Calf Island that Flapping Eagle discovers for himself in *Grimus* and the conference of freaks and mutants that Saleem convenes telepathically inside his skull in *Midnight's Children*. Both places of belonging have similarities. Firstly, they are highly diversified in terms of the social types they contain and they represent an imaginative attempt to conceive of a utopian social structure that will accommodate such diversity. Secondly, both imaginary collectivities are troubled by the question of meaning: Saleem is concerned to discover what the Midnight's Children are for, and the occupants of Calf Island attempt to exclude the realisation that they have no meaning from their consciousnesses by cultivating speciality obsessions. Thirdly and finally, both Calf Island and the Midnight's Children Conference are products of an imagination fed upon science fiction. *Grimus*, as we have seen, borrows from a flourishing sub-genre of 1960s and 1970s reality-busting, parallel-dimension narratives, and *Midnight's*

Children, as a narrative about mutants with special powers led by a telepath who attempts to use them as a force for good, echoes the plots of comic books such as *The X-Men* that Saleem, and indeed Rushdie, luxuriated in as teenagers.[7] A crucial difference remains between the two imagined collectivities, however, for whilst, in the later novel, the device of the Midnight's Children is the means by which Rushdie, using what Robert Potter might have called a 'microcosmic analogy',[8] examines the difficulties involved in finding a national formation that will represent the first generation of independent Indians, in *Grimus,* no specific national history is suggested. Though we are able to see in the device of Calf Island an allegory of nationhood *retrospectively,* the novel itself never licenses this interpretative leap, and so remains a non-specific meditation on 'the human condition'.

It is this limitation of *Grimus* that many reviewers and critics have emphasised. Catherine Cundy argues that though *Grimus* is about alienation, 'The alienation is not as yet politicised, the transformation is still more of a fantastic than a social nature'.[9] Timothy Brennan, in a similar vein, suggests that '*Grimus* fails even though it is carried off with professional brilliance simply because it lacks *habitus*'.[10] 'It doesn't know where it is', Brennan memorably asserts, but '"tries on" cultures like used clothing'.[11] This critique is a potent one, and its accuracy can be measured by the quantity of readers who express doubts about *Grimus,* or who, at least, rate it poorly in comparison to Rushdie's subsequent works. Not all critics are dismissive of *Grimus,* however. Ib Johansen has argued that though *Grimus* does not attain the dizzying heights of accomplishment that Rushdie attains in *Midnight's Children* and *The Satanic Verses* (few novels do) it is nevertheless 'worth studying for its own sake as a formal experiment'.[12] Likewise, Uma Parameswaran has argued that, whilst the novels Rushdie completed in the 1980s have 'enriched … post-colonial literature', his first novel *Grimus* gives an indication that there is another literary tradition that Rushdie might yet enrich, and to which, she predicts, he will return in later writings (a prediction that is partially borne out by *Fury*).[13]

Brennan is certainly correct in his observation that one of

the defining aesthetic characteristics of *Grimus* is its tendency to draw, eclectically and indiscriminately, upon numerous cultural reference points from numerous periods. *Grimus* borrows scenarios freely from classical Sufi allegory, Renaissance epic Italian poetry, the modern European and American Gothic novel, the nineteenth-century Russian naturalistic novel, the American Western, Norse mythology and Amerindian folklore, to cite the major examples.[14] As a partial response to Brennan, however, we might observe that the intertextual allusiveness of *Grimus* is not *entirely* gratuitous, but springs, with a fair degree of logic, from the plot of the novel, since it is one of the novel's central conceits that the shape of Flapping Eagle's quest, and the alternative dimension of Calf Island upon which almost all of the 'generic pastiche' scenarios occur, have been imagined into existence ('conceptualised') by one of the characters in the fiction, the megalomaniac and myth-obsessed Grimus. Grimus has achieved this impressive feat by using an otherworldly piece of technology named the Stone Rose that has been created by the Gorfs of Thera; a race of conceptualist philosophers who structure their reality by playing a complex anagrammatical language game called 'the Divine Game of Order' (G, 64–5). Given this plot it is easy to see why Flapping Eagle's life takes on the lineaments of familiar myths and why Calf Island is imagined in popular generic terms. The technology of the Gorfs works by rearranging *that which is* to create new orderings of 'given materials', so when Grimus imagines Calf Island into existence and gives shape to Flapping Eagle's life (and thus shape to the novel) he does so by rearranging the imaginative models that he already has to hand: namely, his favourite myths and generic narrative scenarios. Both Calf Island and Flapping Eagle's life, according to this reading, may be seen as a speculative embodiment of the idea that when human beings imagine a world – either as fictionalisers or as megalomaniacs – they do so not by reference to objective reality but by reference to the structures of comprehension that have been made available to them by pre-existing narratives.

If this reading is correct, it becomes possible to see the novel as a covert analysis of the forms of popular post-structuralist theory that were current in the 1970s. Like the Gorfs of Thera, French critical theorists of the late 1960s had described reality as a textual construct forged out of pre-existing languages or structures of thought. Like the 'Gorfs', moreover, these theorists had argued that when we engage in a creative linguistic act all that we are doing is rearranging earlier acts of creation and expression. Roland Barthes, for instance, in his influential 1968 essay 'The Death of the Author' had argued that 'life never does more than imitate the book' and that 'the writer can only imitate a gesture that is always anterior, never original'.[15] These arguments are only a whisper away from the Gorfic assertion that reality is constructed by thought forms and can be transformed by the anagrammatical rearrangement of these thought forms.[16]

This self-conscious allusion to French theory suggests an analytical or speculative approach to post-structuralist thought. On the one hand, *Grimus is* a post-structuralist inspired text in which the fictional world is self-consciously compiled out of innumerable pre-texts and intertexts; on the other hand, the world created by the character Grimus (whose actions the novel by no means endorses) also becomes a means of posing the question: if post-structuralist thought does describe reality as it is, what is that reality like and what are its implications for the human condition? The answer, if it is embodied in the nightmarish and dystopian 'reality' of Calf Island, is not an affirmative one, for Calf Island is, firstly, a suffocating and stagnating world in which the populace remain trapped inside the structures of consciouness that they brought with them when they arrived; and, secondly, it is a world that, because it is not rooted in any known reality (in Grimus-speak it is a dimension that has been conceptualised without reference to an object) is destined to dissolve into nothingness at the end of the novel. Roughly speaking these two characteristics of Calf Island correspond to the two principal anxieties that beset post-structuralist thought, and that have preoccupied Rushdie in one way or another throughout his career: the anxiety that, if it is only ever possible to recycle languages, concepts, images that are already in existence, then it becomes impossible to imagine ways in which (as Rushdie later phrases the question in *The Satanic Verses*) newness can enter the world; and the anxiety that, if our notions of reality are constituted solely out of discourse, then there is no reality 'outside of discourse' by which we can measure the validity (or otherwise) of the worlds we create.

Such anxieties, of course, are partly aesthetic – questions posed by a young artist who is endeavouring to discover 'a suitable voice to speak in' (G, 32). They are also political anxieties, however, since they concern the nature of individual agency, and the capacity of individuals to challenge the cultural and political structures within which they find themselves and by which they are partly, perhaps wholly, determined. That Rushdie is aware of this political dimension to his aesthetic speculations is apparent in the sub-strand of *Grimus* that imitates the Russian naturalistic novel. This sub-strand centres upon the pre-revolutionary Russian aristocratic family the Cherkassovs, who are striving to maintain the life of privilege they knew before they came to the island. Also on the island, however, is the Marxist revolutionary P. S. Moonshy, who, true to his political beliefs, is their avowed enemy, and regularly appears outside their house full of Marxist spleen and slogans ('Liberty is herself in chains ... The transgressors shall face a terrible vengeance'; G, 140–1). For the most part of the novel it appears as if Moonshy's politicised hatred of the Cherkassovs is genuine. However, once the 'system' within which they all live and operate comes under threat because of the danger posed to the whole social apparatus by Flapping Eagle, it becomes apparent that the enmity of Marxist revolutionary for aristocratic elite is merely one of the mechanisms by which the system perpetuates itself. Moonshy closes ranks with the Cherkassovs against Flapping Eagle, and, after the death of the servant employed to attend to the needs of the idiot son, becomes minder and servant in his place. 'Moonshy differed from the rest only in choice of obsession', Flapping Eagle realises, 'He was Opposition Man. That was what gave him the strength to question the shaky edifice on which rested the sanity of K. He questioned, but he was a part of it' (G, 150).

This sub-plot reflects *in little* upon the central narrative concerning Flapping Eagle's quest. For much of his journey Flapping Eagle believes that he is acting according to his own free will. When he reaches Grimus's home, however, it is revealed to him that his entire adventure, from the moment he left home to his confrontation with Grimus, has been plotted by the magician. Even his revolutionary desire to destroy Grimus and liberate the people of Calf Island, Flapping Eagle discovers, is part of Grimus's plan to complete the mythic structure of his life by making Flapping Eagle his 'death'. Flapping Eagle's act of resistance is, thus, like Moonshy's, because it becomes nothing more than a confirmation of Grimus's absolutist agendas.

In both respects these narratives operate as concise allegories of the suspicions that Marxist critics have voiced concerning the political efficacy of post-structuralist discourses. Aijaz Ahmad's scornful *précis* of Michel Foucault's conception of power relations, according to which 'whatever claims to be a *fact* is none other than a truth-*effect* produced by the ruse of discourse, and … whatever claims to resist Power is already constituted as Power', is minutely realised in the fates of Flapping Eagle and Moonshy.[17] Likewise, the logic of the novel seems to reflect the charge levelled against postmodernism and post-structuralism by the Marxist critic Fredric Jameson, who, worrying that his own identification of postmodernism as a 'cultural dominant' serves to render any criticism of it futile, comes to identify one of the central paradoxes of contemporary endeavours to explore the ways in which power pervades a system. '[I]t is certain', he writes:

> that there is a strange quasi-Sartrean irony – a 'winner loses' logic – which tends to surround any effort to describe a 'system', a totalising dynamic, as these are detected in the movement of contemporary society. What happens is that the more powerful the vision of some increasingly total system or logic – the Foucault of the prisons book is the obvious example – the more powerless the reader comes to feel. Insofar as the theorist wins, therefore, by constructing an increasingly closed and terrifying machine, to that very degree he loses, since the critical capacity of

his work is thereby paralysed, and the impulses of nega-
tion and revolt, not to speak of those of social transformation, are increasingly perceived as vain and trivial in the
face of the model itself.[18]

At this early stage of Rushdie's career it is hard to determine
whether this observation of the ineffectuality of the resistance offered by Flapping Eagle and Moonshy to the Foucauldian system that Grimus has implemented is an effect of the
novel's post-structuralist logic or whether, like Jameson's own
study, it constitutes a critique of post-structuralism's implications for political commitment. Certainly, the representation
of the futility of resistance as practised by characters such as
Moonshy and Flapping Eagle seems to endorse the very forms
of political quietism that Rushdie later criticises in George
Orwell's *Nineteen Eighty-four*; a novel in which, in Rushdie's
own words, 'the secret book of the dissidents turns out to have
been written by the Thought Police' (IHL, 97). The fact, however,
that the futility of Moonshy's and Flapping Eagle's attempts to
resist the structures that have determined their actions occurs
only within the dystopic worlds constructed by Grimus using
the technologies of the Gorfs may also suggest that Rushdie
intends to invite readers to be suspicious of such philosophies.
We might, perhaps, conclude that Rushdie is engaged in a
cautious balancing act in *Grimus* in which a distinction is drawn
between two different forms of post-structuralist thought, one
of which may be regarded as politically enabling, the other of
which may not. This balancing act is apparent in the distinction
drawn in the novel between the orthodox 'conceptualism' practised by the Gorfs, and the misuses of it by the renegade Gorf
Koax which results in the creation of a dimension that has insuf-
ficient contact with reality. In the orthodox version of Gorfic
conceptualism, the 'statement of the dota' – *I think therefore it
is* – is 'intended to mean simply that nothing could exist without
the presence of a cognitive intellect to perceive its existence' (G,
66). This interpretation of the statement is relatively uncontentious: it suggests that the objective world can only ever be
mediated by a perceiving subject and is, as a result, constructed

by the perceptual knowledges that that subject brings to bear. This statement, however, is corrupted by the renegade Gorf Koax and made to say something quite different: 'that anything of which such an intellect could conceive *must therefore exist*' (G, 66). This modification of the postulate results in the more philosophically radical position: that human perceptions create the world; that there do not need to be 'given materials' outside of the structures of perception in order for those structures to be ontologically validated. The former argument, *Grimus* implies in both its textuality and its narrative, is self-evident: we engage with an independently existing material world using the structures of thought and structures of narrative that we have available to us. The latter argument represents a dangerous form of self-delusion, because it detaches human actions from a material reality, and so relieves human beings of the need for a responsibility to that reality. It is this philosophical misuse of the Gorfs' original position that is the principal target of Rushdie's speculative critique when he constructs the imperfectly imagined, and hence unstable, world of Calf Island.

Grimus, in this respect, is engaged in a complex exploration of the philosophical and aesthetic vogues that were current in the decade during which it was being written. More to the point, it sets out to explore (if not to resolve) the political questions that are raised by those philosophical vogues. Contrary to some of the more strident critiques of the novel, we might therefore argue, *Grimus* is a fiction that applies its speculative methods to an analysis of the intellectual climate from which it springs.

Even if we argue that *Grimus* is a speculatively engaged fiction, however, it remains the case that the intellectual explorations conducted in this fiction remain abstract, because they are never explicitly connected to a coherent, identifiable, historical moment. Brennan and Cundy, as we have seen, have objected to the novel on this basis. The most vigorous critic of the novel in this regard, however, is Rushdie himself, who, in later years, has spurned the first flowering of his talent as a work of artistic and intellectual cowardice. 'The thing that I disliked about my first novel' he told Rani Dharker in interview in 1983, 'was that it's a complete fantasy. It's not placed in a real place, some imaginary island[,] and after finishing it, after some distance had been established from it, it seemed to me that it was not interesting really' (SRI, 52). '[F]antasy', Rushdie adds, extending this expression of personal dissatisfaction with his novel into a more general reflection on the role of fantasy in fiction, 'is not interesting when you separate it from actuality, it's only interesting as a mode of dealing with actuality' (SRI, 52).

Given such sentiments it is perhaps unsurprising that we find Rushdie's narrator, at the very outset of his second novel, *Midnight's Children*, unambiguously turning his back on fantastical, unplaced, atemporal registers, in favour of a text that is carefully located in an identifiable geographical place and rooted in a moment in time so specific that it can be pinpointed to the second:

> I was born in the city of Bombay ... once upon a time. No, that won't do, there's no getting away from the date: I was born in Doctor Narlikar's Nursing Home on August 15th, 1947. And the time? The time matters, too. Well then: at night. No, it's important to be more ... On the stroke of midnight, as a matter of fact. Clock-hands joined palms in respectful greeting as I came. (MC, 11)

The significance of this second is, of course, paramount – both in the recent history of the Indian sub-continent with which *Midnight's Children* concerns itself and in the story of Saleem Sinai's life, which the novel proposes to use to trace a path through this history. For India, it is the moment at which it won independence from Britain; for Saleem it is the moment of his birth, a fact that ensures that he, the narrative that he tells, and the novel that Rushdie writes, are all, unlike *Grimus*, 'handcuffed to history' (MC, 11). From the very outset, then, this is a novel that, though it draws frequently on fantastical registers, announces its locality, its resistance to the abstracted illusions of 'once upon a time', and its *difference* from Rushdie's first novel, which sold only a few hundred copies and which, mortifyingly for such an ambitious writer, disappeared without trace.

The narrative of *Midnight's Children* is told retrospectively, as Saleem reconstructs the events of his biography for the benefit of a single auditor, Padma, his occasional lover and a worker in the pickle factory to which he has come to end his days. The novel's setting thus alternates between a fictional present, in which Saleem intervenes authorially to reflect upon the process of writing, and a fictional past, in which Saleem's family saga unfolds against (or within) the backdrop of Indian national life. This mock-epic saga, as mock-epic epic sagas will be, is diverse, both in the scope of the events it fictionalises ('intertwined lives events miracles places rumours') and in the forms of narration it draws upon (reportage, fairy tale, satire, realism). At the 'fantastic heart' of the narrative, however, is the tale of the Midnight's Children themselves – those who, like Saleem, were born at the hour of Independence, and whose fates, like his, are indissolubly linked to those of their country (MC, 192). Each of these children, Saleem reveals, has, by virtue of their fortuitous (or perhaps, given the course the novel follows, unfortuitous) time of birth, a mysterious magical gift. Some are so beautiful they cause blindness, some can transform themselves into werewolves, some can change sex at will. The two most powerful of the Midnight's Children, however, are those born at the exact moment of midnight: Saleem himself, whose telepathic abilities enable him to provide a mental forum in which the group can 'meet' (Saleem describes himself as a 'radio' receiver, but these days he seems more like an Internet 'chat room'); and Shiva, Saleem's double, with whom he was swapped at birth, and whom Saleem struggles to exclude from the group, thus denying him his rightful inheritance for a second time.

If Saleem's magical abilities suggest empathy and an ability to bring people together through communication and mutual agreement, Shiva, his opposite, is possessed of phenomenal physical strength and believes in rule by force. Hence when he and Saleem are engaged in an extended philosophical conflict over the form that the Midnight's Children Conference should take (also, implicitly, a debate concerning the form of post-Independence India) they come to radically different conclusions. Saleem takes up the familiar liberal position that the group should be 'something more like a, you know, sort of loose federation of equals, all points of view given free expression' (MC, 215). Shiva, predictably contrary, argues that 'gangs gotta have bosses', and that the only rule that should apply to the Midnight's Children – as with all collectivities – is militaristic and authoritarian: 'Everybody does what I say or I squeeze the shit outa them with my knees' (MC, 215). If the novel has any one argument to make, it is that Saleem's hopes for the Midnight's Children Conference and for India, expounded so optimistically in 1957, have been, by 1977, comprehensively disappointed.

On this level, the message offered by *Midnight's Children* is a pessimistic one. The Midnight's Children Conference, like India, fails to find a form that will allow all its members to co-exist harmoniously, and avoid civil strife. The pessimism is offset, however, by the fact that the three most potent of the Midnight's Children, Parvati the Witch, Saleem and Shiva, have produced between them a son symbolically named Aadam (Shiva being the biological parent, Saleem the adoptive). At the start of the novel another Aadam, Saleem's grandfather, had suffered a fall from grace in the idyllic garden state of Kashmir. The mythic logic of the narrative suggests that this second Aadam embodies the hope for future redemption and regeneration; of a new and better start for the children of Independent India. 'We, the children of Independence', notes Saleem in the penultimate episode:

> rushed wildly and too fast into our future; he [Aadam], Emergency-born, will be is already, more cautious, biding his time; but when he acts, he will be impossible to resist. Already, he is stronger, harder, more resolute than I. (MC, 410)

The function of the first generation of Midnight's Children, Saleem thus realises, was to be destroyed, but out of its destruction, the hope for a better future springs. *Midnight's Children*, in this sense, can be seen as an attempt to provide a mythologisation of post-Independence India not dissimilar to the mythologisation of postwar Europe provided by T. S. Eliot in *The Waste Land*; a poem in which, broadly speaking, a realisation of the barrenness of hope for the present generation gives way to the possibility of future regeneration. Like Eliot's 'hooded man' of *The Waste Land*, Saleem might be construed as a modern Indian Fisher King – a figure who has received a sexual wound (his castration) that has rendered him incapable of regenerating his lands (MC, 191). Unlike the Fisher King of *The Waste Land*, however, it is clear that Saleem (and indeed Saleem's successors) will never manage to forge a new totality out of the multitudinous fragments that constitute his history and the history of the nation. At the start of the novel Saleem may believe that he can assemble the confused mass of stories 'jostling and shoving' inside of him into a narrative that has 'meaning' (MC, 11). By the novel's conclusion, however, it has become apparent that the fragments cannot be assembled into a meaningful whole, and that Saleem, like Lifafa Das, will end up defeated by the 'hyperbolic formula' (MC, 75).

In one sense, this means that *Midnight's Children* is much less hopeful than *The Waste Land*: Saleem will never become the 'saviour' of the nation by shoring fragments up against his ruin to make some sense of 'the immense panorama of futility and anarchy which is contemporary history'.[19] In another sense, however, Saleem's failure, whilst a tragedy for him, represents, for Rushdie, a successful overcoming of the Eliotian nostalgia for totality, and the tyrant's need to impose form and order upon that which has no inherent order. Whilst Saleem is unsuccessful in his attempt to provide a form both for his life and for the life of post-Independence India, therefore, *Midnight's Children* itself presents the possibility of narrating the nation in all its complexity, without the need to 'beautify'; to eliminate variety, difference, perplexity in the interests of a totalising vision. It is for this reason that Rushdie argues that, though 'the story of Saleem does indeed lead him to despair', the novel itself is not a despairing one:

> the story is told in a manner designed to echo, as closely as my abilities allowed, the Indian talent for non-stop self regeneration. This is why the narrative constantly throws up new stories, why it 'teems'. The form – multitudinous,

hinting at the infinite possibilities of the country – is the optimistic counterweight to Saleem's personal tragedy. I do not think that a book written in such a manner can really be called a despairing work. (IHL, 16)

In some respects this refusal of a totalising aesthetic, and the declaration of a war on totality, allies Rushdie with the post-modernists. Like Jean-François Lyotard, he strives to imagine a form of representation that 'denies itself the solace of good forms, the consensus of a taste which would make it possible to share collectively the nostalgia for the unattainable'.[20] Rushdie himself, however, has repeatedly insisted that his refusal to 'totalise' is not a product of abstract speculation but springs from a particular conception of the composition of the Indian sub-continent, and from a desire to resist 'singular' conceptions of Indian national identity. Rather than think of his resistance to classical form as something that derives exclusively from a post-modernist sensibility, in other words, Rushdie would have us believe that his choice of fictional form derives principally from his desire to negotiate a concept of nationhood and national identity that is diverse, disseminatory and does not 'add up' to a single story of a single people or a single tradition.

Rushdie's concern, in *Midnight's Children*, to fictionalise an experience of recent Indian history suggests that his novel might potentially be considered as a form of historical fiction. Certainly, *Midnight's Children* has elements in it that identify it as a historical text. It brings within its compass a selection of the major events in modern Indian history, including the Amritsar massacre (1919), the 'Quit India' resolution (1942), Indian Independence and partition (1947), the Bombay language marches (1956), the Indo-Chinese war (1962), the death of Nehru (1964), the brief Prime Ministership of Lal Bahadur Shastri (1964–65), the Indo-Pakistani wars of 1965 and 1971, the first Prime Ministership of Indira Gandhi (1966–77), Indira Gandhi's 'emergency' suspension of normal democratic processes (1975–77), and the defeat of Indira Gandhi's Congress Party by the newly formed Janata Morcha party in 1977. Perhaps more importantly,

Midnight's Children is a novel that is preoccupied at the level of ideas by history and historicity, by the ways in which history is recorded, by the techniques with which a period is conjured and contained (or not contained), and by the ways in which the individual 'historiographer' understands (or misunderstands) his relationship with his material. In all these respects *Midnight's Children* seems to conform to the broad definition of the historical novel offered by Avrom Fleishman in his influential study of the genre *The English Historical Novel: Walter Scott to Virginia Woolf*. 'What makes a historical novel historical', according to Fleishman, 'is the active presence of a concept of history as a shaping force', and *Midnight's Children* (though its narrator Saleem sometimes labours under the delusion that he is a shaper of history rather than a subject of history) reflects an awareness throughout that individual lives and national experiences are the products of material processes, and, as such, are shaped by history.[21]

Harry Shaw's contention in *The Forms of Historical Fiction* that historical novels 'foreground' history by representing 'historical milieux' with a significant degree of probability also seems to allow for a definition of *Midnight's Children* as a historical fiction, since Rushdie's novel not only foregrounds a sense of history but gives its locations (Bombay, Kashmir, Delhi, for instance) sufficient 'probability' to allow readers to believe that historically real times and places are being described.[22] Of course it may be objected that the probability of Rushdie's locations is compromised by his simultaneous use of fabulism, anachronism and historical error. Importantly, however, Shaw also insists that the criterion of 'probability' does not mean straightforward 'fidelity to the external world that a work represents', but can 'also depend upon how consistently a work follows its own rules and patterns'.[23] *Midnight's Children* may incorporate purposeful 'mistakes of historical facts', but it does so in order to veraciously represent how an individual might have understood and misunderstood a viable historical moment. Likewise, *Midnight's Children* may incorporate elements of fantasy, but the fantasy is always designed to make comment upon historically real situations, periods or places. In these senses *Midnight's Children* remains historical because it is consistent to the criteria of historical veracity that it sets up within itself.

The identification of *Midnight's Children* as a historical narrative is, to some extent, supported by parallels between Rushdie's novel and established works of historical fiction such as Walter Scott's genre-defining historical novel *Waverley* (1814). Not only does Scott, like Rushdie, make free use of fantasy and wilful anachronism, there are also revealing structural similarities between the two fictions. Both are, to borrow Rushdie's own phrase, books 'about one person's passage through history' (SRI, 25), both use a youthful and unreliable protagonist to gain a unique perspective on historical events and both are *Bildungsroman* or 'coming of age' novels, in which historical material is transformed into biography, or in which biography is used in an attempt to control and order history.[24] In both cases, moreover, the novels set out to thematise the relationship between the individual hero and the broader national and collective experiences through which he lives; a quality that, for a number of commentators, is at the very core of the definition of the historical novel.[25]

The similarity between the two writers, strikingly, extends not just to structural and formal definitions of the novel but also to subject matter and political significance. Sir Walter Scott, in his day, was, like Rushdie, exploring periods of cultural transition that resulted from colonial (particularly English colonial) activities. Scott's *Waverley*, notably, concerns the shifting power relations between Jacobite supporters of the Stuart line and the forces of modernity represented by the English Hanoverians. In his later novel *Ivanhoe* (1819), likewise, Scott makes dramatic capital out of the clash between indigenous Saxon culture in medieval England and the culture of the occupying Normans. Rushdie's fiction, comparably, locates itself in the period of transition between the colonial occupation of India by the British and India's and Pakistan's emergence as a post-colonial states. Different though the periods that Scott and Rushdie treat inevitably are, and different though the kinds of political negotiations involved must be, both writers are interested in how competing cultural interests relate to one another, and in the kinds of accommodation these interests find, or fail to find. In both cases, moreover, it is the hybridisation of culture that results from the colonial and post-colonial collision of cultural forms that is seen as the dominant and defining characteristic of the period being represented. *Ivanhoe* describes the hybridisation of English culture after the invasion of Saxon England by the Normans, and *Waverley* describes the hybridisation of Jacobite Highland Scotland in the face of British Hanoverian ascendancy. Likewise, Rushdie's novels describe the intensified hybridisation of an already hybrid Indian national culture after the colonisation of India by the British, and the further hybridisation of British culture both in India during the colonial period and in Britain as a result of post-colonial migrations.

The shared interest of both writers in the theme of cultural hybridisation is most apparent in the figures of their heroes, who are frequently presented as products, quite literally, of the cultural and political confusion that is characteristic of their time. Waverley, through his father, and initially through his army commission, owes obedience to the Hanoverian king, but has considerable sympathies, through his uncle and his own romantic inclinations, with the Scottish Jacobites. He therefore becomes the mediating figure who is able to provide a focal point for the assimilation of the Stuart loyalists into the current Hanoverian regime. *Ivanhoe*, similarly, reveals the dominant cultural conflict of medieval England, as Scott sees it, by making its titular character an outcast Saxon, who has been disinherited by his father for his loyal service to the Norman king, Richard I. Ivanhoe's re-assimilation into society depends upon his capacity to reconcile the militant Saxon insurgency represented by his father Cedric with the more chivalric and tolerant elements of the Norman regime represented by Richard.

Rushdie's protagonists also tend to descend from the two (or more) cultural camps that Rushdie feels define their historical and political moment. In *Midnight's Children* Saleem is the biological child of Methwold, the departing English coloniser, and Wanita, a low-class Hindu; he is raised by Amina and Ahmed, bourgeois Indian Muslims, and he later adopts various father figures, including his uncle Zulfikar, a General in the Pakistani army. Likewise, Omar Khayam, the 'peripheral' hero of *Shame* (S, 24), is the product of an illicit union between a departing English sahib and one of three possible Indian mothers. Whilst Rushdie, like Scott, uses hybridised heroes as a means of comprehending cultural transition, however, the allegiances of Rushdie's protagonists are both more complex and more ambiguous than Scott's. The allegiances of Scott's heroes are divided along fairly straightforward binary lines, between two competing causes (though class as well as culture sometimes complicates the relation). They are, moreover, allegiances that may be reconciled – or assimilated – into a new sense of cultural wholeness in the long term. Hence, Ivanhoe fuses Saxon and Norman interests in order to achieve a more composite sense of an 'English' identity; Waverley fuses English and Scottish interests in order to achieve a more composite sense of 'British' identity, and these new forms of composite identity remain opposed to 'other' forms of cultural identity that, for Scott, are beyond the pale. Englishness in *Ivanhoe*, for instance, though a hybrid category in itself, is still defined in radical opposition to the 'foreignness' of the Saracens that Richard has been fighting in the Holy Land or the Jewishness of the character Isaac of York.

Rushdie's heroes, in contrast to this, are defined by multiple allegiances, of class, culture and gender, not all of which are certain, and not all of which help to clarify cultural identity. Saleem, unlike Waverley, is not sure whom he should claim as a father, or how to organise the different aspects of his cultural identity. The effect of this complication and multiplication of cultural allegiance in Rushdie is to produce forms of identity that cannot be reduced to any singular conception of self. For Rushdie, there is no 'new' coherent form of identity that can be set, once more, in opposition to other coherent forms of identity. Cultural diversity in Rushdie's fictions never amounts to something, but remains inexhaustibly (though often fruitfully) perplexing.

The differences and consonances between Scott and Rushdie's understanding of the ways in which competing cultural interests become hybridised are also revealed by their mutual fascination with the theme of translation – that mechanism by which it becomes possible to communicate across borders of language and culture. Rushdie is struggling with the post-colonial problem of representing India and Pakistan in the linguistic medium of English. Scott, in the Scottish fictions, is struggling with the problem of translating the Highland clans, their cultures, languages and customs, for a contemporary British readership. In the work of both writers the problem of communicating between sites of cultural difference is explored through the act of translating individual words or cultural arte-facts such as poems. In a scene of *Waverley* that has excited much commentary, the young Englishman Waverley, whilst on a visit to the Highlands, thinks he hears his name mentioned in a heroic epic poem being sung by a Scots bard in Gaelic and asks his host, Fergus Mac-Ivor, for an explication of the song. Fergus declines, on the basis that his sister, Flora, can explain such things better than he can, and suggests that they visit Flora to request a rendition. Flora, after initially arguing that these songs cannot possibly interest an English stranger, consents, with the following qualification:

> Some of these [poems] are said to be very ancient, and if they are ever translated into any of the languages of civilised Europe, cannot fail to produce a deep and general sensation. Others are more modern, the composition of those family bards whom the chieftains of more distin-guished name and power retain as the poet and historians of their tribe. These, of course, possess various degrees of merit; but much of it must evaporate in translation, or be lost on those who do not sympathise with the feelings of the poet.[26]

Similar concerns about cultural translatability are apparent in Rushdie's fiction – but most evident (if we may leap forward momentarily) in *Shame*, the novel in which the narrator describes himself as a 'translated man' because he has been 'borne across' (the literal meaning of 'translated', Rushdie tells us) from one culture to another. This act of translation, in the narrator's view, means that something has been lost – he is not the person he was when he set out – but he clings to the notion that something has also been gained: 'The broken glass is not merely a mirror of nostalgia. It is also … a useful tool with which to work in the present' (IHL, 12). This experience of translation is also embodied in a more literal sense in the novel in its attention to individual Urdu words that are untranslatable but that the novel attempts to communicate a sense of. Most significant amongst these words is *Sharam*, the Urdu word that is inadequately rendered in English as Shame, and that Rushdie attempts to explicate in the writing of the novel itself, which is titled *Shame*, and which features various modifications on the concept of Shamefulness that seem, for Rushdie, to be illustrative of the culture about which he is writing. The novel thus becomes a kind of extended act of translation, in which a cultural, historical and political experience of Pakistan is 'carried over' into English where it becomes 'not-quite-Pakistan': a fictional country that is not the same as the original, but that has validity in its own right as a work of imaginative reinvention. In this lies the similarity, and subtle differences between Scott and Rushdie's conception of translation – for both writers a third thing is created, not the same as that which was originally the case. In both cases, a metaphor for the give and take, the loss and gain, of cultural transition is found in the act of translation. For Scott, however, translation is only capable of making a record – an inadequate record – of a culture that would be otherwise lost to history. The translated poems can thus never be anything more than romance. Rushdie is more interested in creating new dimensions for cultures that co-exist in the present. The culture being translated is not lost to history – a form of pastness that must be assimilated with the contemporary in order to survive in memory – but is current, co-existing with the contemporary, and very much alive to history (it is lost only to the extent that the 'translated man', the migrant, no longer experiences that culture as 'home').

It might be argued, on this basis, that Rushdie and Scott are effectively writing about different things: Scott is writing about our capacity to comprehend cultures that no longer exist, whilst Rushdie is writing about our capacity to represent different cultures that co-exist in the present. This distinction, however, is based on an illusion engineered by Scott, for the Highland tribes that Waverley meets are very much of the present, it is only that the logic of Scott's novel requires that they should be relegated to the past, because they have, in his eyes, become outmoded in the face of English colonial hegemony. What Scott is in fact expressing is the *desire* that signs of difference that might conflict with the normative culture established as 'modern' should be consigned to the picturesque graveyard of Romance, in order to eliminate any threat to the commercial 'progress' that modernity was making possible in Scotland in the early nineteenth century. In this sense Scott and Rushdie are dealing with identical manifestations of cultural resistance to colonialism, but valuing those forms of cultural resistance in different ways. Both are concerned with locations of culture that resist the 'modernity' brought about by English colonialism, but, whereas in Scott's fiction these anti-colonial discourses are consigned to the past (as Romance, as the Gothic), in Rushdie's work the anti-colonial discourses that 'progressive' colonial history would like to consign to the past consistently return in order that they can actively threaten colonialist claims to hegemony.

The distinction between these two approaches to colonialism is perhaps illustrated most vividly in each novelist's attitude to the English language. For Scott, in the opening pages of *Ivanhoe*, English is presented as the language that makes possible a fortuitous fusion of cultural influences. After the conquest of William of Normandy, Scott notes:

> Four generations had not sufficed to blend the hostile blood of the Normans and the Anglo-Saxons, or to unite, by common language and mutual interests, two hostile races, one of which still felt the elation of triumph, while the other groaned under all the consequences of defeat.

By sheer pressure of time, however:

the necessary intercourse between the lords of the soil, and those oppressed inferior beings by whom the soil was cultivated, occasioned the gradual formation of a dialect, compounded betwixt the French and the Anglo-Saxon, in which they could render themselves mutually intelligible to each other, and from this necessity arose by degrees the structure of our present English language, in which the speech of the victors and the vanquished have been so happily blended together.[27]

In some limited senses this description of the fusion of languages of coloniser and colonised is parallel to the representations, by Indian-English novelists, of the relationship between Indian idiom and literary English. They too argue that the process of colonisation has given rise to a new linguistic register, neither Indian nor English but something in between. In Scott's account of the creation of English, however, language becomes a site of coalescence, wherein the antagonistic cultures of coloniser and colonised may begin to fuse into a single culture. The meeting of the languages, in this capacity, since it serves to defuse cultural conflict and pave the way for cultural accommodation, is a sign of the decline of political opposition and the attainment of consensus. For Rushdie and other Indian novelists who write in English, by contrast, post-colonial writers actively intervene in the language of the coloniser in order to 'carve out large territories for themselves within its frontiers' (IHL, 64). '[W]e can't simply use the language in the way the British did; ... it needs remaking for our own purposes', Rushdie argues:

Those of us who do use English do so in spite of our ambiguity towards it, or perhaps because of that, perhaps because we can find in that linguistic struggle a reflection of other struggles taking place in the real world, struggles between the cultures within ourselves and the influences at work upon our societies. To conquer English may be to complete the process of making ourselves free. (IHL, 17).

This talk of struggle is very different from Scott's vision of beneficent commingling. Whilst for Scott, the anterior culture is translated to the colonising culture in order that it might be preserved as a site of touristic nostalgia, in Rushdie the once-colonised culture is presented, with far more agency, as a force that can translate itself into the colonising culture in order that it might have a transformatory effect upon that culture. Interestingly, Rushdie still talks of the relationship between Indian and English as a 'post-colonial dialectic' (IHL, 65) – a development whereby a new thing is produced by the fusion of two older things. But there is a crucial difference in Rushdie's understanding of the dialectic, and the dialectic presented by Scott in the Preface to *Ivanhoe*. Indian idiom does not disappear into English, neither does the creation of Indian-English eliminate other forms of English available, as is the case with Scott's Norman French and Anglo-Saxon. Rather, the meeting of Indian idiom and English language creates another dimension to both languages that will exist alongside, and in creative antagonism with, them. Rushdie's dialectic does not, thus, eliminate difference but proliferates it – tending towards greater social complexity rather than less. And 'if history creates complexities', as Rushdie notes, 'let us not try to simplify them' (IHL, 65).

In broad terms, then, whilst Scott and Rushdie share an interest in moments of cultural transition, in which national culture, language and personal identity become conflicted by variant interests and allegiances, Scott promotes an Enlightenment view of history as a series of assimilations of once potent sites of difference, whilst Rushdie promotes an anti-Enlightenment historiography that is determined to deconstruct Enlightenment conceptions of cultural coherence and historical progress. Rushdie does this for a number of reasons, but primarily because the Enlightenment pattern of 'progress' was used by nineteenth-century European colonisers to support and justify their conquest of, and attempted assimilation of, other cultures seen as 'backward' or less civilised. Mythologies of endings, in this context, have tended to justify acts of colonialism and accompanying acts of violence. In Scott's vision of history the destruction and personal suffering resulting from colonial collision is regrettable, but necessary, because 'history' is a narrative that needs to get from one place (less advanced) to another place (more advanced). Thus, the decimation of the Highland tribes, whilst a tragic narrative in its own right, becomes comprehensible, even desirable, according to a broader, Whig vision of history as a march towards Hanoverian modernity. This aspect of Scott's work is expressed concisely by Georg Lukács in his study of the historical novel. Scott, he argues, is not blind to the suffering incurred in the dialectical advances of history, he has 'seen the endless field of ruin, wrecked existences, wrecked or wasted heroic, human endeavour, broken social formations etc.', but he presents these forms of suffering as 'the necessary preconditions of the end result'.[28] Rushdie, by contrast, whilst recognising these forms of suffering as characteristic of human history, particularly colonial history in which a self-styled modernising culture takes it upon itself to 'civilise' cultures that are presented as 'less advanced', sees these historical calamities not as 'necessary preconditions' but as violent interventions by an aggressive force. He sees them as violent interventions rather than necessary preconditions, moreover, because he does not recognise the importance of the ideologically construed 'end result' that these events are necessary preconditions of.

Tragedy in *Shame*

Upon completing *Midnight's Children* Rushdie shifted his focus from a pan-Indian fiction of South Asia in the twentieth century to a more localised response to Pakistani politics in the 1970s and early 1980s. Specifically, Rushdie's *Shame* traces a fiction-alised, and heavily fantasised, path through the rise to political power of Zulfikar Ali Bhutto (who appears as Iskander Harappa), Bhutto's appointment of Zia ul-Haq (Raza Hyder) as his army chief of staff in 1976, Zia's deposition of Bhutto after the army was called in to quell street rioting in July 1977, the execution of Bhutto on the charge of ordering a political assassination, and the 'Islamisation' programme that Zia introduced once he had taken power in Pakistan. *Shame* was written at the height of this 'Islamisation' programme, and much of the bitter, brooding anger of the novel can be explained by this fact. The satire, however, is not directed at Zia alone, for his serious erosion of the civil rights of women and for his politicised misuse of Islam.[1] It is directed also at Bhutto, who is held responsible for compromising the democratic process sufficiently to allow the military to regain power.[2] *Shame* is thus a double satire on a pair of 'conjoined opposites' – the playboy and the puritan, the socialist democrat and the autocratic dictator – who are seen as two sides of the same coin: a Jekyll and Hyde of authoritarian politics.[3]

In some respects this focus on Pakistani politics makes *Shame* a companion piece to *Midnight's Children*: a 'Pakistani' fiction to complement the earlier 'Indian' fiction. The two novels, however, also differ significantly in form and in atmosphere. *Midnight's*

Children, is an ebullient, over-reaching, over-crowded fiction in which the excesses of the text strain against the limits of sentence, chapter and book. *Shame*, by contrast, is a cramped, claustrophobic, even paranoid, fiction, haunted by the narratives that it is unable to tell, and oppressive in its unrelenting focus on the narrow social strata with which the novel deals. In formal terms, moreover, whilst *Midnight's Children* has one narrator who struggles to incorporate everything into his text; *Shame* is a fiction of multiple points of view, none of which has primacy, and none of which will enable the reader to orientate himself or herself in relation to the fiction. The result is that whilst in *Midnight's Children* the reader feels overwhelmed with the possibilities, the numinousness, of the text; in *Shame* the reader feels trapped in a network of textuality and narrative dead ends. According to Rushdie, this is an effect of his different feelings concerning the two nations with which he was dealing.

> *Midnight's Children* was a book that was deliberately con-
> structed to be very open; *Shame* describes a very closed
> society. And that has to do, I suppose broadly, with the differ-
> ences in my perception of India and Pakistan. If the one
> society asks for an open sort of approach, the other demands
> a closed one – and so *Shame* is a closed system. (SRI, 63)

The emphasis on enclosure, entrapment and alienation that Rushdie sets out to create in *Shame* in support of his politi-cised commentary upon Pakistan's leaders also demands a shift in generic allegiance. *Midnight's Children*, broadly, may be described as a historical fiction that draws upon carnivalesque and comic modes; *Shame*, by contrast, is more obviously indebted to the darker genres of the Gothic and of tragedy. More particularly, the novel recalls both classical Greek tragedy and Senecan revenge tragedy in its depiction of the violent decline of once noble 'houses' and in its representation of a corrupt 'court' culture that is unable to contain the cycles of violence that are unleashed by the immoral actions of the protagonists.

The intertextual relationship between *Shame* and tragic narrative gives the novel a number of its distinctive features.

Like tragic drama, the fiction develops in five discreet sections
('acts') towards an apocalyptic conclusion; it has a pervasive
atmosphere of inevitable fatality; and it features men of power
whose actions and whose overreaching pride bring destruction to
themselves and to their families. *Shame* also includes a number
of more minor figures that echo conventional character types
in tragic narrative: for instance, Maulana Dawood, the ancient
divine, plays the role of the Machiavellian tempter, or malcon-
tent, whose wicked and subversive suggestions help to lead the
hero astray. He also, after his death, plays the role of the 'good
angel' who sits on Raza Hyder's right shoulder and attempts to
direct him along the path of 'righteousness', a device derived
from the medieval 'psychomachia' in which angelic and devilish
advisers vie for the soul of the protagonist.

Further tragical paradigms for the plot of *Shame* are
provided by Shakespeare. *Macbeth* is recalled both in the three
witchy figures (Omar's mothers) with whom the novel, like the
play, begins, and in the central plot, concerning the murder of a
head of state by an ambitious underling, who is then haunted,
literally and metaphorically, by his deeds. The novel also reper-
forms the tragedy of *Julius Caesar*, which offers a dramatic
prefiguration of the plot-line in which the protégé of a political
leader becomes his assassin.

Rushdie summons the spirit of tragedy in *Shame* for a
number of reasons. In the first place the strong intertextual
bond between Rushdie's novel and tragic narrative serves to
reinforce the impression of a society that is 'out of joint'. Just as
the ghost in *Hamlet* gives an indication that something is rotten
in the state of Denmark, so the various uncanny horrors of
Shame suggest that something is rotten in the state of Pakistan.
Tragic parallels are also used in *Shame* to reinforce Rushdie's
assertion that Pakistan is 'a miracle that went wrong': a tragic
betrayal of the fairy tale hopes that had attended Independence
in the Indian sub-continent in 1947 (S, 87). Centrally, however,
Rushdie draws on tragedy not in order to affirm the model of
tragic action but to undercut it by revealing the extent to which
his own protagonists fall short of the heroic ideal established

in depictions of men such as Caesar and Hamlet. Conventionally, the hero of tragedy is ennobled by his suffering, and puri
fied by his death. In Rushdie's tragedy of clowns, by contrast,
as in Marlowe's buffoon-tragedy *Dr Faustus*, the fiction takes
its power, ultimately, from a refusal, rather than a fulfilment, of
tragical expectations.[4] '[I]t seemed to me that what you had in
Pakistan was a tragedy being enacted by people who were not
tragic figures', Rushdie explained to Kumkum Sangari in the
year of *Shame*'s publication:

> The Zia-Bhutto relationship is tragic ... but the figures
> haven't the stature you can associate with high tragedy.
> And this did have a very wide application outside Pakistan.
> It seems to me that one of the characteristics of public
> life in the present age is that everywhere you look in the
> world you have situations which you can only call trag-
> edies on a very grand scale, but the leading actors who're
> playing out these tragedies are buffoons ... So in *Shame*,
> the plot is almost unrelieved tragedy, but written in the
> language of a farce. (SRI, 65)

Tragedy in *Shame* thus becomes an aspect of Rushdie's political
satire, its function being to make comment on the moral and
political failings of those with power in Pakistan by indicating,
frequently with a blackly comic effect, the shortfall between
tragic grandeur and the deadly banalities of corrupt uses of
power.

Tragedy is not always undercut in *Shame*, however. On occasion it is employed, undiluted, as a means of registering the real
suffering that is caused by misuses of power. This is particularly
the case in the narratives of the women, who are the subjects,
but, arguably, not always the victims, of the tyrannical actions
of the clownish men. One of the key images of the novel is the
series of eighteen shawls that Rani Harappa weaves whilst under
house arrest and sends to her daughter Arjumand (a fictional
figuration of Benazir Bhutto) when she too begins to contem-
plate a political career.[5] These shawls, like the thirty jars of pickle
that Saleem makes in *Midnight's Children*, are receptacles of
memory but, unlike Saleem's pickles, they are not about hope

for the future, but about anger and despair for the past. Titled 'The Shamelessness of Iskander the Great', they operate as a kind of woven series of political cartoons depicting the life and violent crimes of Rani's husband Iskander: his libertinage, his obscenities, his violence, his disregard for human rights, his strangulation of Pakistan and his contempt for democracy. Perhaps most forcefully of all, the seventeenth shawl exposes his murderous use of the military to suppress separatist insurgency in the north west of the country. This last shawl, readers are told, is 'all in scarlet, scarlet and nothing but scarlet' (S, 194) but there is, finally:

> not enough scarlet thread on earth to show the blood, the people hanging upside down with dogs at their open guts, the people grinning lifelessly with bullet-holes for second mouths, the people united in the worm-feast of that shawl of flesh and death. (S, 195)

This strategy for exposing tyranny employed by Rani echoes that of Ovid's Philomela from the *Metamorphosis* who 'wove a scarlet design on a white ground, which pictured the wrong she had suffered' at the hands of Tereus.[6] Through Philomela, moreover, Rushdie alludes to yet another revenge tragedy, Shakespeare's *Titus Andronicus* (1594), which employs Ovid's tale of Philomela and Tereus as a source for the story of Lavinia, who must resort to drawing the wrongs done to her in the sand, holding a stick in her mouth, because her other organs of communication have been removed.[7] Both these allusions place Rani in the company of those women in classical myth and in Elizabethan and Jacobean revenge tragedies who have been figuratively silenced by corrupt and hypocritical patriarchal regimes and have been forced to find aesthetic means (writing, painting, embroidering) of responding to their oppressors.

Some feminists critics have found fault with Rushdie's apparently sadistic catalogue of annihilated or servile women in *Shame*. Catherine Cundy, for instance, argues that *Shame* provides 'yet another instance of the blend of confusion, frustration and even outright hostility towards the relative autonomy of women which surfaces in Rushdie's fiction'.[8] Inderpal Grewal, likewise, contends that Rushdie's exclusive focus in *Shame* on women who have been defeated by oppression tends to imply that women in Pakistan under Zia were only the passive victims of male power when in fact there was a potent and active network of women's resistance groups, such as the Women's Action Forum, that sought to challenge 'the Zia regime's interpretation of the Qur'an'.[9] 'Rushdie's narrative', Grewal writes, 'though admittedly fragmented, fails to account for the very useful and powerful practices of opposition that are occurring in Pakistan today, practices which have been part of the history of women in both Pakistan and India'.[10] A vigorous critique of Rushdie's representation of women in *Shame* is also offered by Aijaz Ahmad, in *In Theory*, in which it is argued that the political hopelessness of the novel is reflected in the hopelessness of its female characters. What we find in *Shame*, Ahmad argues:

> is a gallery of women who are frigid and desexualised (Arjumand, the 'Virgin Ironpants'), demented and moronic (the twenty-odd years of Zinobia's childhood), dulled into nullity (Farah), driven to despair (Rani, Bilquìs) or suicide (Good News Hyder), or embody sheer surreal incoherence and loss of individual identity (the Shakil sisters). Throughout, every woman, without exception, is represented through a system of imageries which is sexually overdetermined; the frustration of erotic need, which drives some to frenzy and others to nullity, appears in every case to be the central fact of a woman's existence.[11]

If women are the symbolic underclass of *Shame*, and are meant to give readers an indication of the effects of power on the oppressed, Ahmad concludes, then *Shame* must be regarded as a fiction of despair, for there is no room, in such a presentation, for the promise of change and transformation.

Several points may be made that address different aspects of these arguments. Firstly, we might note that Rushdie at no point suggests that he is representing all women in Pakistan, or indeed trying to make a point about women's existence generally – rather he focuses purposefully and exclusively upon a single, and very narrow, class of Pakistani society (limited to only two families). Any generalised conclusions he comes to, therefore, if he comes to any generalised conclusions, can only be generalisations about that class. Secondly, and connectedly, we might also affirm again that the fact that Rushdie represents this narrow cross-section of women as politically disempowered because of its complicity (owing to its class affiliations) with corruption and hypocrisy does not mean that he disallows or undermines the attempts of other women in Pakistan, outside of his narrow focus, to empower themselves and seek a more active oppositional role. Indeed, a sustained and scathing attack upon the grotesque inequities of a patriarchal ruling elite might even help to inspire and enable such oppositional movements. Thirdly, we might question whether or not it is true that Rushdie does present all the women in the novel as disempowered. Rani Harrapa, as we have seen, is the one character in the novel, male or female, who is able to speak out in a potent and affecting way against corruption and criminality. Ahmad dismisses this act of resistance as something that only allows her a 'dignity of resignation'.[12] But how persuasive is this argument? For Rushdie she is the only character who is allowed to speak the 'truth' – which is surely a form of empowerment in an environment dominated almost exclusively by deviousness and misrepresentation (SRI, 61). A more persuasive critical evaluation of this incident is made by Grewal, who argues that Rushdie gives Rani a measure of power in allowing her to produce her shawls, but that he simultaneously denies her the equivalent powers of self-definition and expression that he allows himself as novelist. '[T]he carefully constructed coalition' between women and the marginalized figure of the writer, writes Grewal:

> breaks down when the narrative reveals that the writer has powers and abilities that the women do not possess. There is shown to be a great difference in the speaking-out of the novelist and of the women; Rushdie the novelist/ narrator does make himself heard, whereas none of the female characters manages to do so.[13]

But here too the criticism is open to debate. Far from being made less powerful than Rushdie as the writer, Rani's act of representation seems to be the *symbolic equivalent* of the act of the writer, as is often the case with the figure of the weaver in fiction. Rather than suggesting that Rani's act of representation is less significant than the novelist's act of representation, it is equally plausible that Rushdie is using Rani's act to explore the capacity of the artist to critique (or fail to critique) those with political power using representation. If this is the case he is using her as a means of examining his own situation as writer, not as a means of establishing his own act of representation as distinct from hers: she like him can show atrocities but do nothing about them, she like him is a satirist who exposes the crimes of the mighty but is unable to act more directly.

The female figure that Ahmad is inevitably most interested in, since she is, as he observes 'The crux of the matter', is Sufiya Zinobia, 'the beast'.[14] For Ahmad, the figure of Sufiya provides clinching evidence of the hopelessness and nihilism of Rushdie's aesthetic. She is presented from the start, he notes, 'as the very embodiment of the principle of redemption' – and yet she is made permanently and irrevocably mentally retarded.[15] Any possibility of redemption is, therefore, hamstrung from the outset: 'The novel … becomes incapable of communicating to us, in whatever grotesque forms, the *process* whereby a woman's intellectual and emotional abilities may be sapped, or regained.'[16] Once more, however, this seems to miss the point of the novel, since it is not *about* those processes of development but the tragic end point – or endgame – that results from the failure of those processes. As such, it is designed to operate not as a description of how repression can be confirmed or resisted but as a warning about the terrible consequences of political repression if it is *not* resisted.[17] This is not the same as saying that such consequences are inevitable or that political repression is inescapable: Sufiya represents the outcome of one possible process, but, by implication, her condition need not hold if that situation does not exist (as a fictional figure, after all, her condition is metaphorical and not, as Ahmad argues, medical).

Whilst the description of Rushdie's novel as a warning against a particular kind of political process identifies it as, broadly, dystopian – like most dystopias, and indeed like most tragedies, the fiction remains, perversely and paradoxically, hopeful. Hopefulness, however, is pitched beyond the pages of the fiction into some unspecified future. In the fictional world of *Shame* there can be no hope for Sufiya, there can be only destruction, and despair; but the novel none the less expresses the hope that there could be a world in which Sufiya Zinobia does not need to suffer in the way that she does, in which democratically elected governments do not become indistinguishable from military dictatorships, in which those without power are not erased from the consciousness of those with power. There is no indication what this society might be like, other than the negative condition that it will lack those features Rushdie finds undesirable in current social organisations, neither is there any suggestion that it is possible or desirable to conceive of and embody a perfect form of social organisation, since, for Rushdie, the attempt to achieve perfection will result only in intolerance of difference. Nevertheless, the condemnation of imperfection – of that which has the capacity to make us feel shamed – is expressive of the utopian hope that a society might exist in which such abuses of liberty are removed.

Satire in *The Satanic Verses*

O my body, make of me always a man who questions!
(Frantz Fanon, 1952)[1]

So I went on with my devilment, changing verses. (Salman
Rushdie, 1988, SV, 368)

In 1988, after a short creative detour to Nicaragua in his travelogue *The Jaguar Smile*, Rushdie published his fourth novel, *The
Satanic Verses*. Like *Midnight's Children* and *Shame* before it,
The Satanic Verses is a strongly satirical text that takes, as one
of its dominant socio-political agendas, the condemnation of the
abuse of power and authority. Unlike the two earlier novels,
however, *The Verses* shifts its attention away from the abuses
committed by South Asian political leaders towards the abuses
that flourished under Margaret Thatcher's Prime Ministerial
watch in 1980s Britain. Specifically the novel, in its dominant
narrative line, sets out to explore (or expose) the impact upon
Britain's minority communities of lingering Falklands-era
jingoism, and of systematic, institutionalised racism in organisations such as the police force and the media.

This aspect of the novel's politics is to the fore in the scenes
that concern one of the novel's two main protagonists, Sala-
huddin Chamchawala, the Bombay-born actor who has, after an
English public school education, settled in England, endeavoured
to become 'a goodandproper Englishman' (SV, 43), and angli-
cised his name to 'Saladin Chamcha' (the surname of which,
by unfortunate but revealing linguistic accident, translates from
Hindi and Urdu as 'spoon', an idiom for a sycophantic toady).

Chamcha, in this incarnation, is representative of a class of migrants well-theorised in discursive accounts of post-colonial diasporic identities. He is a near relative of the psychologically traumatised 'native intellectual' in Frantz Fanon's writings, who has internalised the racism of a dominant white culture to such a degree that he attempts a 'hallucinatory whitening'.[2] In this role he is also a descendant of earlier fictional avatars of the compliant migrant, such as the 'mimic men' of V. S. Naipaul's 1967 novel of that name who 'become what [they] see of [themselves] in the eyes of others', or Harris in Samuel Selvon's *The Lonely Londoners* (1956) who likes 'English customs', dresses like 'some Englishman going to work in the city' and is ashamed of the behaviour of his compatriots ('Only thing,' Selvon's narrator wryly observes, 'Harris face black').[3] Like these earlier figures in fiction, Saladin is regularly confronted with evidence of British racism. In his career as an actor he is relegated to 'voice-over' roles, partly because of the skills in mimicry that his cultural location has compelled him to develop but also because 'his face is the wrong colour' for British televisions (SV, 61). His contact with the profession of advertising, moreover, forces the covert racism of the industry upon his attention. When the grotesque Thatcherite media executive Hal Valance sets out to demonstrate to Saladin that advertising is an industry in which people 'of the tinted persuasion' do not customarily fare well, the ingrained prejudice of the profession is made starkly apparent. 'Let me tell you some facts', Hal offers:

> Within the last three months, we re-shot a peanut-butter poster because it researched better without the black kid in the background. We re-recorded a building society jingle because T'Chairman thought the singer sounded black, even though he was white as a sodding sheet, and even though, the year before, we'd used a black boy who, luckily for him, didn't suffer from an excess of soul. We were told by a major airline that we couldn't use any blacks in their ads, even though they were actually employees of the airline. (SV, 267)

Saladin's naive vision of a benevolent England, the reader learns, has survived years of contact with such racism. However, a terminal blow is delivered to his faith in this myth of England at the start of *The Satanic Verses*, which begins *in medias res* with Saladin and his co-protagonist Gibreel Farishta entering England (re-entering in Saladin's case) after plummeting from an exploding aeroplane to land on Hastings beach, site of an earlier conquest of the isles in 1066. Saladin's unorthodox re-entry into the UK signifies a precipitous expulsion from the Eden of his comfortable middle-class life in England, and his entry into a lurid fallen world in which he is able, finally, to see England – or specifically London – as it is experienced by less economically fortunate migrants than himself: an England that is 'visible' for those who are prepared to look for it, but remains largely 'unseen' by the wilfully blind citizens of the modern metropolis. In this hellish world below Saladin encounters the Black Maria police van in which, mysteriously transmogrified into a satanic goat-man by his fall, he is subjected to grotesque police abuse: punched in the testicles, graphically insulted, and made to eat his own excrement. The extremity of this abuse, combined with the unavoidable physical manifestations of his 'macabre demoniasis' (SV, 159) combine to provide the greatest challenge that Chamcha's dream of English civility has yet faced. Beaten viciously and transformed into what racist white percep-tions have made of him, Saladin's desperate assertions that there is no room in 'moderate and common-sensical' England 'for such a police van' (SV, 158), ring increasingly hollow, and the stage is set for the radical revision in his sense of cultural identity that occurs later in the novel. Propelled by events into another world, or at least another vision of the same world, Saladin begins an educational odyssey that takes him first to The Shaandaar Café, where he reluctantly encounters his 'own people' (SV, 253), who are shown both suffering from and celebrating their migrant lives, then 'underground' to Club Hot Wax, where wax effigies of racist politicians such as Oswald Mosley and Enoch Powell are ritually melted on a nightly basis, and where wax effigies of Asian and Afro-Caribbean men and women who have made a significant contribution to British culture *'since-de-Rome-*

Occupation' are revered (SV, 292). Club Hot Wax is the closest Chamcha comes to radical Black Power politics; and here Rushdie makes a tangential obeisance, albeit through pastiche and gentle satire, to more hard-line anti-racist writers such as the poet Linton Kwesi Johnson.

Saladin, however, remains an unwilling student of his experiences, which in turn enables Rushdie to maintain an analytical distance from the various political stances that Saladin is confronted with. As a devil figure Saladin is annexed as an emblem of resistance by a black youth culture seeking to reclaim traditional models of oppositionality; but he makes it clear that he is being appropriated against his will ('This isn't what I wanted. This is not what I meant, at all', Saladin protests, with a revealing echo of T. S. Eliot's Prufrock).[4] Likewise, when Saladin attends a political meeting in support of a black activist who has been arrested for multiple rape on trumped-up charges, he softens to the idea of grass-roots activism, but remains suspicious of the slanted and historically dubious rhetoric employed by the movement's leaders (SV, 414–16). Saladin's path, like Rushdie's own, is destined to be the 'third way' between extremes. He renounces the 'uncle Tomism' of his early career and so ceases to be a mimic man, but he does not rush headlong into radical opposition to the idea of England *tout court*. Rather he discovers that it is possible to become neither an 'assimilationist' nor a radical 'nativist' but to embrace what Bhabha calls (in reference to *The Satanic Verses*) the 'liminality of migrant experience'; a discovery that allows him to live within the experience of his multiple identity without striving to reduce that multiplicity to artificial certainties.[5] His moment of epiphany, if such it is, occurs whilst he is channel hopping and sees a 'chimeran graft' of 'two trees bred into one' on the television programme *Gardener's World*. 'If such a tree were possible', Chamcha reflects, 'then so was he; he, too, could cohere, send down roots, survive' (SV, 406).

The transformation of Saladin Chamcha into a devil-goat, and the concurrent transformation of his co-protagonist, Gibreel Farishta, into an angel, associates *The Satanic Verses* closely with

a specific sub-genre of the satire, the Menippean, which characteristically employs fantastic scenarios and improbable transmu
tations to give its characters new perspectives upon the familiar
world. As Philip Engblom has argued in an essay on 'carnivalization' and 'dialogicality' in Rushdie's novels, *The Satanic Verses*
includes 'every one of the menippean elements' enumerated by
Mikhail Bakhtin in the influential definition of the genre that
appears in *Problems of Dostoevsky's Poetics*: it is comic, it makes
free use of fantasy, it combines fantasy with 'slum naturalism',
it finds methods of observing from unusual points of view (from
mountain tops or through the eyes of angels and devils), it uses
the abnormal states of madness and dream to challenge ideas of
'epic and tragic wholeness', it sets the scandalous and 'profane'
against the normative and holy, it engages in 'abrupt transi-
tions', it is 'multi-styled and multi-toned [in] nature', it does not
obey classical literary rules or naturalistic linguistic conventions
and it is, finally, resolutely concerned to 'unravel and evaluate
the general spirit and direction of evolving contemporary life'.[6]
Centrally, however, *The Satanic Verses* is Menippean because
it fulfils the most essential qualification of Menippean satire as
defined by Bakhtin: it sets out to use fantastic fictional scenarios
as a means of interrogating ideas, and it subordinates all other
aesthetic features, including characterisation, plot, narrative
form, and even ethical restraint, to this overriding goal.

There are two central, and concurrently realised, acts of speculative intellectual enquiry taking place in *The Satanic Verses*.
In the first place the novel conducts a searching philosophical
investigation of the impact of migration upon individual identity. It sets out to discover what migrant life has been like in
Britain in the second half of the twentieth century, and it poses
what might be regarded as the principal philosophical question
concerning the migrant experience, modern or otherwise: does
the act of crossing over frontiers create the self anew and destroy
the prior self, or does the old self remain the same, even as identity is reshaped and remoulded by new experiences? This question is given a classical formulation in *The Verses* by Muhammad
Sufyan, the intellectually intrepid proprietor of the Shaandaar

Café, who finds an analogy for the experience of the modern migrant in the rival descriptions of metamorphosis offered by the Latin authors Lucretius and Ovid. According to Sufyan, the migrant is either like the mutating self presented by Lucretius in *De Rerum Natura* which by going 'out of its frontiers ... brings immediate death to its old self'; or the migrant is like the metamorph portrayed by 'poet Ovid' in the *Metamorphoses* which like 'yielding wax', can be 'stamped with new designs' without ever changing its essential self (SV, 276). Rushdie also poses this conundrum in a characteristically Menippean fashion using the rhetorical device of *syncrisis*: the establishment of '*pro et contra*' positions that are placed in a dialogue by the narrative.[7] On the one hand, the narrative gives us Saladin Chamcha – the integrationist chameleon who has staged an oedipal rejection of father and fatherland in order that he might be fully assimilated, all difference erased, into the new homeland of Britain. On the other hand, the narrative gives us Gibreel Farishta, engaged in a grander oedipal battle with God, who arrives on Hastings beach like William of Normandy, intent on some reverse colonisation, and enters into a disorientating battle with his host culture that culminates with his blowing a trumpet to bring down the city's walls during a fictionalised version of the Brixton and Southall riots (both of which locations are fused into Rushdie's 'Brick-hall').[8] If Chamcha, according to the analogy offered by Sufyan, is a Lucretian migrant because he seeks to bring death to his old Indian self, Gibreel is like the transformed beings that appear in Ovid because he is moulded into new shapes by his English encounter but remains unerringly scornful of all things English. One character, in Rushdie's terms, is 'seeking to be transformed into the foreignness he admires', the other prefers 'contemptuously, to transform' (SV, 426). Neither is fully at ease with himself, neither succeeds in finding an 'ideal' cultural location – but through the experiences of them both Rushdie manages to reflect upon the issues that the migrant must face, and the kinds of resolutions that he might (or might not) find. Gibreel, it transpires, does not survive because he is unable to reconcile the conflicting elements of his old self, and because he cannot replace his old self with a new self: 'He can neither return to the love of God, nor succeed in replacing it by earthly love' (IHL, 398). Saladin meanwhile finds that he is unable to erase his old self completely, and survives only because he is ultimately able to abandon his dream of total transformation and return, in part at least, 'to his roots' (IHL, 398). The solution to the conundrum, Rushdie appears to suggest, lies in neither the models given by Lucretius nor the model offered by Ovid, but in both. The self changes and it remains the same, or, rather, elements of it change, and elements of it are transformed; some aspects of identity are translated, and some remain untranslatable, and the trick, for the successful migrant, is to find a way of holding such an alarming, unsteady, multiple and irreconcilable sense of the selfhood together.

There are, in this respect, no final answers to the questions raised in *The Satanic Verses*, there are only negotiations of complex realities that cannot be reduced to coherent either/or solutions. 'Anybody ever tries to tell how this most beautiful and most evil of planets is somehow homogeneous, composed only of reconcilable elements, that it all *adds up*', Rushdie's character Otto Cone explains:

> you get on the phone to the straitjacket tailor … The world is incompatible, just never forget it … Ghosts, Nazis, saints, all alive at the same time; in one spot, blissful happiness, while down the road, the inferno. You can't ask for a wider place. (SV, 295)

Otto Cone's conclusions, based upon this hypothesis, are not optimistic. In the irreconcilability of different factions he sees only collision. 'The modern city', he lectures his bored family:

> is the locus classicus of incompatible realities. Lives that have no business mingling with one another sit side by side on the omnibus … And as long as that's all, they pass in the night, jostling on Tube stations … it's not so bad. But of they meet! It's uranium and plutonium, each makes the other decompose, boom. (SV, 314)

This world-view is to some extent confirmed in the novel, which does indeed show competing worlds in collision; most obviously in the street riots in which the diverse communities of a nascent multicultural London meet in destructive conflict. Rushdie, however, also offers more optimistic possibilities based upon the same world view. It is possible, *The Verses* sets out to demonstrate, that divergent realities can co-exist without necessarily coming into contention; that, indeed, the co-existence of divergent realities can be culturally and aesthetically productive, even as they simultaneously bring about disruptive forms of change. This possibility is exemplified by the novel itself, which engineers a convergence of diverse realities, but which continues to exist none the less as a functioning entity. It is also embodied in Rushdie's complex vision of London as a city that, even as it embodies these rather hellish possibilities, is, simultaneously, and for the same reasons, a beloved component of Rushdie's 'love-song to our mongrel selves' (IHL, 394). Migration and cultural mixing may cause collision, as Cone argues, and as the riots seem to demonstrate, but nothing is ever single and simple for Rushdie. Change is painful because it brings death, but it is also productive, because it brings about new life; and migrancy, as a species of change, is interpreted in precisely these terms. It is disruptive and transformative, both for the host culture and for the migrant, but it is also energising and reinvigorating because migrants 'impose their needs on their new earth, bringing their own coherence to the new-found land, imagining it afresh' (SV, 458). In this lies one of Rushdie's central theses concerning migrancy in this novel and elsewhere: that 'however ambiguous and shifting this ground may be, it is not an infertile territory' (IHL, 15).

The second subject of Menippean enquiry in *The Satanic Verses* also concerns the experience of a splitting of allegiance, a loss of certainty, the entry into multiplicity and the removal of *grounding* from between the feet. In this instance, however, the act of splitting comes about not purely because of a loss of homeland but because of an additional loss of faith. In this case the character of Gibreel Farishta is central, because his narrative charts his sudden loss of faith in Allah, and his subsequent traumatised hallucination of a series of visions in which he imagines himself to be the Angel Gabriel delivering revelation to various inspired personages.[9]

The questions posed in this second act of enquiry are questions about the nature of religious revelation. What is revelation? How is it received? Who gives out revelations? And how can we know that the revelation comes from a reliable source? These acts of interrogation are conducted predominantly, though not exclusively, in the four inset 'dream' chapters of the novel, which alternate with the scenes set in London and Bombay, and help create the novel's contrapunctual structure.[10] Each of the dream scenarios concerns an act of revelation of one kind or another. The scenes set in Jahilia offer a fictionalised representation (or travesty) of the revelation of Qur'anic scripture to Muhammad/Mahound in a transformed version of seventh-century Arabia. The scene concerning an exiled, Khomeini-like Imam living in contemporary London shows the Imam conjuring up Gibreel/Gabriel to assist him in his mental fight against the female goddess Al-Lat whom he regards as being representative of the notion of History. Finally, the narrative centred upon the 'Butterfly Girl' Ayesha concerns a young girl living in contemporary India who receives the instruction from Gabriel/Gibreel that she should lead her village on a pilgrimage to Mecca over the Arabian Sea.[11]

Rushdie presents each of these scenes as independent narratives that exist in their own right, *and* as dreams that appear to be products of the increasingly disorientated imagination of Gibreel. The result is a series of ontologically uncertain fictional interventions, which leave the reader unsure about whether the text is meant to be experienced as dream or reality. The act of hesitation between possibilities, experienced by the reader when confronted with these episodes, is arguably meant to duplicate the experience of hesitation experienced by the recipient of revelation when confronted by a vision: is the angel real or is it a dream? In practice, however, Rushdie leaves little room for any real intellectual hesitation about the veracity of the visions experienced by Mahound or Ayesha. The characters may sincerely believe that they are seeing the Archangel Gabriel and receiving instruction from him, but, Rushdie repeatedly implies, their belief rests upon unstable ground because they have no means of knowing whether their vision proceeds from God, the devil, a demented actor or – and this is what Rushdie ultimately means readers to understand – their own desires. Rushdie's interrogation, in this respect, is conducted from a relentlessly secular perspective that aims to expose the experience of revelation as being, at best, sincere but delusional and, at worst, self-serving and cynical.

Central to Rushdie's fictional premise in these interrogations is the apocryphal incident of the 'satanic verses' that has independent existence in Islamic tradition. The incident is recorded by two early Islamic authorities, Al-Tabari and Ibn Sa'd, and concerns verses that were 'delivered' to Muhammad in the course of the revelation of the fifty-third chapter of the Qur'an.[12] These verses appear to allow a semi-divine or intercessionary status to three pagan goddesses, Al-'Lat, Al-'Uzza and Manat, who were worshipped in Mecca prior to its conversion to Islam. Muhammad, according to the story, initially believed these verses to be the true word of God, and delivered them to the people of Mecca. A later revelation, however, showed that the acceptance of Al-'Lat, Al-'Uzza and Manat had been inspired by Satan, and the verses were expunged from the sacred text.[13]

The validity of this incident is heavily contested by Muslim scholars. Some, such as M. M. Ahsan, believe that the story is the product of an Orientalist conspiracy designed to 'to cast doubt on the teachings of Islam by challenging the authenticity of the Qur'an'.[14] Others grant the story apocryphal currency, arguing that it offers a useful (but not a sacred) insight into the character of the Prophet and the traditions surrounding him. Shabbir Akhtar, for instance, suggests that 'the incident of the satanic verses is actually a tribute both to the scrupulous honesty of a Muslim tradition that recorded such a potentially damaging event and also to the integrity and sincerity of Muhammad as God's spokesman'.[15] In Rushdie's hands the story is used to very different ends since it provides support for his fictional thesis that the Prophet (or at least his shadow-self Mahound) is not, as he ought to be, a passive recipient of the message, but is using his 'revelations of convenience' as a means of achieving his own ends (SV, 365). In Rushdie's provocative rewriting of the incident, Mahound delivers the contested verses in order to guarantee that he and his disciples 'will be tolerated, even officially recognised' (SV, 105), and then engineers the retraction when he becomes aware of the impact his compromise is having on his credibility.

Even the most dispassionate of readers will perceive that such episodes will offend believers – and not just believers in Islam but believers in all faiths, since what is at stake in the novel is the credibility of the act of revelation itself. *The Satanic Verses* is a blasphemous text on many levels. It offends against the sacred orthodoxies of religious creeds; it also commits several acts of what Sara Suleri identifies as 'cultural heresy' – 'acts of historical or cultural severance' that constitute 'blasphemies' against established secular perspectives.[16] The question to be asked of the novel, therefore, becomes not whether it is blasphemous – blasphemy is part of the novel's intention – but what we believe the function of Rushdie's blasphemy to be, and whether or not we believe such blasphemy to be justifiable. To what end does Rushdie's blasphemy work? Is the blasphemy gratuitous, or does it have a constructive social, political or even aesthetic function? Is the blasphemy simply designed to shock, upset and, more cynically, sell more novels, or does it have a viable, artistically justifiable, *raison d'être*? Obviously connected to this field of enquiry are a host of further questions that touch upon the nature and function of literature itself. Is there a place for blasphemy in the arts? Should such acts of blasphemy be allowed, or should they be subject to censorship in order for religious sensibilities not to be offended?

There is not space here to deal extensively with such complex questions, which have become increasingly topical as multiculturalism has brought different cultural codes into contact with one another (we need look no further than the political squall that surrounded the 2004 production of the play *Behzti* by

Gurpreet Kaur Bhatti, or the international furore that attended on the publication of a series of satirical cartoons depicting the Prophet Muhammad in the Danish newspaper *Jyllands-Posten* in 2005).[17] There is, however, space to briefly account for Rushdie's justification of his use of what he rather cautiously terms 'dissent' (IHL, 395). For many of his critics, it is axiomatic that the subject areas Rushdie interrogates should not be submitted to satirical interrogation, and, indeed, should be protected, morally and legally, from such forms of criticism. To use the shock tactics of the carnivalesque menippea to unsettle the sacred truths of Islam, even if the intent is playful, is, for some, an offence so great that it demands the ultimate punishment. Rushdie's defence of his novel, however, rests upon the demand that no ideas and ideologies should be immunised from intellectual testing, particularly if that intellectual testing takes place in the context of a literary tradition such as the menippea that has fulfilled this social function for centuries. 'A poet's work', as the satirist Baal explains in *The Satanic Verses*, is 'To name the unnameable, to point at frauds, to take sides, start arguments, shape the world and stop it from going to sleep' (SV, 97), and Rushdie, in the tradition of such poets, set out to do just that.

This element of Rushdie's defence may be regarded as relatively innocuous, since it applies not specifically to the tenets of Islam but to ideological systems more generally. It would, however, be disingenuous to suggest that Rushdie does not also believe that certain accepted 'truths' within Islam need to be tested because he wants to contest the validity of those truths. Indeed in *The Satanic Verses* Rushdie uses the narrative of Mahound to satirise monolithic and ahistorical interpretations of Islamic law, and to offer a surreptitious critique of the positioning of women in certain (but by no means all) manifestations of the faith. The continuing adherence to such interpretations, Rushdie suggests, is the result of a refusal to accept that the evolution of the holy book was an event in history, and that the book was subject to the ideological and cultural assumptions of the period in which it was written. The Qur'an, in Rushdie's view, was revealed at a time that has given it distinctive ideological characteristics and it ought, therefore, 'to be fascinating to Muslims everywhere to see how deeply their beloved book is a product of [that] place and time'.[18] 'Few Muslims', however, according to Rushdie, 'have been permitted to study their religious book in this way' because:

> the insistence within Islam that the Koranic text is the infallible, uncreated word of God renders analytical scholarly discourse all but impossible. Why would God be influenced by the socioeconomics of 7th-century Arabia, after all? Why would the messenger's personal circumstances have anything to do with the Message?[19]

The Verses returns the Qur'an to the historical conditions of its making, in order to show that it reflects a historically contingent set of ideological belief systems that ought to be open to critique *as* ideological systems. It is only by recognising such historicity, in Rushdie's view, that it will become possible for Islam to 'move beyond tradition' and 'bring the core concepts of Islam into the modern age'.[20]

These arguments, whilst illustrating Rushdie's motivations for critiquing certain interpretations of Islam in *The Satanic Verses* simultaneously reveal the unbridgeable gulf that exists between his own point of view and those that object to *The Verses* on an orthodox religious basis. As a cultural materialist Rushdie sees the Qur'an as a historical document that can be subjected to ideological analysis of the kind that underpins his reconstruction of Muhammad's life in *The Verses*. Orthodox Muslims, however, believe that the Qur'an is an immutable document of absolute authority because it is 'the word of god revealed through the angel Gabriel'.[21] To deny this is to deny one of the fundamental tenets of the faith; which is why Shabbir Akhtar argues that 'Any Muslim who fails to be offended by Rushdie's book ceases on account of that fact, to be a Muslim'.[22] The fact that Rushdie offends those who would see the Qur'an as a literal text, however, does not mean that Rushdie has no sympathy with Islamic thought more broadly. On the contrary, as Sara Suleri has argued in her outstanding reading of the novel, 'Rushdie has written a deeply Islamic book' that performs 'an act

of curious faith' by choosing 'disloyalty' as a means of drama-
tising 'its continuing obsession with the metaphors Islam makes
available'.[23] *The Verses*, she agrees, is written from a secular
perspective; this perspective, however, is not identical to the
secularism of the liberal West because Rushdie's is an 'Islamic
secularism' conceived from the point of view of an insider of the
faith.[24] 'Rather than confine a reading of the text to the somewhat unhelpful oppositions between fundamentalism and secularism, therefore', Suleri proposes:

> To move beyond the obvious good and evil implicit in such
> easy binarism to suggest instead that *The Satanic Verses*
> is, from a cultural point of view, a work of meticulous reli-
> gious attentiveness … [that enables] Rushdie to extend
> – with urgency and fidelity – his engagement with both
> cultural self-definition and Islamic historiography.[25]

The very fact that the novel needs to commit the act of blasphemy, Suleri goes on to argue, demonstrates Rushdie's ongoing
attachment to the cultural system of Islam, because 'blasphemy
can be articulated only within the compass of belief'.[26] Rushdie's
act of betrayal should therefore be read not as a simple insult or
as a simple renunciation but as an act of 'archaic devotion' that
seeks to desecrate a cultural tradition in order that that cultural
tradition might be revisited and renewed.[27]

'To be born again … first you have to die', Gibreel Farishta
sings as he plummets, like Satan, from the heavens at the start
of the novel (SV, 3). His observation applies to the experience of
the migrant in the first instance, since both he and Saladin are
about to suffer a rebirth as a result of their entry into England.
The phrase also serves to connect the novel's two principal intellectual concerns, however, because it applies equally to Rushdie's interrogation of Islam. Rushdie commits an act of betrayal
against Islam in *The Satanic Verses*, which may also be read as
a symbolic form of assassination. According to Suleri, however,
he does so as a 'gesture of recuperative devotion' because this
little death is designed to bring about a renewal and a rebirth
of the cultural system that this religious faith has generated.[28]
Rushdie thus blasphemes against religious faith in his œdipal act

of defiance, but this 'desacralizing of religion', for Suleri, simultaneously effects 'a resacrilizing' of Islamic history.[29] The act of renunciation that takes place in *The Satanic Verses* is, in this sense, a simultaneous gesture of recommitment and return. Just as Saladin renounces his father in order to return to him, and just as he leaves India in order to learn how to become an Indian again, Rushdie departs dramatically from the official narratives of Islam, in order that he can return to the tradition and make it his own.

Pessoptimistic fictions:
Haroun and the Sea of Stories
and *The Moor's Last Sigh*

> In real life the Guppees would lose the war. They're a
> shambles. (Salman Rushdie, 1998)[1]

> Forget Mumbai. I remember Bombay. (Salman Rushdie,
> 1999, GBF, 158)

At the midnight moment of Independence the new Indian Prime
Minister, Jawaharlal Nehru, made a now famous address to the
nation that has remained a testament to the optimism of the
times. In this speech, which is cited several times in *Midnight's
Children*, Nehru gives voice to his desire to create a secular,
democratic, tolerant, pluralist and socially just nation – 'the noble
mansion of free India where all her children may dwell'.[2] 'We
are citizens of a great country on the verge of a bold advance',
he announced from the Red Fort in New Delhi:

> and we have to live up to that high standard. All of us, to
> whatever religion we may belong, are equally the children
> of India with equal rights, privileges and obligations. We
> cannot encourage communalism or narrow-mindedness,
> for no nation can be great whose people are narrow in
> thought or in action.[3]

One of the principal aims of Rushdie's *Midnight's Children*
is to ask whether the first generation of independent Indians
lived up to Nehru's hopes for the newly created nation state or
squandered their opportunities. The answer the novel gives is
ambivalent. On the one hand, the image of India that emerges
is a broadly affirmative one that emphasises the nation's 'talent
for non-stop self-regeneration' (IHL, 16). On the other hand,

specific unfolding political developments led Rushdie to paint a much gloomier picture. India, the world's largest democracy, is shown lurching into fratricidal wars with Pakistan, losing its democratic rights at the hands of manipulative political leaders and fragmenting into violently opposed communal factions. The nation's allegorical representatives, meanwhile – the Midnight's Children – fail to find a meaningful role for themselves as a secular, multi-faithed institution, and end up imprisoned, mutilated and, finally, 'sperectomised' – drained of the hope that the Nehruvian idea of India had initially fostered. These were not, as Rushdie later argued, optimistic times, and the novel, as a political assessment on Indian affairs, reflects that lack of optimism. *Midnight's Children* ends, however, with the hope that the children of the children of Independence will make a better job of it. 'We, the children of Independence', as Saleem notes in the penultimate episode, 'rushed wildly and too fast into our future', the next generation 'Emergency-born, will be is already, more cautious, biding [its] time' (MC, 410). *Midnight's Children*, in this respect, may be said to conclude in a pessoptimistic spirit: pessimistic, to the extent that its narrator, Saleem, has failed in his efforts to redeem the nation and must end his days in a state of pathetic decline; optimistic to the extent that Saleem sees, in his young son Aadam, the lineaments of a future hope.

Writing in 1987, six years after the publication of *Midnight's Children*, Rushdie had come to believe that both the pessimism and the optimism of this conclusion were misjudged: the optimism because it was overly naive, the pessimism because it was insufficiently bleak. 'It's a sad truth', Rushdie writes:

> that nobody finds the novel's ending pessimistic anymore, because what has happened in India since 1981 is so much darker than I had imagined. If anything, the book's last pages, with their suggestion of a new, more pragmatic generation rising up to take over from the midnight children, now seem absurdly, romantic. (IHL, 33)

Rushdie's sixth novel, *The Moor's Last Sigh*, written fourteen years after *Midnight's Children*, may be seen as the fictional embodiment of this darker, less forgiving assessment of India's post-Independence political life. Here, much of the ebullience that characterised *Midnight's Children* has evaporated in the heat of communitarian violence and rampant political corruption, whilst the political resolution that the next generation was supposed to have embodied has been diverted into rapacious (and ultimately disastrous) stock market speculation and commodity fetishism. Greed, cynicism, aggression, malaise and ennui have become the determining characteristics of this generation, and where *Midnight's Children* saw such factors at work, but located, in the diverse Indian populace, a spirit of resistance to the corruption and tyranny practised by the nations rulers, here the politics of the people on the street and their shady manipulators have become just as divisive, just as cynical, bitter and twisted as the politics imposed from above.

The Moor's Last Sigh, like *Midnight's Children*, traces the family history of its protagonist back to the early years of the twentieth century. From the start, however, it is clear that the later novel is interested in different aspects of that history. Where *Midnight's Children*, broadly speaking, was a novel about the Emergency of the late 1970s, *The Moor's Last Sigh*, in a conspicuous departure from the concerns of the earlier Indian fiction, dismisses the Emergency in two deliberately cursory sentences: 'The Emergency ended. Life went on' (MLS, 235). Since, moreover, the novel's protagonist Moraes Zogoiby does not, like Saleem, crack up in 1977, his fictional experience of India extends considerably further than his predecessor's, reaching into the 1980s and early 1990s to glance at 'the disintegration of the post-Emergency, anti-Indira coalition government' (MLS, 261), the return of Mrs Gandhi to power in 1980 (which proves, for Rushdie, that 'there was no final morality in affairs of state, only Relativity') (MLS, 272), the death of her eldest son and right-hand man, Sanjay, in an air crash in the same year (MLS, 274) and the assassination of Mrs Gandhi by her Sikh bodyguards in 1984 after she had given orders for Indian troops to storm the Sikh Golden Temple to arrest the militant separatists who were seeking sanctuary there. The vicious anti-Sikh riots that followed in New Delhi in November are mentioned briefly in the novel

(MLS, 309). This is, however, one element in a broader consideration of the rise of Hindu nationalist opposition to Congress and the Nehru–Gandhi dynasty in the form of the Bharatiya Janata Party (BJP) on the national level, and parties such as the Shiv Sena (Maharashtra) on the regional level. In *The Moor* this latter party is represented as Mumbai's Axis, under the leadership of Raman 'Mainduck' Fielding, a thinly veiled caricature of the leader of the Shiv Sena, Bal Thackeray, also an ex-cartoonist and also a man with an English novelist's surname.[4]

The Shiv Sena, according to Aijaz Ahmad, has 'undergone many incarnations'.[5] Its members have appeared 'as anti-communist goon squads; as sons of the soil and self-styled representatives of the Maratha community in Maharashtra, saving the homeland from migrants from other parts of India; and as rabid Hindu communalists'.[6] 'In all its guises', Ahmad observes, 'it has been deeply involved with the crime underworld of Bombay and devoted to terror as a means to power'.[7] Each of these incarnations is reflected in Rushdie's fictional reconstruction, in which the hero, Moraes Zogoiby, becomes, for a time, one of Mainduck's henchmen – assisting him in breaking textile mill strikes in 1982 and 1983 by following 'union-wallah dross, activist scruff and Communist scum' down back alleys to beat them up (MLS, 306), and by aiding him in his quest to rid India of its minorities by persecuting Muslims and 'out-caste unfortunates, untouchables or Harijans or Dalits ... who had in their vanity thought to escape the caste system by converting to Islam' (MLS, 308). This forceful and frequently shocking portrait of neo-fascist communalist politics in India inevitably caused grumbles of discontent from those at whom it was aimed. Bal Thackeray, without reading the novel, declared that Rushdie had 'no business' writing about such matters when he had 'no motherland', and anxious distributors delayed releasing the novel in Bombay (CSR, 167). Commentators more sympathetic to Rushdie observed that the experience of the *fatwa* had not deterred him from writing about highly sensitive political situations.[8]

The BJP was formed in 1980 from the right-wing elements of the fragmenting Janata Party, a coalition of opposition groups formed in 1976 to resist Indira Gandhi's 'Emergency'. Its stated aim of transforming India into a Hindu state gained it increasing political support throughout the 1980s, and after the 1989 elections it took office as part of a coalition government consisting of the Communists and the Janata Dal party under V. P Singh. The anti-Sikh and anti-Muslim rhetoric of the party contributed to a sharp rise in communal tensions, culminating in violent disagreements concerning the ownership of the location of the Babri Masjid at Ayodhya in Uttar Pradesh, a sixteenth-century Mughal mosque constructed, according to some Hindu groups, on the site of a temple marking the birthplace of Ram, the hero of the Hindu epic *The Ramayana*. In 1989 and 1990 the BJP and associated organisations (the 'Sangh Parivar' or 'family of parties') had attempted to claim the site back without success, but, after the election of the BJP to power in Uttar Pradesh, on 6 December 1992 a gang of *kar sevaks*, militant Hindu 'volunteers' under the auspices of the BJP, demolished the Babri Masjid and launched a series of attacks on the Muslim community.[9] It was in the aftermath of this assault that Rushdie conceived and wrote *The Moor's Last Sigh*, and the novel is profoundly marked by the event. Rushdie's response is characteristically satirical: the leaders of the BJP and Shiv Sena are, like Bhutto and Zia before them, lambasted as 'clowns ... Burlesque buffoons, drafted into history's theatre on account of the lack of greater men' (MLS, 352). Rushdie also responds to the claims made by the BJP and the Shiv Sena at the mythological level, by contesting their own arguments about the exclusivity of the mythic traditions of India. Central to the claims of the proponents of *hindutva* is the belief that India has a single dominant tradition and that sites such as that of the Babri Masjid can therefore be claimed by a single community. Rushdie, whose work is characterised at the mythological level by attempts to demonstrate the interdependence of Hindu and Muslim narrative traditions, is at particular pains to demonstrate that the BJP's reconstruction of a holistic Hindu-Indian tradition is both a falsification of Indian cultural history and a falsification of Hinduism itself. In the first place Rushdie argues that the true significance of sites such as that of the Babri Masjid should be that they expresses the shared history of Muslims and Hindus in India, hence the novel's repeated use of palimpsestic images of layering and co-existence. In the second place Rushdie points out that the Hindu 'Lord Ram' – who is being presented by the BJP as a god of absolutist claims – is in fact 'the avatar of Vishnu … most metamorphic of the gods' (MLS, 351). 'The true "rule of Ram"', Moraes Zogoiby reflects in the novel:

> should therefore, surely, be premised on the mutating, inconstant, shape-shifting realities of human nature – and not only human nature, but divine as well. This thing being advocated in the great god's name flew in the face of his essence as well as ours. – But when the boulder of history begins to roll, nobody is interested in discussing such fragile points. (MLS, 351)

The sense that *The Moor's Last Sigh* imparts of the inescapability of violence and the inevitability of decline license, in the novel, a return to the kind of imagery that characterised Rushdie's third novel *Shame* – with its recurrent motifs of a house in decline, of monstrous physical defects, and of double identities. Just as, in the earlier fiction, the mental disability and incipient violence of Sufiya allegorised the corruption of Pakistan and the erosion of the values of civility; so in the later work the hyperactive growth of Moraes and his more conscious resort to graphic brutality signify the accelerating deterioration of Indian politics. In both works it is Rushdie's central conceit that 'Civilisation is the sleight of hand that conceals our natures from ourselves', and that 'our natures' will periodically rupture the veneer of civility with grotesque results (MLS, 365). The conflation of images in *Shame* and *The Moor's Last Sigh* suggests that, where Rushdie, at an earlier stage of his career placed India and Pakistan in opposition to one another, the former being associated with abundance and escape, the latter singularity and closure, here, in the later part of his career, he is increasingly seeing Indian and Pakistani political developments in similar terms.

The shift from the relative optimism of *Midnight's Children* towards the pessimistic register of *The Moor's Last Sigh* is also apparent in the shift of tone between *The Moor's Last Sigh* and Rushdie's previous work, *Haroun and the Sea of Stories*. This shift is all the more striking because the narratives of *Haroun* and *The Moor* are, in the very broadest sense, about similar things: the conflict between a pluralist and tolerant society and a monolithic and intolerant political order. In *Haroun and the Sea of Stories* this conflict appears in the guise of fantasy. The Guppees, a wonderfully various community of talkative creatures, have to defend themselves against the depredations of a monomaniac cartoon villain, Khattam Shud, who is trying to destroy their story sea because he sees it as a manifestation of a world of ideas he is unable to control. In *The Moor's Last Sigh*, the same conflict is replayed on both the novel's temporal plains. In the fiction's present, as we have seen, Rushdie dramatises a struggle between the 'superabundant, heterogeneous' Bombay of his childhood and the idea of 'Mumbai' peddaled in the 1980s and 1990s by the Shiv Sena (IHL, 32). In the historical period to which the novel repeatedly alludes, moreover, a comparable struggle is recorded between the variform culture that flourished in Moorish Spain between the eighth and the fifteenth centuries, and the repressive monomania of the re-conquering monarchs, Isabella of Castile and Ferdinand II of Aragon, who reclaimed southern Spain for Catholicism in 1492. '[W]hat happened in the Arab period in southern Spain, in Andalusia,' Rushdie explains to Charlie Rose:

> was that a kind of composite culture grew up. Although the Muslim sultans were the rulers, there were Christians and Jews and Muslims living side by side for hundreds of years, and their cultures affected each other. So the Muslims were no longer completely Muslim and likewise the others … And then this was destroyed by what you might call Christian fundamentalism, by the re-conquering Catholic kings. Now, it seemed to me that the world I come from, India, the world this book comes out of, is also a composite culture. It's also a place where there's a Hindu majority, but there are many different cultures – Hindu, Christian, Muslim, Jewish, et cetera – forming this kind of melange,

> this kind of composite entity, which is the world I grew up
> in and which I find very rich and pleasurable ... There is a
> kind of threat to that composite culture now coming from
> a new kind of fundamentalism, which is basically Hindu
> fundamentalism, the fundamentalism of the majority.
> (CSR, 202–3).

The respective outcomes of *Haroun*'s fantastic version of such a struggle and *The Moor*'s historicised account are predictably diverse. *Haroun* depicts the representatives of pluralism, the Guppees, managing, with the assistance of the intrepid young Haroun, to defeat the tyrant Khattam Shud, and to preserve their multi-form society and its impressively various 'story sea'. *The Moor*, by contrast, rooted in bleaker historical fact, is much less hopeful when it comes to its assessments of human society's prospects for peace and equality. The novel's narrative of the past results in the surrender of the Alhambra to a victorious Ferdinand and Isabella, and the flight from Granada of the last Moorish sultan Boabdil (giving the *ultimo suspirio* after which the novel is named) (MLS, 78–83). Meanwhile, Rushdie's depiction of the contemporary political scenario, of which the historical narrative is paradigmatic, expresses the fear that tolerance of cultural diversity in India will be increasingly eroded in coming decades. If the Moor Boabdil, long ago, gave his last sigh upon departing from the Alhambra, Rushdie warns, this too might be the fate of the modern Moor in India confronted with the tenacity of the proponents of *hindutva*.[10]

The differences in outcome in *Haroun and the Sea of Stories* and *The Moor's Last Sigh* are, of course, the result not of some radical four-year turnaround in Rushdie's assessment of the political scenario but of the generic differences between the two texts. *The Moor* is a satirical historical novel, the generic logic of which allows Rushdie to project what he calls a 'grownup knowledge ... of India and of this world' (CSR, 200). *Haroun*, by contrast, is a utopian fantasy that is aimed largely at a children's book market and that, in consequence, demands the relatively artificial aesthetic convention of a happy ending.[11] The optimism of *Haroun*, we might conclude, is not characteristic of Rushdie's political philosophy, but emerges *against* his own inclination. By contrast, the worldly pessimism – some would say realism – of *The Moor* is more in tune with the Voltareian instinct apparent in most of Rushdie's writing to brutally disabuse his readership of any illusions they may have about the benevolence of the world.

The fact that there are generic differences between *Haroun* and *The Moor*, however, does not obscure the comparability of intention in both texts, that intention being to celebrate the values Rushdie cares most about, namely, 'the values of pluralism and multiplicity and being many things and not being narrow, not defining your culture or yourself too narrowly' (CSR, 207). In *Haroun* this is done directly, through a depiction of triumphal overcoming. In *The Moor* Rushdie aims to reaffirm those same values of pluralism *by negative example*, through an outraged representation of the vulnerability of pluralism to fanaticism. Whilst one novel is utopian and optimistic and the other apocalyptic and pessimistic, therefore, their end point is the same: to advocate the moral imperatives of 'freedom, tolerance, living side-by-side with difference' and to emphasise the necessity 'of guarding against that attack, that intolerant, narrow spectrum' (CSR, 207).

This coincidence of concern between *Haroun* and *The Moor's Last Sigh* is also apparent in the shared formal preoccupations of both texts; in particular, in their mutual drive to create spectacularly complex intertextual webs of cross-cultural allusions. *Haroun*, in the space of its two hundred pages duplicates the narrative complexity of the story sea it depicts by drawing freely upon a range on narrative pre-texts, including European, Middle Eastern and Indian fairy tale, pop music lyrics, English children's classics, Indian cinema, Persian poetry, political allegory and science fiction. *The Moor's Last Sigh*, likewise, interweaves references to a vertiginous range of fictions, films and art-works, including Dalí and Buñuel's *Chien Andalou* (MLS, 148–9), *The Wizard of Oz* (MLS, 304–5), Oscar Wilde's *Picture of Dorian Gray* (see SRI, 204), Shakespeare's *Othello* (MLS, 224–5 and 430), *The Merchant of Venice* (MLS, 89 and 114–15), fairy tales from diverse cultural sources, Mehboob Khan's

Bharat Mata (MLS, 137–9), and Cervantes's *Don Quixote* (from which the name Benengali is taken).[12] None of these references is purely gratuitous, as each serves specific functions in the text, as scholars have already begun to demonstrate. Jonathan Greenberg, for instance, has argued that Rushdie uses *Othello* because 'the textually ambiguous nature of the Shakespearean original offers a model for how literary texts can accumulate meaning as they travel through space and time'; Justyna Deszcz asserts that Rushdie uses fairy tale in *The Moor's Last Sigh* as a utopian means of imagining 'how dominant social structures could be changed into more congenial ones'; and Stephen Henighan explores the ways in which Rushdie uses Latin American literature to demonstrate the existence of a shared Hispanic/Indian 'magic realist counter tradition'.[13]

Taken as a fact in itself, however, the intertextuality of these fictions also forms part of a broad argument Rushdie is seeking to make about cultural identity, namely that it is not determined by one influence alone, but develops through a complex process of hybridisation and exchange; that communal segregation, cultural supremacism, walls of force, apartheids and suchlike are falsifications of the historically verifiable, mongrel nature of human community. In embodying this viewpoint intertextually in *The Moor's Last Sigh* as well as in *Haroun* Rushdie is effectively carrying some of the formal optimism of the earlier novella into the later 'grownup' work; for if it is the case that, at the level of plot, Rushdie chooses, in *The Moor*, to depict 'the tragedy of multiplicity destroyed by singularity, the defeat of Many by One' (MLS, 408), it is also the case that the sheer polyphony of Rushdie's textuality simultaneously tends to assert that the plural and profligate sensibility will somehow persist in the structures of the individual imagination and in the perennially resurgent forces of art.[14]

The most obvious representative of the pluralist sensibility in *The Moor's Last Sigh* is the flamboyant, middle-class, socialite painter Aurora Zogoiby, whose artwork, like Rushdie's writing, is palimpsestic in style and hybrid in its sources. Aurora is clearly a figure of considerable sympathy in the novel, since it is her vision of India that Rushdie seeks ultimately to affirm – an India in which 'Jews, Christians, Muslims, Parsis, Sikhs, Buddhists, Jains' are allowed to co-exist peacefully in the same aesthetic space (MLS, 227). Whilst *The Moor* celebrates pluralism through Aurora and her work, however, it is also possible to detect in the novel a developing criticism of certain forms of pluralism, and certain uses to which pluralism may be put. This is apparent in the implicit contrasts between the artwork of Aurora and the work of her sometime friend, the Portuguese Indian painter Vasco da Gama, who also makes use of eclecticism and hybridity, but to radically different effect. Aurora's 'hyperabundant caval-cade' (MLS, 84) of imagery is motivated by a desire to represent her own embattled emotional reality and the complex cultural mix of the Indian nation. Hence when she, as a child, paints 'the great swarm of being itself' on her bedroom walls she does so by making this 'swarm' emerge from specific contexts: from her own family saga, from the convoluted past of the sub-continent, and from the landscape of 'Mother India with her garishness and her inexhaustible motion' (MLS, 59–60). When Vasco da Gama paints an equivalent 'swarm' on Moraes's bedroom walls, by contrast, it is motivated solely by his 'fondness for imaginary worlds whose only natural law was his own sovereign whimsi-cality' (MLS, 173):

> There were talking roosters, booted pussies and flying red-caped Wonder Dogs; also great galleries of more local heroes, for he gave us … djinns on carpets and thieves in giant pitchers and a man in the claws of a giant bird. He gave us story-oceans and abracadabras, Panchatantra fables and new lamps for old. (MLS, 152)

In juxtaposing the work of these two painters Rushdie seems to be making the same distinction that is implicitly drawn by Zeenat Vakil in *The Satanic Verses* between eclecticism that is 'historically validated' and eclecticism that is 'free floating', moti-vated by play alone (a fact that might explain Zeenat's reappear-ance in *The Moor's Last Sigh* as curator of Aurora's exhibition and author of Bhabha-esque monographs (MLS, 329)). Aurora's eclecticism is of the former variety, since it is justified by its social rootedness, and by its awareness of historical paradigms. Vasco's is of the latter variety since the welter of allusions in his work are made in the interests of kitsch pastiche, not of drawing politically and historically viable parallels between divergent cultural moments. This much is apparent in the detached, simulacra fortress he builds for himself at Benengali – a location, created like Calf Island in *Grimus* without sufficient regard for material realities, 'to which people came to forget themselves – or, more accurately, to lose themselves in themselves, to live in a kind of dream' (MLS, 402).

The different fates of the works of each artist give an indication of Rushdie's views concerning the social and political viability of each aesthetic mode. Aurora's fondness for contentious satirical statements leads her headfirst into a number of ideological controversies and makes her the target of a series of waspish critics. Her work is presented as a form of politicised agitation, product of a 'fucked-up dissident mind-set' (MLS, 206), that aims, as Rushdie believes the artist's work should aim, 'to point at frauds, to take sides, start arguments, shape the world and stop it from going to sleep' (SV, 97). Vasco's flattened-out style, meanwhile, makes him into a tremendous commercial success because it is unthreatening and easy to peddle on the global market. It is, however, ideologically vacuous. '[A]t once pyrotechnic and banal', Moraes notes in a snide aside, it looks good in airports (MLS, 160).

Vasco's cynical exploitation of eclecticism for commercial gain prepares readers for the recognition, developed in the latter half of the novel, that pluralism may be used for shallow and manipulative ends as well as socially constructive ones. This is particularly apparent in the depiction of Adam Braganza, the 'fast-track Infobahini' who emerges as the rising star of Abraham Zogoiby's Siodicorp corporation (MLS, 359). Adam demonstrates that, in the fast-moving, high-tech atmosphere of modern business, change and transformation are essential to survival. He is, for instance, adept at rebranding companies, changing their names and appearances in order to relaunch them 'into the world market' in 'snappier' guises (MLS, 342).

He also maintains a position for himself at the cutting-edge by practising 'the chameleon arts' – transforming himself continuously in order to 'bewitch and woo' (MLS, 354). All this change, however, is – as Rushdie puts it – 'affectless' (MLS, 343). In *The Satanic Verses*, when Muhammad 'rebrands' himself by taking the name Mahound, he does so for personally (and politically) empowering ends: to adopt the name that Europeans have used to denigrate him, 'To turn insults into strengths' (SV, 93). Likewise, when Rushdie refers to himself as 'chameleon … chimera … shape-shifter' in his essay 'One Thousand Days in a Balloon', he sees these qualities as politically enabling, because they are a dimension of his 'mischievous, iconoclastic, out-of-step, clown-[instinct]' (IHL, 438). In Adam's world of fiscal flux, by contrast, equivalent transformations are designed not to alter social structures or to precipitate real change in personal relations, but only to *repackage* them, leaving inequitable economic systems at best untouched, more authoritarian at worst. His desire to engender 'we-feeling', for instance, is a product not of progressive social responsibility but of his intent to 'optimise manpower utilisation' (MLS, 342). Likewise, his insistence that Siodicorp become a 'listening corporation' is a recipe not for greater understanding between management and workers but for greater managerial control (MLS, 343).

It is significant, in light of this characterisation, that Adam Braganza is the son of Saleem Sinai from *Midnight's Children* now grown into adulthood. Adam, or Aadam, it will be remembered, represented Saleem's hope for the future of Independent India. It is a bitter irony, on Rushdie's part, that Adam has grown up to be a shallow fool, who has swapped political idealism for financial greed and who has submurged the quest for meaning in dynamic-sounding but vacuous business-speak. The new generation, as Saleem predicted, has arrived full of brash confidence and a desire to take over the world, but it cares 'nothing for old-timers' concerns' for political justice and social organisation (MLS, 343). It is concerned only with money and self-promotion.

Adam's female equivalent in the novel is Uma Sarasvati: an Eve who compliments his status as first man of the new 'me' generation. Like Adam she is a plural entity, and like Adam she uses her pluralism to destructive effect – systematically deceiving Moraes and his family, and finally destroying the vital connection between Moraes and his mother by tape-recording him cursing Aurora during bouts of engineered love play. '[I]n the matter of Uma Sarasvati,' as Moraes realises too late, 'it had been the pluralist Uma with her multiple selves, her highly inventive commitment to the infinite malleability of the real, her modernistically provisional sense of truth, who had turned out to be the bad egg' (MLS, 272). The damage that Uma does to the 'pluralist philosophy' on which Aurora has raised Moraes and his siblings causes them all to reassess their faith in the hybrid, and, finally, leads to a transformation in Aurora's eclectic aesthetic practice. The figure of the Moor in her paintings, at one time the embodiment of 'Palimpstine', the place where 'worlds collide' to 'flow in and out of one another' (MLS, 226), ultimately comes to lose 'his previous metaphorical rôle as a unifier of opposites, a standard-bearer of pluralism', ceases 'to stand as a symbol – however approximate – of the new nation' and is 'transformed, instead, into a semi-allegorical figure of decay' (MLS, 303). Aurora, we are told:

> had apparently decided that the ideas of impurity, cultural admixture and mélange which had been, for most of her creative life, the closest things she had found to a notion of the Good, were in fact capable of distortion, and contained a potential for darkness as well as for light. This 'black Moor' was a new imagining of the idea of the hybrid – a Baudelairean flower, it would not be too far fetched to suggest, of evil. (MLS, 303)

This suspicion of pluralism is not entirely without precedent in Rushdie's work. Uma's unstable character is foreshadowed in the maniacal mythical assemblages of Grimus, in the schizoid disharmonies of Eliot Crane in the short story 'The Harmony of the Spheres' (EW, 123–46), and in the pornographic, worm-tongued whisperings of Chamcha on the telephone to Gibreel in The Satanic Verses. In company of these forebears, Uma becomes one of a network of characters in Rushdie's writing who represent a failed hybridisation: a multiplicity of identity that is the result of madness, instability or immorality rather than a finely balanced, materially realistic and ideologically grounded sense of the hybrid nature of the self. She is the 'shallow protean[s], forever shifting shape' described in *The Ground Beneath Her Feet*, and not the transformatory migrant for whom a 'principle of uncertainty' is 'a measure of certainty' and a 'gauge of the solidity of the ground' (GBF: 462).

Though Rushdie's suspicion of Uma has precedent and antecedent, however, his critique of rootless pluralism in *The Moor* seems more sustained and vituperative than elsewhere. The principal reason for this is that Rushdie's satire in *The Moor* is directed as much at liberal cosmopolitans in India who have sought to accommodate the fanatical right as it is at the fanatical right themselves. Hence, the 'pluralists' of the novel, whether they are represented affirmatively or critically by Rushdie, are, at one point or another, compromised by their association with the far right. Aurora is rumoured to have had an affair with Raman Fielding, Moraes works for him, Uma is associated with the MA, and the operatives of Siodicorp are happy to make use of MA street thugs in their business processes. Hence, too, the principal villain of the novel turns out to be not Raman Fielding, the totalitarian bigot and natural successor to Rushdie's children's villain Khattam Shud, but Abraham Zogoiby, the capitalist businessman in whose hands Rushdie's 'cosmopolitan ideal' is transformed into what Rachel Trousdale has called a 'faceless globalism'.[15] 'Rushdie's critiques of the Shiv Sena in *The Moor's Last Sigh* drew cries of outrage in Bombay', as Trousdale notes in her important article on the novel:

> But they might have been even more incensed had they realised that they are not the real enemy in the [book]. Rushdie's critique is wider ranging and more subtle than an attack on an easily parodied neo-fascist organization. Rushdie objects to the Sena's goals and methods, but he also uses his history of the Sena's origins to offer a critique of the pitfalls of his own position ... the Sena are ... created by a failed cosmopolitanism, and the eventual destruc-

tion of Bombay comes from the same source. When the ideal of inclusivity remains a rhetorical goal rather than a reality, the result may be one of two terrible extremes: the violent, bigoted communalism of the Shiv Sena and the destructive, exploitative internationalism of the Da Gama-Zogoiby Axis.[16]

Towards the conclusion of *The Moor's Last Sigh*, as Trousdale suggests, the city of Bombay (now renamed Mumbai by the Hindu right) is symbolically assaulted by a series of terrorist bombs. During this assault a number of characters who appeared in Rushdie's earlier Bombay fictions are violently killed: Zeenat Vakil, from the Bombay scenes of *The Satanic Verses* is blown up along with most of Aurora's work, Adam Braganza of *Midnight's Children* meets his untimely end, as does Lord Khusro, the boy-mahaguru who was Saleem's childhood friend Cyrus Dubash. The significance of these events is not hard to perceive. Rushdie feels that the Bombay of his earlier fictions is in the process of being eradicated, and this is his obituary for that earlier incarnation of Bombay.[17] There is additional significance, however, in the fact that it is not clear where these devastating bombs have come from. It could have been Abraham Zogoiby who 'lit the fuse', Moraes speculates, or maybe it was the goon 'Scar', but ultimately the actual bomber becomes irrelevant because all Bombayites are implicated in the political and capitalist processes that have brought violence to the city (MLS, 372). 'The explosions were our own evil', sighs Moraes. 'We have chopped away our own legs, we engineered our own fall. And now can only weep, at the last, for what we were too enfeebled, too corrupt, too little, too contemptible, to defend' (MLS, 372–3).

The pop novel in the age of globalisation: *The Ground Beneath Her Feet* and *Fury*

> It's time you finally high-tailed it out of the British Empire.
> (Salman Rushdie, 1999, GBF, 330)
>
> Eat me, America. (Salman Rushdie, 2001, F, 44)

Rushdie's bitter critique of Abraham's cynical business practices in *The Moor's Last Sigh* tends, overwhelmingly, to emphasise the destructive effects of rapacious economic globalism in India. Corruption, hypocrisy, violent crime and secret links with back-alley politics are daily fare for the super-capitalist Abraham, and all resources available are placed at the service of his mock-Satanic ambitions to own the city of Bombay, and, in owning it, eradicate any local character it might once have had. Rushdie's following two novels, *The Ground Beneath Her Feet* and *Fury*, also take globalisation as a central theme. These latter fictions, however, tend to reflect more ambivalently upon the subject, since they focus upon global mass culture – a phenomenon in which Rushdie is able to discover egalitarian and utopian impulses flourishing alongside the darker machinations of international capital flows. On the one hand, in these novels Rushdie is clearly aware that mass popular culture is driven by, even complicit with, what Shaul Bassi calls 'consumeristic ideology'.[1] On the other hand, he is simultaneously concerned to argue that, despite this implication in capitalist economics, global mass culture has sufficient ideological autonomy and cultural complexity to offer a critique of the very same economic processes that have brought it in to being.

Globalisation is a term that has been used extensively in recent decades to refer to the growing interconnectedness of world economic, political and social systems. In Anthony Giddens's influential definition, globalisation involves 'the intensification of worldwide social relations which link distant localities in such a way that local happenings are shaped by events occurring many miles away and vice versa'.[2] Theorists of globalisation differ on the subject of when globalisation begins. Some argue that it is, exclusively, a late twentieth-century phenomenon, sparked by the internationalisation of politics and economics since the Second World War, and the growing capacity of communication systems to operate on a worldwide scale. Others date globalisation back as far as the invention of printing and paper, the emergence of language, even to the first human movements across the globe.[3] Rushdie, in *The Ground*, gestures towards this more long-term form of globalisation in his attention to mythic narratives that have circulated globally for centuries, achieving numerous different localised expressions in the process. The parallels that William Methwold and Darius Xeres Cama discover (via the work of Max Müller and Georges Dumézil) between the myths of ancient Greece and the Sanskrit myths of Vedic India are a vivid indication that there have been information flows across national borders for as long as there have been people to carry information from one place to another. Rushdie, however, also suggests in *The Ground* that global interconnections between divergent localities have gained a distinctive new character in the contemporary period because the world is *speeding up*. Where once it took centuries for information to circulate between distant cultures, it now takes moments; and where once the local had time to absorb, digest and transform materials that arrived from other locales, now information arrives in such overwhelming quantities, and with such powerful economic backing, that the collisions between the local and the global have become more visible than ever before.

This new relationship between the global and the local has given rise to a series of questions that have preoccupied cultural theorists with an interest in identity and ethnicity in the modern world. These questions, characteristically, concern the nature of global culture, and the role that is played by local forms of cultural identity in global contexts: By what is global mass culture driven? Whose world view does it favour? Is it truly global? Or is it the view of one power structure writ on a global scale? Are marginal local cultural influences subsumed entirely into global mass culture, or do cultural differences remain apparent? Does the local have any power to transform the global, or does the global always transform the local? Stuart Hall in his essays on the subject addresses precisely these questions, and so offers a convenient point of reference for the study of Rushdie's approach to the globalisation of culture in *The Ground* and *Fury*. Like Rushdie, Hall believes that globalisation advances, as capitalism advances, upon 'contradictory terrain'.[4] To the extent that it has brought divergent cultures into inter-animating relationships on a scale never before possible, eroded parochial borderlines and created forms of hybridisation that have given new life to art, Rushdie's work reflects globalisation as a dynamic transformatory force. To the extent, however, that it is produced by a long, inequitable history of imperial activity led from the global North, enables the ever-more-effective exploitation of subaltern classes and Third-World nations by those with economic power, and secures the increasing homogenisation of culture into brand names and recognisable commodities, his work reflects more critically upon the subject.

Central to Hall's essay is a recognition of the fact that global mass culture is driven by the West, and so represents an extension of Western power. 'Western technology, the concentration of capital, the concentration of techniques, the concentration of advanced labour in the Western societies', Hall argues, 'remain the driving powerhouse of this global mass culture', and in this sense, global mass culture 'is centered in the West and ... always speaks English'.[5] Hall, in this regard, is aligned with those globalisation 'sceptics' who argue that the concept of globalisation is:

> primarily an ideological construction; a convenient myth which, in part, helps justify and legitimize the neoliberal global project, that is, the creation of a global free market and the consolidation of Anglo-American capitalism within the world's major economic regions.[6]

Whilst recognising this economic reality, however, Hall also points out that Anglo American dominance of the mediation and dissemination of global mass culture does not necessarily entail absolute dominance of the cultural products themselves. Hence, though global mass culture may speak in English, it no longer speaks in an English that has been fully authorised by England and America:

> It speaks English as an international language which is quite a different thing. It speaks a variety of broken forms of English: English as it has been invaded, and as it has hegemonized a variety of other languages without being able to exclude them from it.[7]

The global can thus be transformed by the local; or rather, the local interrupts the global to interpolate its own way of speaking, singing, its own way of looking. Globalisation, in this sense, allows new localities access to a terrain of representation that was once the exclusive playing field of only a few localities.

The entry of localised modes of expression and perception into the arena of global representation, however, is, as Stuart Hall goes on to argue, by no means an automatic guarantee that the local will be represented *as* local. Globalisation may give localised modes of expression greater exposure, greater international *presence* than ever before, but the globalisation of local forms of representation often occurs as a mechanism of 'its peculiar form of homogenisation' – its drive to 'recognise and absorb ... differences within the larger, overarching framework' that remains 'essentially an American conception of the world'.[8] The analogy Hall offers in explication of this idea is the now familiar culinary one. On the one hand globalised capitalism has given us the power to be able to eat 'exotic cuisine' on an unprecedented scale – 'to eat fifteen different cuisines in any one week, not to eat one'.[9] On the other hand, it is clear that, exotic cuisines are not being eaten by the poor in Calcutta but by the rich in Manhattan, and that the precondition for their consumption in Manhattan is that they have been removed from those cultural contexts in which their differences are meaningful. '[I]n order to maintain its global position', Hall observes:

capital has had to negotiate and by negotiate I mean it had to incorporate and partly reflect the differences it was trying to overcome. It had to try to get hold of, and neutralise, to some degree, the differences. It is trying to constitute a world in which things are different. And that is the pleasure of it but the differences do not matter. [10]

These observations give rise to a question, that, for Hall, is clearly central to the problem of representing difference in the context of globalised mass culture. '[I]s this', he asks:

simply the final triumph, the closure of history by the West? ... Is this the final moment of a global post-modern where it now gets hold of everybody, of everything, where there is no difference it cannot contain, no otherness it cannot speak, no marginality which it cannot take pleasure out of?[11]

This conclusion, Hall confesses, is 'tempting', but ultimately he dismisses it as a form of 'ideological post-modernism' that says 'I can't see round the edge of it and so history must have just ended'.[12] Instead, Hall argues, we must see globalisation, not just from the inside – from the perspective of the global itself, which sees nothing but absorption – but also from the outside; from the perspective of the local that uses the process of globalisation to tell 'the story from the bottom up, instead of from the top down'.[13] 'After all', Hall argues, 'it would be an extremely odd and peculiar history of [the late] twentieth century if we were not to say that the most profound cultural revolution has come about as a consequence of the margins coming into representation'.[14]

In *The Ground Beneath Her Feet* Rushdie explores the relationship between the 'local' productions of the individual artist and global economic flows by meditating upon the related phenomena of popular music, pop celebrity and photo-journalism. Like Stuart Hall, Rushdie argues that popular mass culture is an American-led phenomenon, made possible by the massive concentration of wealth, power and technological means in the West. This hegemonsing role of American popular music is vividly illustrated in the novel when, after American troops are shown withdrawing ignominiously from Vietnam (renamed Indochina in the parallel dimension of the fiction), rock and roll is described as one of those 'real warriors of America' that moves in like a Trojan horse to complete the job that the military had failed to do. 'Where soldiers had failed,' Rai notes with heavy irony, 'U.S. values – that is, greenbacks, set to music – had triumphed ... Let the music play. Let freedom ring. Hail, hail, rock 'n' roll' (GBF, 441). Simultaneously, however, even as he shows rock and roll's complicity in the process of mediating American capitalism to the world, Rushdie is at pains to offer readers a more complex picture of American-led global mass culture. Principally, he seeks to demonstrate that mass cultural media such as popular music cannot be said to be owned by any one nation, because the cultural influences that have come together to create it are drawn from diverse centres of culture in complex power relations. This point is made effectively in *The Ground* via the concise if flippant technological history of the medium offered by the defiantly lower-case 'rock journalist' lil dagover:

> When the slaves came across the sea and were forbidden to use their drums ... they listened to the music of the Irish slave drivers, the three-chord Celtic folk songs, and turned it into the blues. And after the end of slavery they got their drums back and that was r&b, and white kids took that from them *and added amplification* and that was the birth of rock 'n' roll. Which went back across the ocean to England and Europe and got transformed by the Beatles ... and that stereo mutation came back to America and became VTO et cetera. (GBF, 545)

Given such a cross-cultural history, Rushdie implicitly avers, this supposedly American medium cannot be said to embody Americanness in any simple sense. Neither can it be said to reflect a *one-way* channel of power, since its formation – circulating between those with power and those without – has been a result of dynamic claims and counter-claims. The slaves may have been introduced to the music of the Irish slave drivers as a result of highly inequitable power relations, but their appropriation and transformation of that music allowed them, in some measure, to reassert their own power (what Hall calls the 'weak power' of the margins). Likewise, America may now have claimed the musical forms that have resulted from these cross-cultural meetings as its own, but these claims are being made by bands such as Rushdie's fictional rock group VTO, which reflects an inherent complexity in American culture because its two lead members, Ormus Cama and Vina Apsara, are Indian in origin. If American popular music is culturally complex in its origins and in its current mediations, Rushdie seems to ask, then how can it be said to carry a homogeneous or non-complex idea of American power? Music, like all art forms, almost certainly has a role to play in hegemonic processes; but it is also sufficiently complex in itself, sufficiently manifold and ambivalent in its cultural locations, that it can simultaneously be used to contest these processes.

The idea that American music is too complex in its cultural location to be described as a mediator of American power in any simple sense is allegorised in the rather fanciful sub-plot concerning Ormus Cama and his twin Gayomart. Gayomart, readers learn, has died in the womb, but this has not prevented Ormus communing with him, because Ormus turns out 'to be what the ancients called a psychopomp' – a latter day Orpheus who is 'concerned with the retrieval of lost souls, the souls of the beloved dead' (GBF, 53–4). From these ghostly communions with his dead brother, Ormus claims, he hears all pop music hits 'in advance', long before he hears them from their American sources (GBF, 96): 'Sitting on the top step of his dreamworld, staring into the dark … searching out his lost sibling, his shadow self, who is down there somewhere in the blackness', Ormus Cama apprehends mumbled versions of tracks that he will later know to be 'Heartbreak Hotel' or 'Blue Suede Shoes' (GBF, 99).

The twin narrative fulfils several functions in the novel. It forges an allusive link between Ormus Cama and Elvis Presley, who also had a twin brother who died *in utero*. It also helps Rushdie establish one of the novel's guiding conceits, that there are two worlds, a 'real' world and an 'other' world, existing in parallel with one another (the 'twist' being that the real world for the novel's characters is the 'other' world for its readers). Principally, however, the narrative of Ormus and his twin is designed to demonstrate that 'the genius of Ormus Cama did not emerge in response to, or in imitation of, America' because it was mysteriously fostered by his Indian twin whilst he was still living in Bombay (GBF, 95). The 'early music' of Ormus, as Rai the photographer-narrator observes, 'was not of the West, except in the sense that the West was in Bombay from the beginning, impure old Bombay where West, East, North and South had always been scrambled, like codes, like eggs'. (GBF, 95–6).

Some critics of *The Ground* have found the argument embedded in this episode less than persuasive. Christopher Rollason, for instance, having teased out many of the musical allusions in the novel, argues that the Gayomart subplot is a 'piece of trickery' designed to conceal the fact that Rushdie is actually describing 'a textbook case of mainstream Anglo-American 60s/70s stadium rock, bereft of any "Asian" input'.[15] 'We could have had an Indian Buena Vista Social Club,' Rollason complains, 'what we get is VTO, playing born-in-the-USA rock'n'roll while laying claim to an Asian "authenticity" that derives from literary sleight-of-hand alone'.[16] An alternative view is expressed by Shaul Bassi who, in a later article on the novel, takes issue with Rollason's argument by pointing out that Rushdie, in using the device of the dead twin, is not striving for a representation of elusive authenticity but is making an argument for the impossibility of authenticity. '[T]his is not a gratuitous gimmick', she contends, but

> another parodic take on authenticity, which is a recurrent trope of a novel teeming with forgeries, scams, hoaxes, and, contiguously, ghosts, apparitions, doubles ... What is authenticity, asks Rushdie? Do we really know where culture comes from ...?[17]

A revealing contender for a real-life paradigm for VTO, Bassi goes on to argue, is the band Queen, fronted by Farrokh Bulsara, better known as Freddie Mercury. Mercury, like Ormus Cama, was from a Parsi family. He was born in Zanzibar and spent some of his youth in Bombay; and yet Queen, as Bassi notes, were 'deficient in visible ethnic markers'.[18] Rushdie's VTO, in Bassi's view, should be understood as a band of this type, rather than a band of the radical or ethnic variety. 'Like Freddie Mercury, Ormus Cama … is no herald of some politically correct message'; 'His story rather embodies all the contradictions of the globalisation of culture, extolled by some, demonised by others'.[19]

There is an element of truth in both Rollason's and Bassi's arguments. As Rollason suggests, the musical work of VTO never seems interesting enough to persuade readers that it is anything other than a rather banal, run of the mill, stadium rock band. Vina and Ormus may come from India, but the music they produce, so far as it is possible to tell, does not use Indian musical traditions or influences in any dynamic or transformatory sense. At the same time, however, it is clear that Rushdie never intends to claim that VTO are culturally radical, or that Ormus and Vina actively seek to present a radicalised Indian identity. Rushdie's argument is merely that global popular culture – like all cultures – is a complex and ambivalent phenomenon, that cannot be owned by any one nation, and that cannot be used to express the values or beliefs of any one power complex. In India critics of pop music may argue that it is 'one of those viruses with which the almighty West has infected the East, one of the great weapons of cultural imperialism, against which all right-minded persons must fight' (GBF, 95); but, by giving his mainstream American pop band Indian singers who have re-localised American pop via Bombay, Rushdie is posing the question: how is it possible to claim that, in such a hybridised, cross-cultural medium, power moves in only one direction?

It is also necessary to observe that American economic and political power is not Rushdie's only – or indeed primary – object of analysis in *The Ground*. As with many of Rushdie's earlier novels, the political energies of the novel are directed predominantly towards a critique of regimes and ideologies that are, in one form or another, culturally segregationist. Indeed, when Rushdie sets about describing what he regards as the positive (self-consciously utopian) political impact of the globalisation of Vina's music, it is not its capacity to resist American cultural imperialism he focuses upon, but the threat it poses to the guardians of religious, political or ethnic purity. '[I]n death', as Rai records, Vina becomes a potent political force because her symbolic transcendence of 'all frontiers: of race, skin, religion, language, history, nation, class' angers oppressive rulers and inspires resistance against them.

> In some countries there are generals and clerics who, alarmed by the Vina phenomenon, by its otherness and globality, seek to shut it down, issuing commands and threats. These prove useless. Inspissated women in sexually segregated societies cast off their veils, the soldiers of oppression lay down their guns, the members of racially disadvantaged peoples burst out from their ghettos, their townships, their slums, the rusty iron curtain is torn. Vina has blown down the walls, and this has made her dangerous. (GBF, 480)

Rushdie's celebration of pop music, in this passage, is as much a celebration of its capacity to resist what Hall calls 'exclusivist and defensive' forms of localism as it is a celebration of its capacity to give voice to politically progressive forms of localism.[20] Indeed, pop music becomes a form worthy of celebration for Rushdie precisely because he believes that it does two things simultaneously: it is able to reflect differentiated localised forms of identity on the global stage, yet at the same time the inherently hybridised nature of the medium works against those prejudicial forms of localism that seek to respond to globalised American power by asserting the purity of their own cultural identities. The medium of rock and roll – as constructed in Rushdie's fiction at least – thus seems to offer him the best of both worlds: on the one hand it takes from the local an enabling sense of a complex intercultural self that is able to survive in global contexts, on the other hand, it is a utopian form that takes from the global an energising refusal of absolute boundaries. Rock and roll, in *The Ground*, thus takes up the mantle of the phenomena that have served similar functions in Rushdie's earlier works. Like the oral narrative tradition as it is represented in *Haroun and the Sea of Stories,* pop music is depicted as a fundamentally democratic, inherently hybrid, boundary crossing form that tends by nature to resist monolithic interpretations of cultural identity. Indeed, like the novel form itself, pop music is imagined as a dialogical and heteroglossic aesthetic medium that is by definition antagonistic to singular conceptions of self and society. *The Ground Beneath Her Feet,* in this sense, is not just a novel about pop music; pop music is also about the novel.

Rushdie's subsequent novel *Fury* departs from *The Ground* in a number of respects. The *salaam* to Bombay that Rushdie makes progressively in *The Moor* and *The Ground* appears to be absolute in his eighth novel, since the protagonist's Bombay childhood is barely explored. Indeed, as a result of abuse Malik Solanka has suffered in his childhood, memories of Bombay are actively suppressed until late in the narrative. Correspondingly, Rushdie also makes a formal shift away from the diachronic narrative method of *The Ground,* which like many novels by Rushdie bridges several generations and several historical periods, towards a synchronic narrative arrangement in which the story moves laterally between four parallel locations: New York, Hampstead, the imaginary island of Lilliput-Blefuscu, and the fantasy world of Galileo-1.[21] These departures, however, work in tandem with a number of continued themes. The novel's exploration of repressed violence, which finds sudden outlet in serial murders, continues a narrative line that can be traced back, through Cyril Cama's murders in *The Ground* to the murders committed by Sufiya in *Shame.* Likewise, the use of narratives drawn from Greek myth as paradigms for the narratives of contemporary protagonists, apparent in the uses made of the Orpheus narrative in *The Ground,* recurs in the comparisons Rushdie makes between Solanka's three lovers and the avenging Furies of classical myth. Love itself, indeed, is a recurring theme, evidenced by the fact that Rushdie appears to be endeavouring to trump the love triangle of *The Ground* with the evermore complex love quadrangle that is depicted in *Fury.*

Centrally, however, *Fury* extends the concerns introduced in *The Ground* by taking the power of US-led global capitalism as its cardinal theme. Indeed, one of the primary ideological concerns of the novel is to trace an epochal shift away from the era of global interconnection brought about by British colonialism towards the era of globalisation brought about by American economic imperialism. This shift is symbolised effectively in a resonant scene in which Malik Solanka meets an advertising copywriter who asks him for his opinion concerning a corporate-image campaign for American Express. The advertisements in this campaign depict 'images of famous city skylines at sunset' and bear the copy line 'THE SUN NEVER SETS ON AMERICAN EXPRESS INTERNATIONAL BANKING CORPORATION' (F, 35). The immediate point of this campaign is fairly evident: there is 'always an American Express office open somewhere in the world' (F, 35–6). The advertisement's full significance, however, lies in the fact that American Express now feels itself to be in a position to appropriate for itself jingoistic slogans that were once associated with British imperialism. Once upon a time it was the British who could claim that they had an empire of such broad geographical spread that, somewhere in the world, the sun would be shining on a British dominion. Now the logic of corporate expansion has allowed American-based companies to make identical claims. There could hardly be a more expressive illustration of the fact that there has been a shift in power away from Britain towards America, and away from direct colonisation spearheaded by military might towards an indirect colonisation led by the logic of the market. The shift in power from Britain to America has not just entailed a *displacement* of British authority, however: the British past has been actively devoured by the American present, its fragmentary remains becoming the fodder for a new and larger imperium. No wonder, perhaps, that the British Prime Minister is named 'Tony Ozymandias' (F, 256). Like Shelley's Ozymandias, the 'King of Kings' in the 1817 sonnet, he represents something that was once mighty but that now lies in dust and ruins.

Consumption of every sort becomes a central theme in this novel, which opens with a vivid and dynamic depiction of a consumer 'golden age' at work on the streets of America:

> The city boiled with money ... New restaurants opened every hour, Stores, dealerships, galleries struggled to satisfy the skyrocketing demand for ever more recherché produce: limited-edition olive oils, three-hundred-dollar corkscrews, customised Humvees ... outsider art, feather-light shawls made from the chin-fluff of extinct mountain goats. (F, 3)

In this frenzy of consumption, Solanka observes, cultures of all descriptions go down the gullet of US-led multinational capitalism – whether they are the marginalised cultures represented in the work of the 'outsider' artists, or the dominant cultures of once proud civilisations such as ancient Greece or imperial Rome. 'Everyone was an American now,' Solanka gloomily observes, 'or at least Americanized':

> Indians, Iranians, Uzbeks, Japanese, Lilliputians, all. America was the world's playing field, its rule book, umpire and ball. Even anti-Americanism was Americanism in disguise, conceding, as it did, that America was the only game in town and the matter of America the only business in hand. (F, 87)

Solanka, it transpires has direct personal experience of the 'omnivorous power' of consumer capital (F, 44). Some years before, after becoming disillusioned with his academic life at King's College, Cambridge ('its narrowness, infighting and ultimate provincialism'), he had created a doll by the name of Little Brain, and developed a series of late-night television programmes in which the doll interviews great philosophers (F, 15). Contrary to expectations, the series had become a cult hit and been moved to prime time, but in the process Solanka had lost creative control of his progeny. From being a 'highbrow' format, in which the protagonist can 'hold her own with Erasmus or Schopenhauer', the show has been transformed by an anonymous crowd of ghost-writers into a banal comedy presided over by a 'tawdry celebrity' with 'the intellect of a slightly over-average chimpanzee' (F, 98). Solanka, enraged but impotent in the face of this theft, has come to despise Little Brain, but, though he has walked away from the project, he has not forsworn the royalty money that pours into his bank account. He is, as a result, 'compromised by greed', and knows that 'What he opposed in [American capitalism] he must also attack in himself' (F, 87).

This tale of an idealistic creator who comes to hate his monstrous and out-of-control creation replays the narrative of Mary Shelley's 1819 novel *Frankenstein*. Indeed, at one point of the novel, Little Brain is referred to as 'Frankendoll' (F, 101). If *Frankenstein* is a parable about the dangers to society of uncontrolled scientific advance, however, *Fury* is a parable about the dangers to the artist of uncontrolled consumer capitalism. Little Brain has become a global phenomenon, but, because she has been globalised 'from above', Solanka has lost control of the moral, intellectual and political meanings of his original work. The responsibility for his loss of control, moreover, is partly his own since it was his own greed – his own implication in the capitalist process – that had led him to relinquish Little Brain to the executives.

Sarah Brouillette has argued that this narrative line in *Fury* reflects anxieties Rushdie feels about his own location as an author.[22] Like Solanka's dolls, Brouillette observes, Rushdie's novels are increasingly mediated by an industry constituted of conglomerate multinationals 'that operate locally through numerous branch offices that are often headquartered in New York'.[23] Like Solanka, therefore, Rushdie too is potentially compromised – 'a suplicant at the feast' of American commerce whose pockets jingle with the coins of the very power structures he seeks to critique (F, 87). In Broullete's view, this injects a degree of uneasiness into the novel. '[W]ith Rushdie's career in mind,' she writes, 'the novel's more significant solipsism is its paranoia about the way mass media make cultural products available for highly politicised forms of appropriation or interpretation that betray the controlling intentions of their authors'.[24] The novel, however, even as it raises such anxieties, also seeks to pre-empt potential criticism by presenting arguments designed to demonstrate that complicity in the capital processes does not automatically negate political autonomy.

These arguments are effectively made on two fronts. Firstly, Rushdie asserts, with Stuart Hall, that, though 'America is the great devourer' (F, 69), those who are subject to devourment can never be fully assimilated. Hence Solanka believes that though Little Brain has made him a slave to American multinational capitalism, he remains in a complex and contradictory relationship with capital that enables him to critique it even as he accepts its coin. 'Yes,' he admits, 'it had seduced him, America; yes, its brilliance aroused him, and its vast potency too, and he was compromised by this seduction', but, he adds crucially, 'that did not mean he could not look it in the eye' (F, 87).

Rushdie also reasserts the autonomy of the individual in the face of American led capitalism by setting against his parable about globalisation from above a counter-parable about globalisation from below. In the present time of the novel Solanka meets a young New Yorker named Mila Milo (an echo of Mira Celano in *The Ground*) whose gang of friends are, it turns out, 'stormtroopers of the technologized future', Internet geniuses sufficiently adept to pose a threat to Bill Gates himself (F, 118–19). Solanka begins a relationship with Mila in which the two of them role-play fantasies that reflect a shared past of childhood abuse. The relationship is doomed, but out of its wreckage comes a grudging collaboration on an Internet relaunch of Solanka's dolls, this time in the form of the Puppet Kings of Galileo-1. Mila, playing the young technological hustler, promises the nervous Solanka that the project, as orchestrated by her, will not be hijacked from on high because the technology of the Internet provides a route to globalisation that cannot be controlled absolutely from above. 'This time you don't lose control', she assures him. 'This time you have a better vehicle than even *existed* when you came up with Little Brain, and you drive it, totally. This is your chance to get right what went wrong before' (F, 178). Once bitten, Solanka is understandably suspicious, especially since he does not trust developing technologies. When the project comes to life, however, Solanka discovers that his imagination is liberated by the medium, and that Mila is correct in her assertion that 'the whole concept of ownership … is … different now' (F, 178). Aesthetic concepts developed through the use of the Internet, he finds, cannot be contained or controlled absolutely by any one interest group, because its functioning is truly dialogical: 'the river of Solanka's imagination [is] fed from a thousand streams' and 'the work never settled, never stopped being a work in progress but remained in a condition of perpetual revolution' (F, 190–1). Solanka also discovers that the formal possibilities for art produced by Internet technologies are non-conventional, and thus tend to favour his own quirky and inspiration-led modes of creation. 'He, who had been so dubious about the coming of the brave new electronic world', we are told:

> was swept off his feet by the possibilities offered by the new technology, with its formal preference for lateral leaps and its relative uninterest in linear progression, a bias that had already bred in its users a greater interest in variation than in chronology. This freedom from the clock, from the tyranny of what happened next, was exhilarating, allowing him to develop his ideas in parallel, without worrying about sequence or step-by-step causation. (F, 186–7)

It is significant that in these observations on the functioning of the Internet Rushdie echoes two phrases from his earlier fictions. Solanka's distaste for 'the tyranny of what happens next' recalls Saleem's efforts to resist being bullied by Padma 'back into … the universe of what-happens-next' in *Midnight's Children* (MC, 39). Likewise, the 'river' of Solanka's imagination that is 'fed from a thousand streams' recalls the 'sea of stories' in *Haroun* that is 'made up of a thousand thousand thousand and one different currents' (HSS, 72). These timely echoes suggest that Rushdie believes that the Internet functions in ways that are not dissimilar from his own fictions: it permits the construction of anti-linear narrative sequences that are comparable to the anti-linear narrative sequences of *Midnight's Children*, and it allows for a degree of narrative interactivity that is also apparent in the complex textualities of *Haroun*. The Internet, in this respect, operates as one more in a long line of metaphors, from the oral narrative tradition in *Haroun* to popular music in *The Ground*, that are designed to be paradigmatic of Rushdie's own writing: heterotopian spaces in which multitudes of influences blend creatively and clash dynamically.

Rushdie's intentions in constructing this specific parallel between his own fictions and the aesthetic productions made possible by the Internet are at least twofold. Firstly, Rushdie is indicating that his own distinctive and individuated style of writing is in no way suppressed or compromised by the mechanics of globalised culture but actively *aided* by them. Secondly, Rushdie is indicating that vehicles of globalisation, such as the Internet (and by implication, mass publishing), do not inevitably produce inane and commodified pap, but may produce complex and contestatory forms, which are expressive of divergent and non-homogenised viewpoints. The Internet may have been brought into being by dominant capitalistic processes that encourage the homogenisation of global culture, *Fury* suggests, but it also, paradoxically, enables the global dissemination of forms of expression that cannot be fully contained by dominant structures of authority.

The difference in authority between the two forms of globalisation that Rushdie describes in *Fury* is marked by another repetition, this time within the novel. In the early stages of the narrative Solanka, reflecting on the tendency of American capital to 'devour' the cultures of classical Greece and Rome, observes that 'Such plundering and jumbling of the storehouse of yesterday's empires, this melting pot or *métissage* of past power, [is] the true indicator of present might' (F, 43). Placed in the context of the sustained satirical reflection on the inequity of US power that takes place in the first quarter of the novel, it is clear that Solanka disapproves 'in his old-fashioned way' of this cultural theft (F, 6). Yet, when Solanka comes to develop his own 'multimedia beast', he not only engages in the same practice but seeks to justify it: 'The ransacking of the world's storehouse of old stories and ancient histories', he notes, 'was entirely legitimate … Transmutation was all' (F, 190). Solanka is not being an unconscionable hypocrite when he says this, because in each case the act of 'plundering' or 'ransacking' the 'storehouse' is done by different parties. In the former case power works from on high to assimilate divergent cultural references. In the latter case power works from the ground up to reclaim the territory that is being predated. In this resides a neat illustration of the distinction drawn by Hall between globalisation from above and globalisation from below. The former introduces the margins into its orbit in order that those margins can be absorbed; the latter results from the margins finding ways of representing themselves.

Rushdie's parable about globalisation is not, however, a naive affirmation of all forms of globalisation from below. It is significant that in the latter part of the novel, Solanka's Puppet Kings of Galileo-1, like Little Brain before them, *are* appropriated and put to uses that Solanka cannot control; this time by a resistance group who are seeking greater political representation for the diasporic Indian population on the imaginary, but Fiji-like, South Pacific island of Lilliput-Blufescu.[25] Solanka is, at least in principle, favourable to the cause of the revolutionaries, since his girlfriend, Neela, is an Indo-Lilliputian, and has spoken passionately about the disenfranchisement of her people by the indigenous 'Elbee' population. As the movement for the enfranchisement of the Indo-Lilliputians is hijacked by an authoritarian and separatist leader, Babur, however, Solanka's attitude to the cause begins to change, and the uses made of his puppet kings begins to seem more sinister. Rather than being used for a cause that promises the enfranchisement of a people who have been dispossessed because of their ethnic origin, it increasingly appears that Solanka's creation is being used to support the ambitions of a tyrant-in-the-making who seeks to crush rather than foster 'democratic principles'. Once more, therefore, having sought his 'redemption in creation', Solanka has seen the 'denizens' of his imagination 'move out into the world and grow monstrous' (F, 246).

As was the case in *The Ground Beneath Her Feet*, therefore, *Fury* enacts a critique not only of capitalistic gloablism but also of intolerant and exclusive localism, and of the capacity of both to appropriate and distort the materials of culture. Indeed, it may be said that in *Fury* Rushdie uses one cultural dynamic to answer back to the extreme manifestations of the other: the globalisation of culture works against cultural isolationism, meanwhile localised cultural expressions continue to work within, and sometimes against, the homogenising forces of globalism. Rushdie thus adopts, in these novels, a familiar position 'in between' alternatives, although in these cases he does not just locate himself 'in between' cultures, but in between the very mechanisms of cultural mediation in the modern world. Whilst earlier novels thus tend to explore the impact upon individuals and communities of the experience of being between multiple traditions, *The Ground* and *Fury* turn more explicitly to consider the impact upon the producer of cultural works of the experience of being caught between the demands of the global market and the imperatives of local self-expression.

Critical overview and conclusion

Timothy Brennan in his critical study *Salman Rushdie and the Third World* identifies Rushdie as being a member of a distinctive and historically original group of writers that has come to prominence in the period following the formal dissolution of the British Empire. These writers are described by Brennan as *Third World cosmopolitans*: migrant intellectuals who are identified with a Western metropolitan elite in terms of class, literary preferences and educational background, but who, by virtue of ethnicity, are also presented by the media and publishing industries as being 'the interpreters and authentic public voices of the Third World'.[1] Such intellectuals, Brennan argues, have come to enjoy a privileged place within the Western, or Westernised, intellectual community because they allow a 'flirtation with change', but they are ultimately accepted and celebrated in the West only because they speak to the West in its own voice: they represent, in Brennan's suggestive oxymoron, a 'familiar strangeness' that allows Western intellectual institutions to incorporate previously marginalised voices, without any actual challenge to their basic preconceptions about literature, culture, class and race.[2]

The complex cultural position occupied by the 'Third World cosmopolitan', Brennan admits, has some distinctive political advantages for the socially progressive writer: it enables him or her to make 'interventions into the cloistered West and its book markets' and, as a result, to speak from locations that non-Western writers have historically only had limited access to.[3] Because an international perspective tends to produce a new outlook on the idea of nationhood, moreover, cosmopolitanism also allows 'fresh thinking about national form, about a new homelessness that is also a worldliness, about a double-edged post-colonial responsibility'.[4] Brennan's study, however, tends to emphasise the limits that a cosmopolitan location imposes upon writing that seeks to be politically transformatory. Though internationalised writers of non-Western origins may be able to achieve unprecedented exposure, Brennan suggests, they do so only at the cost of being conditioned by the Western market for which they write. Likewise, though such writers may engage in some constructive rethinking of the idea of nationhood, this rethinking tends to be 'detached [from] and insensitive [to]' life as it is lived within the nations themselves because cosmopolitan writers are, by definition, writing about nationhood at a distance – physical, emotional, temporal and intellectual.[5] Thus, even though Rushdie is a novelist who writes what Brennan concedes may be a 'literature of combat' – and even though Rushdie may attempt, through his uses of 'oral' narrative techniques and 'popular' forms, to locate what Brennan refers to (via Fanon) as 'the people's "zone of occult sensibility"' – Rushdie's fiction cannot be politically useful to 'the people' in the nations concerning which he writes because 'it is not addressed to them' but to the West.[6]

In Brennan's view this failure to address 'the people' accounts not only for the greatest ideological limitation of Rushdie's work but also for its greatest aesthetic limitation: its emotional disengagement, and its tendency towards 'brilliantly sketched cartoons woven together by an intellectual argument' rather than narratives that follow 'the emotional logic of the characters' lives'.[7] The exception that demonstrates this rule, for Brennan, is *The Satanic Verses*, which differs from previous novels 'Because here Rushdie is dealing with a life not only remembered and longed-for but experienced first-hand':

> England is where Rushdie lives (not India or Pakistan), and so the immediacy of the account takes us away from those snapshots of emotion, and those distanced descriptions of lives actually lived, that fill the pages of the earlier novels.

> Those works were essentially thinking pieces whose only really vivid human interactions took place where the personal narrator spoke directly to the reader ... By contrast, the metafictional strategies of *The Satanic Verses* are not nearly so pronounced; the characters are for the first time people living in the world, acting out their lives in a story of their own. The story is not *about* events, but in them.[8]

This more immediate relationship with his subject matter, for Brennan, produces decisive shifts in Rushdie's approach to two of his major subject areas: the Islamic tradition and Western 'liberalism'. In the case of the former, *The Satanic Verses* (ironically, given its reception) 'no longer simply targets that tradition for rebuke' since, 'as a part of what makes the new immigrant different from the English, it is something can be learned from, even emulated, at the cultural level'.[9] In the case of the latter, Brennan argues, Rushdie ceases to be so messianic about the apparent 'attractions of Western "freedom"', because Western 'liberalism' is revealed to be a hollow prospect when seen in the actual (rather than abstract) political context of Thatcherite Britain.[10]

Whilst Brennan detects these more positive polemical elements in *The Satanic Verses*, however, he also argues that here, as in the earlier novels, Rushdie's political position is compromised – in part because Rushdie's fiction, whilst critical of Thatcherite policies on race, does not, unlike the earlier diasporic novels to which Rushdie is indebted (Samuel Selvon's *Lonely Londoners*, G. V. Desani's *All About H. Hatterr*), operate 'within a larger milieu of union activism [and] community organising'.[11] One of the consequences of this, Brennan suggests, is that the black communities which are represented in *The Satanic Verses* are not presented in a serious or politically effective light. Indeed, Brennan believes that 'The book's characterisations of West Indians (like its characterisation of women) are often embarrassing and offensive':

> Some random examples might include ... the comically stupid and overweight Afro-Caribbean community activist,

Uhuru, given the last name 'Simba' after Tarzan's elephant;
the clownish West Indian Underground employees speaking
dialect as though it were fit for low comedy.[12]

Brennan's critique of Rushdie's representation of the black
community in *The Satanic Verses* is indicative of further critical agenda operative in Brennan's study as a whole. As well
as exposing Rushdie's failure to offer empowering representations of national liberation struggles, *Salman Rushdie and
the Third World* also includes a sustained exposé of Rushdie's
depiction of characters drawn from the less privileged socio-
economic sectors of society. For instance, Brennan maintains
that 'Saleem's occasional revulsion for Padma's bodily smells
and habits' in *Midnight's Children* 'carries to the cultural and
personal level' the kind of 'class tensions' also 'found between
Saleem and Shiva'.[13] Likewise, 'Padma's lower class impulses in
art' (that is, her responses to Saleem's narration) 'symbolise the
fatal immaturity of her class in the struggle for a meaningful
democracy on a legitimately "Indian" terrain'.[14]

Such criticisms carry potent polemical force; though they
do also raise a number of potential objections. The use of names
like 'Simba', for example, is justified explicitly in *The Satanic
Verses* as being part of a politicised strategy of reclaiming
insults. It might also be observed that Brennan's practice of
selecting various characters, identifying them as grotesque, and
then arguing that Rushdie, thereby, represents a whole class
as distasteful or 'cartoonish', seems methodologically dubious
– primarily because Rushdie tends to represent all his characters
as grotesque regardless of their class, or of other social or ethnic
distinctions. Hence Saleem, the middle-class character and autobiographical shadow of Rushdie himself, can be seen to be just
as physically revolting, just as ignorant, just as self-interested
as Padma, or Shiva, or Tai. Also problematic, in this regard, is
the fact that it is not always clear that it is Rushdie the author
who is making judgements about characters. Frequently, observations in Rushdie's novels are filtered through the perceptions
of narrators – or other characters from the text – whose outlook
Rushdie presents as unreliable. We see Padma, for instance, only

through the highly distorting lens of Saleem's perceptions – and we as readers know that Saleem is a 'little rich boy' whose view of the world is shaped (or rather mis-shaped) by his arrogance and the sense of personal superiority given him by his propitious birth.

These are specific quibbles, however, and do not touch upon Brennan's central thesis: that Rushdie's socio-cutural location compromises his viability as a political writer. It is this thesis that has proved the most enduring of Brennan's arguments, and that has provoked some of the most important critical responses to Rushdie's work. Few if any of these critical responses disagree with Brennan's broad location of Rushdie as a migrant, cosmopolitan intellectual (indeed, Rushdie defines himself in this way). The source of disagreement, rather, concerns the degree to which Rushdie's political arguments are undermined by this location, and by the structures of thinking that his location tends to implicate him in.

Perhaps one of the most thoroughgoing defences of Rushdie against Brennan's broad thesis comes from Bishnupriya Ghosh, who argues that, since *Salman Rushdie and the Third World* appeared in the late 1980s, it has become possible to 'confront cosmopolitan privilege without dismissing cosmopolitanism as politically bankrupt'.[15] Her study, *When Borne Across*, accordingly, seeks to identify and explicate a form of *situated* cosmopolitanism that 'despite the glare of international visibility' engages 'in a literary politics that interrupts [its] own global circulation'.[16] This category of writers (which includes Salman Rushdie, Arundhati Roy, Amitav Ghosh, Vikram Chandra and Upamanyu Chatterjee) is, as Brennan might suggest, engaged in 'a canny play to emergent global and local markets for world literatures'; simultaneously, however, it is also part of a 'South Asian progressive discursive formation' that challenges 'both the forms of nationalism reinforced by global flows and the pernicious globalism surfacing in dispersed local contexts'.[17] 'It is', Ghosh maintains, 'a formation that shares ... a social imaginary of sorts: of democratic self-rule, and of contingent cosmopolitics', even though 'Its political articulation is dispersed, defined by the dispersed nature of the common enemy, globalism'.[18]

Conversely, Marxist critics, following Brennan, have, on the whole, endorsed Brennan's thesis, arguing that Rushdie's brand of destabilising cosmopolitan metafiction leaves dominant ideological systems unscathed whilst undermining cohesive programmes of politicised resistance. This argument is made with some force by M. Keith Booker in an essay that appears in the same collection that first introduced Ghosh's arguments: *Critical Essays on Salman Rushdie* (1999), edited by Booker himself. This essay represents something of an about-turn for Booker, who, as he himself remarks, had, in the early stages of his career been sympathetic to the idea that Rushdie was a 'transgressive' writer who, by 'providing historical accounts that are complex, multiple, nonlinear, and unreliable' was 'somehow striking an effective blow against Western scientific historiography and therefore against the bourgeois hegemony that this historiography represents'.[19] The later Booker, however, is increasingly mystified by the idea that the 'exuberant presentation' of the individual memory as 'erratic, confused, and often fabricated ... somehow shakes the mighty ideological foundations upon which the global power of Western capitalism has been built'.[20] On the contrary, Booker argues, the aesthetic complexity of Rushdie's writing, its valorisation of fragmentary modes of perception, and its refusal of rationalist models of history mean that his fictions conform to, and so indirectly reinforce, 'the ideological structures deployed by Western capital during the decades of the Cold War'.[21]

Comparable arguments are also developed by Aijaz Ahmad, whose polemical critique of Salman Rushdie's *Shame* in *In Theory: Classes, Nations, Literatures* remains one of the most provocative denunciations of Rushdie as a political thinker yet to be published. Despite a thriving industry of Rushdie-orientated criticism, literary critics, with the notable exception of Stephen Baker in his *The Fiction of Postmodernity*, have yet to offer a detailed analysis of Ahmad's arguments, or to offer a persuasive defence of Rushdie's position.[22] This is not for lack of commentary, affirmative or negative, on the various positions developed by Ahmad in *In Theory*. Critics have responded abundantly to his condemnation of Rushdie's representation of women in *Shame* and to his interrogation of the privileging of Rushdie's works in metropolitan intellectual orthodoxies. Both these arguments, however, are, for Ahmad, rooted in more fundamental political objections to Rushdie's work that, whilst they are often rehearsed, have yet to receive a sustained response. In Jaina Sanga's study of Rushdie, for instance – excellent as it is in many ways – Ahmad's arguments are summarised, but no detailed reply is made to them; an omission that is surprising, given that Sanga's own broadly post-structuralist view of Rushdie's political significance as a writer would seem to demand a defence of Rushdie against Ahmad. For Sanga, Rushdie's re-utilization of colonial and post-colonial metaphors can be politically effective because it provides a means of 'problematizing entrenched versions of reality'.[23] For Ahmad, however, such an argument is flawed. Change is effected by transformations in material relations and the only thing that can be helpful, in the context of ongoing neo-colonialism in the Third World, is not a challenge to conceptions of 'reality' but a global transformation in the ownership and distribution of capital. 'Very affluent people may come to believe that they have broken free imperialism through acts of reading, writing, lecturing, and so forth', writes Ahmad:

> For human collectivities in the backward zones of capital, however, all relationships with imperialism pass through their own nation-states, and there is simply no way of breaking out of that imperial dominance without struggling for different kinds of national projects and for a revolutionary restructuring of one's own nation-state.[24]

Despite the pre-existence of such arguments, critical studies such as Sanga's and others like it, written from within a broadly post-structuralist academy, do not sufficiently question their own basic post-structuralist assumptions about the political efficacy of transforming metaphors and 'writing back' to established genres. Some critics even go to the extremes of suggesting that novel writing might have a direct and destabilising effect on political dictators. Joel Kuortti, for instance, in one of his monographs on Rushdie's fiction, argues that 'Oppressive rulers can be overthrown by the sheer power of fiction, because it is capable of telling the truth about, exposing, oppression'.[25] From one perspective, such assumptions favour a writer like Rushdie enormously, for it becomes very easy to claim that his works, which also (to some extent) make these post-structuralist assumptions, are works of constructive and credible political thought. From another perspective, however, they do Rushdie a disservice, for they not only make his political arguments seem inane, they also fail to defend him against critiques such as Ahmad's by blithely reproducing arguments made from theoretical positions that Ahmad absolutely rejects.

It is perhaps necessary to consider Ahmad's objections to *Shame* in more detail. To assess *Shame* on his own terms, Ahmad starts by proposing to change the criteria by which the novel is usually discussed. Instead of focusing upon the 'range of questions that may be asked of the texts which are currently in the process of being canonized within [the] categorical counter canon' of 'Third World' fiction – namely, questions which refer to 'representations of colonialism, nationhood, postcoloniality, the typology of rulers, their powers, corruptions, and so forth' – Ahmad sets out to consider those questions which are usually 'subordinated to the primacy of the authorized questions', notably questions concerning 'representations of classes and genders'.[26] Ahmad quickly establishes that *Shame*, for all its multiculturalism in other respects, is resolutely monocultural in terms of class. Rushdie, as his own narrator figure suggests, has 'learned Pakistan by slices' (S, 69); and the slices he has learned – 'because of his own class origin' – are those involving 'the history of the corruptions and criminalities of Pakistani rulers'.[27] This description of the novel, we might note, is not one that Rushdie himself would deny, despite the fact that Ahmad sees it as an ideological flaw in the novel's conception. Indeed, Rushdie has defended the novel against accusations that it oversimplifies the complexity of the Pakistani national experience by arguing that he was only attempting to represent a single – highly privileged – stratum of Pakistani society and did not set out to write about Pakistani society in all its diversity. As he tells Kumkum Sangari:

> The ruling elite in Pakistan today [1984] is a very iden-
> tifiable, tiny microcosm. Even in India you can't say that
> – here it's much more diffuse. Every general that comes to
> power is bought by them, every politician who comes to
> power is part of them, and it's about these people I wanted
> to write. There's a very huge gap between the state and
> the people … That's what I was writing about, not making
> a survey of that society, because how can one condemn a
> nation? It doesn't mean anything to do that. (SRI, 67)

But this is not Ahmad's objection. Ahmad's objection is that in showing only the corrupt strata of Pakistani society Rushdie is failing to show other, more hopeful, dimensions of Pakistan, and so failing to allow for the possibility of resistance to political oppression. In Ahmad's terms:

> Neither the class from which the Pakistani segment of his
> experience is derived, nor the ideological ensemble within
> which [Rushdie] has located his own affiliations, admits, in
> any fundamental degree, the possibility of heroic action;
> between the structure of felt experience and the politico-
> literary affiliation, therefore, the circle is closed. What this
> excludes – 'the missing bits' to which he must 'reconcile'
> himself – is the dailiness of lives lived under oppression,
> and the human bonding – of resistance, of decency, of innu-
> merable heroisms of both ordinary and extraordinary kinds
> – which makes it possible for large numbers of people to
> look each other in the eye, without guilt, with affection and
> solidarity and humour, and makes life, even under oppres-
> sion, endurable and frequently joyous. Of that other kind
> of life his fictions, right up to *The Satanic Verses*, seem to
> be largely ignorant … The infinite bleakness of *Shame*,
> its cage-like quality, is rooted, in other words, in what it
> excludes as much as what it actually comprises.[28]

Once more, the *descriptive* assessment of *Shame* provided by Ahmad here is not necessarily one that Rushdie would contest. For Rushdie, *Shame* is 'about a world that's so locked into itself that it cannot escape from its own logic – and the processes of that logic continue to unfold, generation after generation' (SRI, 67). The similarity between this observation, and Ahmad's own summation of *Shame* as 'a space occupied so entirely by Power that there is no space left for either resistance or its representation' is revealing, since it suggests that the bleakness that Ahmad reads as an accidental revelation of the barrenness of Rushdie's political stance is in fact part of Rushdie's intention.[29] Where the two writers would disagree then, if it is not to be a disagreement over how to describe the novel, must be in their mutual assessments of the *value* of this kind of representation. For Ahmad, such a novel is, at best, politically useless, because it cannot offer a coherent programme for changing that which it criticises, and, at worst, politically obstructive because it breeds passivism and despair by implying that power is monolithic and therefore unassailable. But what does Rushdie believe?

In the interview cited above between Rushdie and Kumkum Sangari, who shares Ahmad's Marxist orientation and who asks similar questions of Rushdie's work, Rushdie is pressed, repeatedly, to resolve just this problem. 'If writing is an act of communication', Sangari observes towards the end of the interview, 'one has to have some idea, however nebulous, of what's on the other side, some commitment to a set of people one is writing for'. Rushdie's response is revealing:

> Writing is a very odd act of communication. It's an act of expression, first, and of communication second ... I have a very intense relationship with the real world and with the fictional world – it's only that there's no reader in it! It's difficult enough trying to translate that world into the one on the page; whether anyone's reading it or not is of no consequence. In that sense, I'm not at all a political novelist. I know you have complained of not finding a coherent political ideology in *Shame* – and in that sense I'm certainly not an ideological writer. (SRI, 71)

In some respects this seems a curious thing to say – Rushdie, if the growing body of criticism about him is to be believed, is an intensely ideological writer, a writer committed to political change, to the transformation of colonial modes of thinking, even a writer capable of threatening tyrants: all this is ideological in the broad sense of the term. What Rushdie means, of course, is that he does not have a specific political (read Marxist) agenda in his writing: he does not conform to *an* ideology. The novel, for Rushdie, is about self-expression, storytelling, question-asking, not about offering or promoting a particular programme for political change. He does not see it as his job, as a novelist, to provide answers, rather, he regards himself, like Graham Greene, as the grit in the state machine that unsettles the machinery but gives no thought to replacing it. We might anticipate that a critic like Ahmad would ask how coherent such a position can be. How significant can any social or political critique be that does not also imply the desirability for, and therefore, some means to achieve, political change? How seriously can we take a fiction that criticises a system for being politically undesirable, if it does not know what politically desirable is, or how we can go about getting there? Rushdie's comment in interview, however, implies that he does not intend his fiction to be significant, or to be taken seriously, in this way. He observes and he records, but he does not propose to do anything about what he sees.

This stance is illuminated further by an essay written by Rushdie a year after the publication of *Shame* about a visit he made to the United States, taking with him for reading material a copy of Lucius Apuleius' second-century satire on the Roman world: *The Golden Ass*. The narrator of *The Golden Ass*, Rushdie tells us (foreshadowing the transformation of his own character Saladin Chamcha into a goat-man):

> is transformed by witchcraft into the tale's eponymous donkey, and his ass's eye view of his age reveals a world of ubiquitous cynicism, great brutality, fearsome sorcery, religious cultism, banditry, murder. Friends betray friends, sisters betray sisters, corpses rise up and accuse their wives of poisoning them. There are omens and curses. (IHL, 365)

This portrait of the Roman world, Rushdie observes, is not dissimilar to the portrait that he, in his role of satirist, would draw of contemporary America:

> There have been several race killings of late, blacks
> murdered by whites sparking revenge-murders by blacks.
> Meanwhile, at the UN building, there's a demonstration
> protesting police violence against blacks in New York City.
> All this is familiar to the ass.
>
> For sorcery, one need look no further than the mumbo-
> jumbo of the Star Wars schemes; cultism and Jerry Falwell
> are everywhere; and as for banditry, Calero and his FDN,
> let's call then the 'Contrabandits', are more dangerous
> than anything in Apuleius's book. (IHL, 365–6)

The list goes on, but what is immediately apparent is the similarity between this Apuleian list of American social and political
abuses and the Apuleian list of Pakistani social and political
abuses offered in *Shame*:

> The business, for instance, of the illegal installation, by
> the richest inhabitants of 'Defence', of covert, subterra-
> nean water pumps that steal water from the neighbour's
> mains ... the Sind Club in Karachi, where there is still a
> sign reading 'Women and Dogs Not Allowed Beyond This
> Point' ... the subtle logic of an industrial programme that
> builds nuclear reactors but cannot develop a refrigerator.
> (S, 69)

Inevitably, the cultural conditions that give rise to the abuses,
and the specific nature of the abuses, differ in both cases, but
the satirical format in which the abuses are presented is the
same: both use the device of the distanced observer to comment,
almost casually, on what he has seen, both present the abuses as
a semi-humorous, exaggeratedly long list designed to contra-
dict the assumptions of moral probity made by the defenders
of the culture. These formal parallels between Rushdie's satirical perception of America and his satirical representation of
Pakistan tell us several things about the nature of Rushdie's
political strategies. Perhaps most significantly, Rushdie's willingness to satirise political corruption in the United States in terms
identical to those he uses for Pakistan (satiric 'equal time' as
Brennan calls it)[30] may serve as a corrective to the oft-expressed
view that Rushdie, in lambasting the Pakistani ruling elite, is

only reconfirming 'Western' orientalist prejudices concerning the 'Eastern' tendency towards tyranny and corruption. In fact Rushdie sees corruption everywhere, not just in the 'East', and his satire is thus multi-directional – a view that gives some credence to the argument expressed in *Shame* that whilst 'not-quite-Pakistan' is the overt subject of his satire, the satire is none the less relevant to all of humanity. What is most useful for the purposes of this argument, however, is that Rushdie goes on, in his essay, to comment on the justice and value of the Apuleian satirical approach: 'The Picture of America emerging from these notes is, of course, in some sense "unfair". What you see depends on where you look. But the Apuleian America does exist, and I make no apology for looking at it' (IHL, 367). This comment might easily be applied to *Shame* if the word 'America' were to be replaced by the word 'Pakistan'. Rushdie knows his satire is partial, he knows that he is looking at Pakistan 'in slices', and is being 'unfair' in his exclusive focus upon the negative aspects of Pakistani political life – but he is unapologetic; those negative aspects exist, so he is not going to be squeamish about putting them in the spotlight. There is, in this sense, no pretence, on Rushdie's part, that satire is just: it is partial and exploitative – but he has the confidence that his readers will understand this. The comment that follows this is even more revealing about the nature of the satirist's art, as Rushdie understands it. Rushdie describes an incident from Apuleius in which the ass/observer/satirist sees a gang of eunuch priests assaulting a labourer (an incident that Rushdie parallels with US aggression in Nicaragua). The ass attempts to shout 'help, help! Rape, rape! Arrest these he-whores', but all that comes out is 'he-whore', 'he-whore'. 'The trouble is,' Rushdie observes resignedly, 'what can a poor ass do? He observes but cannot act' (IHL, 367). Clearly Rushdie is suggesting that he knows that although he has a role as an observer – a voyeur even, like many of his protagonists – he cannot act to change what he sees.

To understand Rushdie's position as a political novelist more accurately, then, we must abandon the idea that Rushdie is, or sets out to be, a politically *transformative* writer, and accept instead that he is, in *Shame* at least, a *reactive* writer, satirising what is, without attempting to offer any coherent blueprints for what should be. This is, to some extent, a concession to Ahmad, who argues all along that Rushdie, whilst he is able to respond locally, savagely and bitterly to existing political situations, is incapable of relieving his peculiarly loveless form of vitriol with any hint of a constructive solution. We do not, however, like Ahmad, need to see this political position as untenable, for we might legitimately maintain that such a position, whilst not in itself constructive, is nevertheless potentially politically *enabling* for the social groups that suffer from the political corruptions about which Rushdie writes. We might argue that a fiction, even though it does not present constructive solutions, may still facil-itate the pursuit within society at large (and by means other than those of writing) of constructive solutions to the problems represented. We might also argue that the omission from the fictionalised representation of those classes and social catego-ries that may be deemed the 'oppressed' does not automatically mean that the interests of those classes are not being served. On the contrary, a sustained and powerful condemnation of oppres-sion, its intolerance, its injustice, its violence, its hypocrisy, its corruption, may be judged just as helpful to the oppressed as any representation of them being 'hopeful'.

Defences of Rushdie's 'novelistic enterprise' on this basis do not need to be made from outside the Marxist critical paradigm. Ahmad's arguments that Rushdie ought to show the objective truth of the social situation echo the arguments levelled against expressionism as a political form by Georg Lukács in the 1930s. Indeed, a number of Ahmad's polemical positions explicitly recall Lukács: his condemnation of the Parisian intelligentsia in the 1960s for seeming 'to believe more in Surrealism than in socialism', for instance, reformulates, for a different period, Lukács's contention that surrealism can have nothing to do with Marxist politics because it 'denies that literature has any refer-ence to objective reality'.[31] Lukács, however, as is well known, did not go unchallenged in these opinions by fellow Marx-ists. Brecht, amongst others, responded by suggesting that the political value of a work of art depends not upon its capacity to imitate existing political scenarios mimetically but upon its capacity to *estrange* the reader or audience from the ideological illusions that bind them to perceive the world as their ruling class requires. The politicised fiction, for Brecht, may thus be 'realistic', even if it is not 'realist', as long as it commits itself to 'discovering the causal complexes of society [and] unmasking the prevailing view of things as the view of those who are in power' – both of which ends Rushdie's fictions, *Shame* included, seem to achieve admirably.[32]

Revealingly, Rushdie cites just this argument in an interview in which he defends his lack of interest in fictional realism. 'I'm not very inclined towards social realism', he tells Una Chaudhuri:

> Not that I don't like realism, but it seems to me that it's a convention that has tried to impose itself as some kind of objective truth. Whereas it's actually only as artificial as everything else. There's an essay or a letter of Brecht's – maybe it's a letter he wrote to Walter Benjamin – where he says that … in order to describe reality you do not have to write realism, because realism is only one rule about reality: there are lots of others. (SRI, 23)

Rushdie is referring here to one of a series of articles written by Brecht in 1938 that he read aloud to Benjamin when seeking his advice as to whether or not they should appear in print. The articles were designed as responses to arguments made by Lukács in *Das Wort*, but were not, finally, published – possibly because of Lukács's influential position in Moscow.[33] Rushdie's awareness of these argumentative exchanges, and his application of Brecht's responses to his own fiction, suggest that there is more of a defence to be made of Rushdie's Marxism than is made by Ahmad when he dismisses it out of hand. For Ahmad it is not credible that Rushdie can claim Marxist sympathies when he is so clearly in the thrall of postmodernist and post-structuralist thinking.[34] One cannot help but think, however, that Ahmad is seeing Rushdie through a distorting lens because he regards him, straightforwardly, as a representative of the Western academic

discourses that have made him into an object of 'exorbitant celebration', a viewpoint that leads him to fail to credit the extent
to which Rushdie resists those discourses.[35] If Ahmad were to
assess Rushdie on his own terms, rather than as an agent of
the postmodern, it might become more apparent that there is
a persuasive and critically intelligent vein of Marxist thinking
that runs through his work – albeit of a Brechtian rather than
a Lukácsian nature. It might also become apparent that, whilst
Rushdie uses a number of the literary techniques associated with
the postmodern, it is by no means clear that he fully conforms to
the ideological positions of postmodernism. The playfulness of
Midnight's Children, for instance, or the grotesques of *Shame*,
may align Rushdie with certain postmodern fictional practices,
but, because these literary devices are also intended to reflect
upon, and have a discursive impact upon, the world that Rushdie
believes to exist outside the book, they do not make Rushdie
into a postmodernist in the fullest sense of the term. As Rushdie
himself has argued, he 'does not accept the postmodernist label'
because postmodernists 'don't accept that literature is referential':

> Post-modernism has entered me, in the sense that it's in the
> air, but I haven't really studied its lexicon or its processes.
> Of course there are useful things about textual analysis
> – about how the text exists in the world, in society, about
> fictiveness and play and the nature of reality – but it's not
> an ideology of fiction to which I subscribe. Because I do
> think books are about the world. (SRI, 69)

Such an argument evidently puts clear water between Rushdie
and the theoreticians such as Derrida and Baudrillard with whom
Ahmad associates him uncomplicatedly. Instead it suggests that
Rushdie is closer, once more, to the theoretical positions of
thinkers like Brecht who argue that, whilst literature does need
to represent social realities to be politically interesting, prob-
lematising the representation of those social realities is a valid
and indeed necessary part of a politicised fictional process.

Arguments concerning the political viability of aggressive
fictional condemnations of those with power have long been

current in critical studies of satire and its functions. There is a venerable tradition of criticism in which such satire has been seen as 'malevolent and destructive, an affront to the dignity of human nature and a threat to the commonwealth'.[36] There is an equally venerable tradition that has seen satire as 'a highly moral art, motivated by the love of virtue and serving as a useful censor of public and private morals'.[37] Ahmad attacks Rushdie's fiction from the former point of view, though he might wish to replace the now politically loaded term 'commonwealth' with something more suggestive of its etymological sense – common (or communal) well-being. Rushdie's fiction, however, may be defended from the latter point of view, so long as we recognise that Rushdie, unlike some satirists, judges immorality not against an absolute and systematic standard of morality but against something that is more negotiable, pragmatic and contingent: the loose and fallible rule of thumb – shame and shamefulness.[38] The political function of Rushdie's fiction, in this sense, is identical to the political value of satire: like most satirists, but most notably Swift, he uses language to mock the follies and frivolities of those who have and who misuse power. Such a stance is, by definition, reactive: it responds to a situation that already exists, and its attitude is one of almost unrelieved scorn for that which it describes. It is not, however, politically ineffectual, for, whilst such satire will not, on its own, change those with power, or change the nature of their power, it is none the less a vital element of our refusal to be passive subjects in the face of power, and, as such, it is a mechanism of human dignity and human resistance. In these terms, at least, whilst Rushdie may not, as Ahmad suggests, show those acts 'which [make] it possible for large numbers of people to look each other in the eye, without guilt, with affection and solidarity and humour, and [make] life, even under oppression, endurable and frequently joyous'; the novel, as an act of carnival satire, *itself* becomes one of those acts.[39] Ahmad is therefore wrong to say that, because *Shame* is hopeless, it is not about hopefulness. In fact, it is driven from start to finish by a kind of hopefulness: the hopefulness that such inequality, such hypocrisy, such violence, should not have been in the first place; the hope that the night-mare world it conjures up might not exist. This means, of course, that the hopefulness of Rushdie's book exists almost exclusively in negative terms – but it does not follow that Rushdie's political message is entirely negative: rather, it means that he hopes to show, by negative example, how political leaders ought not to behave – an ambition that is in principle constructive in its intentions. Again, we can defend Rushdie on this point from within the Marxist critical paradigm by way of Adorno's praise of Beckett for 'responding negatively to a negative reality'.[40] In Beckett's case, as Adorno argues, characters may be represented as isolated, lonely despairing – but this representation still has polemic thrust, because loneliness must be seen as 'a social product'.[41] Comparably, Rushdie's novel, taken on individual points of detail, is indeed about failure, despair, isolation, anni-hilation – but to judge it politically on this basis is to overlook the ways in which the representation of failure, despair, anni-hilation in the novel becomes a desire for the opposite: political processes that combat failure, despair, annihilation in the social and political arenas.

This form of hopefulness is also a constitutive feature of the satirical tradition in fiction; more specifically it is characteristic of Bakhtin's idiosyncratic idea of Menippean satire – the tradition of novelistic prose in which Rushdie writes and which extends from Rabelais to More, Swift, Bulgakov and Grass. For Bakhtin, 'the unfettered and fantastic plots and situations' of Menippean satire 'all serve one goal – to put to the test and to expose ideas and ideologues'.[42] As in Rushdie's *Shame*, therefore, this satire remains a purely responsive form that aims only to condemn that which it sees in the world around it. According to Bakhtin, however, a utopian element enters to the extent that

> the inconclusive present begins to feel closer to the future than to the past, and begins to seek some valorized support in the future, even if this future is as yet pictured merely as a return to the Golden Age of Saturn … with the freedom of Saturnalian laughter.[43]

Such a future hope, as Bakhtin points out, is not a realistic political prospect because unending Saturnalia provides no social or political answers; it is extreme, fantastical and absurd – fun but not functional.[44] Presenting answers for the future is not, however, the political aim of the Menippean satire, so to condemn it on these grounds is to mistake the genre. Menippean satire is intended to be of political use only in the present – for it gives us a means of responding *in the present* to possible or actual political scenarios with spirit, with disgust, with laughter, with outrageous insult, with irreverence. All of which, of course, does not help us find a solution – though it may provide an inspiration.

'The liberty to crudely degrade, to turn inside out the lofty aspects of the world and world views, might sometimes seem shocking', notes Bakhtin, 'But to this exclusive and comic familiarity must be added an intense spirit of inquiry and utopian fantasy'.[45] It is in these terms that we should seek to understand the political value of Rushdie's fictions.

Of course this assessment of the political location of Rushdie's writing remains limited if it is only an assessment of *Shame* – Ahmad's principal subject. Whilst Ahmad takes *Shame* as his focal point, however, he is also seeking to critique what he calls 'Rushdie's novelistic enterprise' more generally. Any response to Ahmad's critique of Rushdie, accordingly, is also one that touches on the political significance of all Rushdie's work.

Nevertheless, it needs to be emphasised that the political significance of Rushdie's writing does change from text to text – not only because his subject matter changes but also because his political location changes. The subject of the variability of Rushdie's politics is treated by Kathryn Hume in a 1995 article on his work.[46] Here Hume argues that, *after* the publication of *Shame*, there is a marked shift in Rushdie's approach to what she regards as the key issue in his writing – how the 'decentred, culturally hybridised' individual can act in politically and ethically significant ways.[47] In his first three novels, *Grimus*, *Midnight's Children* and *Shame*, she suggests, 'Rushdie proposes only one rather tentative answer to the question of how a decentred being can act meaningfully, and that is by writing history'.[48] In *The Satanic Verses* and *Haroun*, however, Hume believes that Rushdie becomes more concerned with finding active 'solutions to decenterment'.[49] In the former, she suggests, Rushdie employs 'his postmodern heroes' – Mishal Sufiyan and Zeenie Vakil – to demonstrate that 'a person without a conventional centre' can act in politically productive ways by working locally, within the community, to achieve specific libertarian and humanitarian ends.[50] In *Haroun*, correspondingly, she argues that Rushdie shifts from an artist-centred argument, which implies that only the re-writer can generate change, towards a reader-focused argument, which suggests that art 'can have some equivalence to political action' if it is able to inspire writers and readers with a 'defiance of the fact-choked simplicities or ideological dictates imposed by tyrants'.[51]

In a more recent article on Rushdie's *Fury* Sarah Brouillette has also argued that readers need to be sensitive to political differences between Rushdie's works, although she – in the tradition of Brennan, Ahmad and Booker – sees Rushdie's socio-cultural location as the key to his politics.[52] For Brouillette the most illuminating shift of priorities is that which occurs between the publication of *The Jaguar Smile* in 1987 and the publication of *Fury* in 2001. Both works, she points out, are linked by their attention to national liberation struggles and to their exploration of the ways in which 'cultural products are used to sell or promote political ideologies'.[53] '[R]eading *Fury* against *The Jaguar Smile*', however, also reveals that between the two fictions:

> [Rushdie] has abandoned a more straightforward adherence to leftist politics sympathetic to resistance movements, as expressed in *The Jaguar Smile*, in favour of representing how those politics are incorporated into contemporary media culture and enshrined in cultural commodities that themselves have no discernible authorship or origins.[54]

The reason for this shift, according to Brouillette, lies in the fact that Rushdie's career, between the late 1980s and early 2000s, has increasingly been determined by his status as a lead author in a publishing industry controlled by multinational corporations. This status, in Brouillette's view has led Rushdie away from

> a general attention to the politics of contemporary nation-formation, particularly within a South Asian context, to a more solipsistic interest in the status of authorship and origins within the field of cultural production for a global market.[55]

Hume's and Brouillette's approaches allow us to identify two distinctive shifts in the political focus of Rushdie's writing. The first occurs in the late 1980s when, in writing *The Jaguar Smile* and *The Satanic Verses*, Rushdie begins to advocate localised political activism alongside his emphasis on a radicalised aesthetic practice. The second occurs in the late 1990s and early 2000s when, in writing *The Ground Beneath Her Feet* and *Fury*, Rushdie turns his attention to the problem of writing politically in the context of global mass culture.

Even as Sarah Brouillette marks a transition between Rushdie's early work and his later work, however, the similarities between her discussion of Rushdie's negotiation of globalisation and Timothy Brennan's early discussion of Rushdie's cosmopolitanism suggest a broad and ongoing trend in critical approaches to Rushdie's writing. For both critics, the central issue in the assessment of the political importance of Rushdie's fiction is the extent to which it is complicit in or compromised by the very processes that it sets out to contest. Correspondingly, in Rushdie's fiction itself, one of the central themes has been the extent to which it is possible to write within but also write back to dominant discursive formations. My own argument has been that Rushdie's location *within and against* dominant aesthetic and ideological formations has meant that he has been able, consistently, to disrupt those formations by adopting denunciatory political rhetorics, but that, because he is unwilling – or perhaps unable – to step outside those discursive formations, he is not a writer who has thought it his role to propose constructive alternatives.

'Freedom to reject is the only freedom', Rushdie's narrator Rai observes aphoristically in *The Ground Beneath Her Feet*,

'Freedom to uphold is dangerous' (GBF, 146). Such are the sentiments of the literary satirist. If these sentiments seem somewhat nihilistic, however, we can add to them Rai's subsequent
dictum, that is characteristically hopeful, but not decisive: 'When
you know what you're against you have taken the first step to
discovering what you're for' (GBF, 223).

Shalimar the Clown

Rushdie's ninth novel, *Shalimar the Clown*, was published in 2005 shortly before this book was completed. Although it is impossible to predict the future trajectory of Rushdie's career, *Shalimar* suggests a new development to the extent that it fuses the interest in US-led globalisation apparent in the novels of his middle period (*The Ground Beneath Her Feet* and *Fury*) with the sustained focus on a South Asian national experience apparent in the novels of his early period (*Midnight's Children* and *Shame*). In this instance Rushdie takes, as his principal subject matter, the state of Kashmir, homeland of his maternal grandfather and one-time favourite location for Rushdie family holidays. Prior to the publication of *Shalimar*, Kashmir has not received sustained attention from Rushdie, though it does loom up, like a troubling ghost, in most of his South Asian fictions. In *Haroun and the Sea of Stories*, for instance, it appears as the shadowy original for the Valley of K, over which corrupt politicians are battling. It also serves as a point of departure for Aadam Aziz when he is cast out of paradise after losing his faith at the start of *Midnight's Children*. In the latter novel the weight of Kashmir's woes is heaped on to the ancient shoulders of the unwashing, expletive-loving Tai the Boatman, who believes himself to be more of a Kashmiri than an Indian, and who takes as his personal motto the political mantra 'Kashmir for the Kashmiris' (MC, 37). With heavy symbolic significance, Tai dies in the year of partition when, 'infuriated by India and Pakistan's struggle over his valley', he walks to Chhamb to stand in between the opposing forces. 'Naturally', readers are told, 'they shot him' (MC, 37).

Shalimar the Clown is, in some respects, Tai's story writ large. Here too we see the annihilation of the idea of Kashmir as it is caught between violent and opposing political interests. Here too it is the ordinary village Kashmiris who suffer and die as a result of antagonisms that are fostered and manipulated by distant national leaders in pursuit of equally distant national ideals. There are, however, also significant differences between the representations of Kashmir in *Midnight's Children* and *Shalimar*. Whilst Tai dies at the point of partition in 1947, the two Kashmiri protagonists of *Shalimar*, Shalimar Noman and Boonyi Kaul, are born at the moment of partition, and so come to act as mirrors of a post-Independence Kashmir in much the same way that Saleem, in the earlier novel, was a mirror for post-Independence India. Whilst in *Midnight's Children* Kashmir is simply presented as the thorn in the side of Indian and Pakistani post-Independence optimism, moreover, in *Shalimar* it has a grander, more global role to play. In the first place, it is offered up as a symbol of the inherent weaknesses of the US-led efforts to establish a global political and economic consensus in the wake of the Second World War. In the second place (and inter-connectedly) it is used to announce the decisive abortion of the idea, promoted by American neo-conservative intellectuals after the conclusion of the Cold War, that history was coming to an end because Western capitalist 'liberal' democracy was triumphing. One form of history may have ended with the collapse of state Communism, the novel reminds us, but US machinations against Russia during the Cold War have also brought new forms of history into being that were now bearing fruit in regions such as Afghanistan and Kashmir. *Shalimar*, in this sense, adds other elements into the mix of South Asian politics that were not – could not have been – present in *Midnight's Children*: the globalisation of the power of the United States after the conclusion of the Cold War, and the evolution of new ideologies of violence such as those given their most grotesque embodiment in the attacks on New York in September 2001. The resulting difference is that where Kashmiriness is shown, in the earlier novel, being gunned down by the opposing forces of Pakistan and India, here it is shown being crushed in a three-way power struggle between US interests, the Indian army and Islamic insurgents from Pakistan.

As is the case in all Rushdie's fictions, the political conflicts with which he is primarily concerned are played out micro-cosmically in the lives of his central characters. In this instance, Western interest in Kashmir is ciphered by the European-born, Jewish American Ambassador to Kashmir, Maximilian Ophuls, who in his younger days has fought for the resistance against the Nazis but who latterly has become a secret nego-tiator for American interests around the globe. His involvement in Kashmir is registered through his impact upon the lives of Boonyi, whom he seduces, impregnates and abandons, and the eponymous Shalimar, her husband, who, embittered by the loss of his wife, becomes involved in guerrilla conflict. Having trained in Afghanistan using weapons that Ophuls has himself provided when the US was covertly arming Islamic terrorists after the Russian invasion in 1979, Shalimar becomes an assassin in Europe and the US, and finally murders Ophuls on the doorstep of his daughter's apartment block.

Ophuls's seduction of Boonyi, and their subsequent rela-tionship – during which he gluts her with goods and comestibles before abandoning her out of hand when he loses interest in her – can clearly be read as an allegory of America's relationship with what Rushdie calls in *The Ground Beneath Her Feet* 'the back yards of the world' (GBF, 420). America's power seduces, its affections imprison, its commodities corrupt, and it abandons once it has taken what it wants. Boonyi is thus a product of America's love for the world, and, when she speaks, she speaks in the voice of Kashmir. 'I am your handiwork made flesh', she tells Ophuls:

> You took beauty and created hideousness ... Look at me. I
> am the meaning of your deeds. I am the meaning of your
> so-called love, your destructive, selfish, wanton love. Look
> at me. Your love looks just like hatred ... I was honest and
> you turned me into your lie. This is not me. This is not me.
> This is you. (SC, 205)

A moment later Rushdie removes the moral high ground from Boonyi by having her revert to 'another, older line of attack': 'I should have known better than to lie with a Jew', she says. 'The Jews are our enemy and I should have known' (SC, 205). Even this, however, is part of Rushdie's argument, for here it becomes apparent that the very thing that Ophuls set out to prevent, racial and religious hatred, has become part of what his machinations have created.

By dwelling on the atrocities of fascism, Rushdie's novel asserts the need to recognise the honourable, even utopian, intentions behind the postwar allied efforts to impose a global consensus. Nazi atrocities, as Ophuls argues in conversation with the historian Gaston Zeller, demanded the creation of a 'new world order', and it was this demand that pointed in the direction of 'the Council of Europe, the International Monetary Fund and the World Bank', indeed, the whole architecture of globalisation imagined into being in New Hampshire at the Bretton Woods conference (SC, 164–5). Simultaneously, however, the novel also asserts the need to recognise that those initially honourable intentions have gone sour, or at least been kidnapped and corrupted by forces more pragmatic and cynical. Hence Max Ophuls, hero of the wartime resistance, whose parents have died in concentration camps and who started his political career as an idealist and optimist, finds himself, at the height of the Cold War, defending the American idea of a free world by manipulating religious factionalism in unstable regions, and engaging in covert, strategic arms deals with the Taliban and al-Qaeda. 'Ambassador Max Ophuls', the narrator drily observes, 'these days was supporting terror activities while calling himself an ambassador for counterterrorism' (SC, 272).

The transformation of Ophuls, from a liberator with unquestionable moral justification into an agent of a new imperial power which, in its turn, presides over the same kinds of moral atrocity that he once fought against, is registered most uncomfortably when he finds himself, suddenly, playing the same kind of role once played by those he despised. 'When Boonyi Noman danced for him in the Dachigam hunting lodge in Kashmir', readers are told:

> he thought of those feathered dead-eyed showgirls wreathed in Nazi cigar smoke, flaunting their gartered thighs. The clothes were different but he recognised the same hard hunger in her stare, the readiness of the survivor to suspend moral judgement in the presence of imagined opportunity. But I'm not a Nazi, he thought. I'm the American ambassador, the guy in the white hat. I'm for God's sake one of the Jews who lived. She swung her hips for him and he thought, And I'm also a married man. She swung her hips again and he ceased to think. (SC, 141)

Rushdie is not here claiming that American neo-imperial activities are identical to the activities of the Nazis in the Second World War, though an unsympathetic reading might seek to interpret this episode thus. More subtly Rushdie is arguing that, whilst the US lacks the malignant and programmatic intent of the fascists, it nevertheless, in the name of self-interest, allows, even encourages, things to happen that are not dissimilar to the things that the Nazis made happen by more direct means. It also tends to look the other way, to wilfully 'forget' what it does with its power, and so is surprised when it finds the rest of the world treating it in the way victims treat an oppressor. Whilst such indirection allows it to maintain the illusion that it is 'the guy in the white hat', Rushdie implies, the stance is clearly a hollow one, because the US, whether it likes it or not, is now sitting in the seat of power. 'The wheel had turned', as Ophuls realises, confronting the fallen Boonyi. 'In this moment of his story he was not the victim. In this moment she, not he, had the right to claim kinship with the lost' (SC, 205).

Shalimar the Clown may be one of Rushdie's most carnivalesque of titles, but it is his least carnival of novels. It is true that it features a village full of circus performers, and it is true that it uses the naming and renaming of characters to emphasise the liminality of identity (though, more often than not, characters fail to remake themselves by the names they select, and discover that names are made for them by circumstance). The novel also features its share of magic realist whimsies: the man who can hear colours, the preacher who is made of iron, giant marmot-like treasure-hunting ants, and (yet again) tele-paths who can read each other's minds. *Shalimar*, however, also lacks the essential levity, the exuberant comedy, that is a crucial feature of the carnivalesque novel, and that has characterised many of Rushdie's works to date. This is, no doubt, partly a result of Rushdie's subject matter: genocidal massacres and the anni-hilation of a way of life. But Rushdie has treated bleak subject matters before, and has always found room for humour. The difference here is that Rushdie sees nothing that allows for hope in contemporary Kashmir. In *Midnight's Children* and *Shame* – bitter though their subjects were – the knowledge remained that India and Pakistan would survive the political abuses that Rushdie was satirising; that there was an *outside* to the fictional world into which a more utopian hopefulness could be projected, even if it was never shown. In *Shalimar* there is no hope for the continuity of the idea of Kashmir outside the fiction. Kasmmiri-ness is annihilated without redemption, and the slogan 'Kashmir for the Kashmiris' becomes a joke, 'a moronic idea' (SC, 101), 'no longer an option' (SC, 311). Given this, it is hardly surprising that *Shalimar* is so relentlessly grim, and that the comedy apparent in Rushdie's earlier novels is visibly, and perhaps intentionally, lacking here.

That said, if there is one redeeming element in *Shalimar*, it resides in the next generation, as was the case in *Midnight's Children*. Kashmir itself may have been annihilated, but the seduction of Kashmir by America has produced a bastard child – India Ophuls a.k.a. Kashmira Noman – a hybrid being, who lives in America and who loves her American father, but who is also in the process of discovering who her father really is, what he has done and who her mother was. Global politics may be such that old Kashmir no longer exists, Kashmira's story tells us, but globalisation has also generated new combinations, new ethnicities, that exist in complex relationships with the power systems that have produced them, and in which the possibility of

new forms of political equilibrium reside – neither fully sympathetic to the US nor in the arms of absolutist militants

Not all of the political stances struck in *Shalimar* are convincing.
It is Rushdie's conceit that Kashmir, prior to the political dramas
that have transformed it in the twentieth century, was a haven,
a paradise, of peaceable village traditions, and multicultural,
multi-faith tolerance. Rushdie demonstrates this by introducing
the Shalimar–Boonyi plot with a potential tragedy. Shalimar is
a Muslim, Boonyi a Hindu, and they consort in secret because
they fear repercussions. The reader, expectations already primed
with an epigraph from *Romeo and Juliet*, immediately jumps
to the conclusion that the star-crossed lovers will come to a bad
end as a result of religious hostility, and that the novel's crisis
will stem from here. These expectations are dashed, however,
when the village decides to overcome its reservations about the
conduct of the relationship and to allow their marriage: 'We are
all brothers and sisters here', Shalimar's father argues:

> There is no Hindu-Muslim issue. Two Kashmiri – two
> Pachigami – youngsters wish to marry, that's all. A love
> match is acceptable to both families and so a marriage
> there will be; both Hindu and Muslim customs will be
> observed. (SC, 110)

Rushdie, in this scenario, clearly intends to invoke and then
undermine tragic expectations in order to make a point: that
Kashmir's problems stem not from inherent Hindu–Muslim
enmity but from a Hindu–Muslim enmity that has been brought
into being by political processes and historical forces. Whilst this
point is well made, however, the assertion that Kashmir, before
the 1940s, was a paradaisical zone of tolerance and harmony, in
which the only conflicts result from squabbles over cooking pots,
seems stretched. This idea of Kashmir, of course, is yet another
entry in the growing list of idealised, multicultural utopias in
Rushdie's fiction that are under threat from the forces of singularity and oppression: Gup in *Haroun and the Sea of Stories*,
Moorish Spain and 'Bombay' in *The Moor's Last Sigh*. In this
respect, the Kashmir of *Shalimar* plays a familiar iconic role

in Rushdie's imaginative universe. The problems in Kashmir, however, seem too present, too rooted in a long history of antipathies, for readers to suspend disbelief sufficiently in the interests of the broader symbolic scheme. Kashmir's religious problems did not spring into being fully formed in 1947, and each time a village elder observes that 'in Kashmir, our stories sit side by side on the same double bill, we eat from the same dishes, we laugh at the same jokes' (SC, 71) the reader's faith in the fiction is tested.

This is a minor observation, however. In general, *Shalimar the Clown* is a fiction of considerable power. The narrative is engaging, the political commentary is astute and provocative, and the female characters (particularly India/Kashmira) are amongst the strongest Rushdie has drawn. Perhaps the most striking feature of the novel is the effectiveness with which Rushdie conveys his sense of outrage at the systematic slaughter carried out in Pachigam by both Islamic insurgents and the Indian army. This outrage reaches a climax twice in the novel, and on both occasions the narrator is left unable to do anything more that ask questions. On the first occasion – after 'a week-long orgy of unprovoked violence' against Kashmiri Hindus during which the Indian army stood by because it helped 'simplify' the situation – the question is 'why'.

> There were six hundred thousand Indian troops in Kashmir but the pogrom of the pandits was not prevented, why was that? Three and a half lakhs of human beings arrived in Jammu as displaced persons and for many months the government did not provide shelters or relief or even register their names, why was that? When the government finally built camps it only allowed for six thousand families to remain in the state, dispersing others around the country where they would be invisible and impotent, why was that? ... There was one bathroom per three hundred persons in many camps why was that ... and the pandits of Kashmir were left to rot in their slum camps, to rot while the army and the insurgency fought over the bloodied and broken valley, to dream of return, to die while dreaming of return, to die after the dream of return died so that they

could not even die dreaming of it, why was that why was
that why was that why was that why was that. (SC, 297)

On the second occasion – after the Indian army take revenge on
the village of Pachigam for managing to hold out against them
for so long – the question is 'who'.

Who lit that fire? Who burned that orchard? Who shot
those brothers who laughed their whole lives long? Who
killed the sarpanch? Who broke his hands? Who broke his
arms? Who broke his ancient neck? Who shackled those
men? Who made those men disappear? Who shot those
boys? Who shot those girls? Who smashed that house?
Who smashed *that* house? Who smashed *that* house? …
Who killed the children? Who whipped the parents? Who
raped that lazy-eyed woman? Who raped that grey-haired
lazy-eyed woman as she screamed about snake vengeance?
Who raped that woman again? Who raped that woman
again? Who raped that woman again? Who raped that
dead woman? Who raped that dead woman again? (SC,
308)

Such question asking is characteristic of Rushdie's fictional
response to political events. Indeed, as we have seen, Rushdie
sees the asking of questions as the principal job of the political novelist. Rushdie does not, however, see it as the job of the
novelist to offer answers, and, in accordance with this belief, no
direct responses are offered to the pertinent questions posed
in *Shalimar the Clown*. This does not mean that *Shalimar* has
nothing to contribute to the assessment of the political scenario
in Kashmir, however. On the contrary Rushdie's question asking
serves at least two constructive political functions. In the first
place, the very act of posing the question, of bearing witness
to atrocity, constitutes a potent political gesture: a demand for
attention and a demand for redress. In the second place Rushdie's question asking also functions as a plea: a plea to the Indian
army not to exploit the situation in Kashmir, a plea to moderate
Muslims to seek to reform their religion, and a plea to European and North American politicians to create a global political
context that helps rather than hinders their progress.

'A curse on both your houses', reads Rushdie's Shake-spearean epigraph. As might be expected from such an epigraph, the novel is one of cursing: it curses its satirical targets comprehensively, from head to toe, just as Boonyi curses Ophuls for his callousness. Rushdie's curses are not mere abuse, however; they are also imperatives. Put your houses in order, he says. Reform, or face mutual destruction.

Notes

Introduction

1 The latter was distributed in Pakistan in 1990, directed by Jan Mohammad. The international guerrillas of the title are the heroes who set out to execute Rushdie – a sinister villain with a private army who tortures the heroine by forcing her to listen to readings of *The Satanic Verses*. The British Board of Film Classification in the United Kingdom was prepared to ban the film – not so much for its blatant misogyny and antisemitism, as for its criminal libel on Rushdie. Rushdie intervened, however, with the request that there should be no censorship in his name. For further comment see the British Film Institute site www.screenonline.org.uk/film/id/460938/ (accessed January 2006), and for a plot summary see 'Shock Cinema Archives' at http://members.aol.com/shockcin/international.html (accessed January 2006).

2 Anita Desai, 'Introduction', in Salman Rushdie, *Midnight's Children* (London: Everyman, 1995): vii.

3 Allan Vorda, 'Stuck on the Margins: An Interview with Kazuo Ishiguro', in *Face to Face: Interviews with Contemporary Novelists* (Houston: Rice University Press, 1993): 8.

4 Aijaz Ahmad, *In Theory: Classes, Nations, Literatures* (London: Verso, 1992): 69.

5 Vorda, 'Stuck': 8.

6 Aparna Mahanta, 'Allegories of the Indian Experience: The Novels of Salman Rushdie', *Economic and Political Weekly* 19.6 (1984): 244. A large portion of this article is reproduced in *Salman Rushdie:* Midnight's Children / The Satanic Verses, *A Reader's Guide to Essential Criticism*, ed. David Smale, Icon Readers' Guides (Cambridge: Icon, 2001): 18–21.

7 Mahanta, 'Allegories': 244.

8 See Ahmad, *In Theory*: 67–71, and M. Keith Booker, *'Midnight's Children*, History and Complexity: Reading Rushdie after the Cold War', in *Critical Essays on Salman Rushdie*, ed. M. Keith Booker (New York: G. K. Hall, 1999): 283–313.

9 Timothy Brennan, *Salman Rushdie and the Third World: Myths of the Nation* (Basingstoke: Macmillan, 1989): 58.

10 Ahmad, *In Theory*: 135.

11 Tabish Khair, *Babu Fictions: Alienation in Contemporary Indian English Novels* (New Delhi: Oxford University Press, 2001): 297.

12 Kumkum Sangari makes this point in an interview with Rushdie (SRI, 70).

13 Graham Huggan, *The Post-Colonial Exotic: Marketing the Margins* (London: Routledge, 2001): 88.

14 *Ibid.*: 73.

Chapter 2

1 Helen Simpson, '"Hackle Raisers", A Conversation between Salman Rushdie and Angela Carter', *Vogue* (August 1985): 169.

2 *Ibid.*

3 George Orwell, 'Inside the Whale', in *Inside the Whale and Other Essays* (Harmondsworth: Penguin, 1957): 43.

4 *Ibid.*: 48–9.

5 See *Formalist Theory*, eds and trans. L. M. O'Toole and Ann Shukman, Russian Poetics in Translation, vol. 4 (Oxford: Holdan, 1977): 35.

6 Simpson, 'Hackle Raisers': 169.

7 *Ibid.*

8 Ahmad makes this point in relation to Rushdie's essay 'Outside the Whale'. Rushdie's critique of Orwell's quietism is a valuable one, for Ahmad, but the same can be argued for Rushdie's essay as Rushdie argues for Orwell's – it contradicts itself by failing to find grounds upon which political action can take place. *In Theory*: 155–6.

9 Catherine Itzin, *Stages of the Revolution* (London: Eyre Methuen, 1980): 196–7.

10 Salman Rushdie, '*Midnight's Children* and *Shame*', *Kunapipi* 7.1 (1985): 17–18.

11 Simpson, 'Hackle Raisers': 169.

12 For a selection of Gramsci's writings in this regard see *A Gramsci Reader: Selected Writings 1916–1935*, ed. David Forges (London: Lawrence and Wishart, 1988): 192–7.

13 Roger Simon, *Gramsci's Political Thought: An Introduction* (London: Lawrence and Wishart, 1991): 28.

14 The Gramsci quotations are cited in Simon, *Gramsci's Political Thought*: 29.

15 Edward Said, *Orientalism* (London: Routledge, 1978): 12.

16 Edward Said, *Culture and Imperialism* (London: Chatto, 1993): 253.

17 Dennis Porter, '*Orientalism* and its Problems', in *Colonial Discourse and Post-Colonial Thoery: A Reader*, eds Patrick Williams and Laura Chrisman (Harlow: Longman, 1994): 151.

18 *Ibid.*

19 Said, *Culture and Imperialism*: 253.

20 *Ibid.*: 295.

21 *Ibid.*: 260.

22 *Ibid.*

23 Homi Bhabha, *The Location of Culture* (London: Routledge, 1994): 107.

24 *Ibid.*: 110.

25 *Ibid.*: 112.

26 *Ibid.*

27 *Ibid.*: 114 and 121.

28 *Ibid.*: 121.

29 Ahmad, *In Theory*: 11.

Chapter 3

1 Quoted in Alastair Pennycook, *English and the Discourses of Colonialism* (London: Routledge, 1998): 78.

2 *Ibid.*: 79.

3 See Gauri Vishwanathan, *Masks of Conquest: Literary Study and British Rule in India* (Delhi: Oxford University Press, 1998): 23 and 41.

4 Thomas Macaulay, 'Minute on Indian Education', in *The Post-Colonial Studies Reader*, eds Bill Ashcroft, Gareth Griffiths and Helen Tiffin (London: Routledge, 1995): 430.

5 Vishwanathan, *Masks*: 26.

6 Mahanta, 'Allegories': 244.

7 George Steiner, 'The Hollow Miracle', in *Language and Silence: Essays on Language, Literature and the Inhuman* (New York: Atheneum, 1982): 101.

8 Cited in Bishnupriya Ghosh, *When Borne Across: Literary Cosmopolitics in the Contemporary Indian Novel* (New Brunswick: Rutgers University Press, 2004): 69.

9 Gurcharan Das, 'A Novelist's Faith', in *Indian English Fiction: 1980–90: An Assessment*, eds Nilufer E. Bharucha and Vilas Sarang, New World Literature 77 (Delhi: B. R. Publishing, 1994): 3.

10 *Ibid.*: 4.

11 Sujata Bhatt, 'A Different History', in *Brunizem* (Manchester, Carcanet, 1988): 37.

12 *Ibid.*

13 See Bhatt, *Brunizem*: 65–6.

14 Steiner, *Language and Silence*: 115.

15 *Ibid.*: 115–16.

16 For Rushdie's thoughts on Grass and his contemporaries see 'Günter Grass', IHL, 273–81, and SAL, 338.

17 Pennycook, *English*: 193.

18 *Ibid.*: 192–3.

19 *Ibid.*: 201.

20 There is no room here to do justice to this potentially complex argument. For the purposes of the current discussion I think it can be agreed that ideological judgements about literary works that are not propagandistic are *relatively independent* of aesthetic value judgements.

21 Bishnupriya Ghosh, 'An Invitation to Indian Postmodernity: Rushdie's English Vernacular as Situated Cultural Hybridity', in Booker, ed., *Critical Essays*: 130.

22 *Ibid.*: 136.

23 *Ibid.*: 130 and 142.

24 *Ihid*: 150

25 Meenakshi Mukherjee, Foreword, Afterword, *Rajmohan's Wife: A Novel*, Bankimchandra Chatterjee (New Delhi: Ravi Dayal, 1996): v–ix and 136–55.

26 Raja Rao, Foreword, *Kanthapura* (London: Allen and Unwin, 1938): 9.

27 *Ibid.*: 9–10.

28 Uma Parameswaran, *The Perforated Sheet: Essays on Salman Rushdie's Art* (New Delhi: Affiliated East–West Press, 1988): 20.

29 Wimal Dissanayake, 'Towards a Decolonized English: South Asian Creativity in Fiction', *World Englishes* 4.2 (1985): 241.

30 Salman Rushdie, 'The Empire Writes Back With a Vengeance', *The Times*, 3 July 1982: 8.

31 Desai, 'Introduction', *Midnight's Children*: vii.

32 See Vishwanathan, *Masks of Conquest*: Chapters 1 and 2.

33 Rushdie, 'The Empire Writes Back': 8.

34 Rushdie, '*Midnight's Children* and *Shame*': 8.

35 *Ibid.*

36 Parry and Lord argued that formulaic repetition in literary texts was an indication that those texts had oral sources. Rushdie applies this principle in reverse by employing formulaic repetition as a literary device to simulate the appearance of orality.

37 Nancy E. Batty, 'The Art of Suspense: Rushdie's 1001 (Mid-) Nights', *Ariel* 18.3 (1987): 49–65.

38 Robert Irwin, *The Arabian Nights: A Companion* (London: Penguin, 1994): 289.

39 Kwame Anthony Appiah, *In My Father's House: Africa in the Philosophy of Culture* (London: Methuen, 1992): 240.

40 Ahmad, *In Theory*: 126.

41 Huggan, *The Postcolonial Exotic*: xi.

42 *Ibid.* Huggan's argument here owes much to Timothy Brennan.

43 Ghosh, *When Borne Across*: 20.

44 *Ibid.*: 61.

45 *Ibid.*

46 *Ibid.*: 82.

47 Mikhail Bakhtin cites Boris Eikhenbaum's definition of *skaz* as 'an *orientation toward the oral form of narration*'. See *The Problems of Dostoevsky's Poetics*, ed. and trans. Caryl Emerson (Minneapolis: University of Minnsota Press, 1984): 191.

48 Rushdie seems to rate Buñuel's work more highly than Dalí's. A Dalí-like figure appears in *The Moor's Last Sigh*, but, whilst the portrait is partially affectionate, it is also, substantially, a satire – particularly upon Dalí's self-aggrandising, capitalistic instincts.

49 *Goopy Gyne Bagha Byne*, dir. Satyajit Ray, Purnima Pictures, 1968. Rushdie's primary reference point is Ray's scenario, but the story is ultimately taken from Satyajit's grandfather, Upendrakisore Ray Chaudhury.

Chapter 4

1 At the very least this list would have to account for the impact upon Rushdie's fictions of precursors such as Laurence Sterne, William Blake, Charles Dickens, James Joyce, Mikhail Bulgakov, G. V. Desani, Günter Grass and Gabriel García Márquez.

2 Rushdie is familiar with Barthes's work. 'I've read some Barthes because he writes quite well', he told David Brooks in 1984 (CSR: 58).

3 Roland Barthes, 'The Death of the Author', trans. Stephen Heath, in *Literature in the Modern World*, ed. Dennis Walder (Oxford: Oxford University Press, 1990): 230.

4 *Ibid.*

5 If there is a place for a writer like Rushdie in Barthes's theory, it is as a reader-author who demythologises traditional *doxas* by re-reading as he or she re-writes.

6 It is tempting to argue that the differences between Rushdie's analysis of the ways in which a text comes into being and the Barthesian analysis may be explained by the difference between the terms 'influence', favoured by Rushdie, and intertextuality, favoured by post-structuralist theory. 'Influence' allows greater emphasis on the idea that imaginative constructions may be originated in one place and flow, in calculable and comprehensible ways, to another. Intertextuality, by contrast, as the term is initially defined by Julia Kristeva, has nothing to do with the elective passage of ideas from one writer to another but is, rather, a condition of language use resulting from the necessary dependence of all semiotic systems

(such as the novel) upon antecedent, pre-existing semiotic systems. To argue, however, on the basis of terminological use, that Rushdie is not an intertextual author is to oversimplify the matter. Rushdie does, in some instances, advance a traditional model of textual relations, in which one coherent and identifiable author in a specifiable geo-political location, inspires another. However, his vision of the text as an oceanic flux, both in his essay on influence and in *Haroun*, suggests that Rushdie, in textual theory and in practice, holds a more radical vision of textuality than that described in his more conventional literary criticism. The story sea, after all, is an authorless soup in which the anonymous folk narrator meets the postmodern scriptor, and in which many voices concert together to create a polyphony that it is impossible to reduce to the comfort of known sources.

7 Graham Allen, *Intertextuality*, The New Critical Idiom (London: Routledge, 2000): 92.

8 *Ibid.*: 36.

9 Mikhail Bakhtin, 'Discourse in the Novel', in *The Dialogic Imagination*, ed. Michael Holquist, trans. Holquist and Caryl Emerson (Austin: University of Texas Press, 1981): 276.

10 *Ibid.*: 292.

11 *Ibid.*

12 *Ibid.*: 294.

13 *Ibid.*

14 Patricia Waugh, 'Modernism, Postmodernism, Feminism: Gender and Autonomy Theory', in *Postmodernism: A Reader*, ed. Patricia Waugh (London: Arnold, 1992): 190.

15 *Ibid.*: 198 and 195.

16 Morag Shiach, *Hélène Cixous* (London: Routledge, 1991): 23. Cixous in 'The Laugh of the Medusa' uses this as a description of how women have behaved in the past ('What woman hasn't flown/stolen') but argues that it is time for a completely new form of women's writing that is not dependent upon past models. Intertextual theory, however, suggests that absolute abandonment (and absolute newness) is impossible and would locate political agency in the prior activity of the *voleur* who must negotiate pre-existing systems. See Hélène Cixous, 'The Laugh of the Medusa', trans. Keith Cohen and Paula Cohen, *New French Feminisms: An Anthology*, eds Elaine Marks and Isabelle de Courtivron (New York: Harvester, 1981): 258.

17 Waugh, 'Modernism': 194.

18 Bhabha, *Location*: 174.

19 *Ibid.*: 185.

20 See 'Simulacra and Simulations' and 'The Gulf War Did Not Take Place', in *Jean Baudrillard: Selected Writings*, ed. Mark Poster (Cambridge: Polity, 2001): 169–87 and 231–53.

21 It is arguable that Rushdie's rejection of Baudrillardian postmodernism is based upon a misunderstanding of Baudrillard. By the time Rushdie comes to write *The Ground Beneath Her Feet* (1999) and *Fury* (2001), it seems, either the misunderstanding has been cleared up, or Rushdie has changed his point of view, for both these novels provide effective examples of the simulated character of contemporary mass-mediated reality. In *Fury*, for instance, a doll created by Malik Solanka becomes a model that characters such as Mila Milo copy, thus becoming copies of copies with no original (F, 90). In *The Ground Beneath Her Feet*, likewise, a meditation on the 'feedback loop' created by globalised mass communication produces a near perfect duplication of the Baudrillardian argument: 'the initial purity of what happens is almost instantly replaced by its televisualisation. Once it's been on tv, people are no longer acting, but *performing*. Not simply grieving, but *performing* grief … This loop is now so tight that it's almost impossible to separate the sound from the echo, the event from the media response to it' (GBF, 484–5).

22 Bakhtin, 'Discourse': 368.

23 *Ibid.*: 368–370.

24 *Ibid.*: 346.

25 George Steiner, 'In a Post-Culture', in *Extraterritorial: Papers on Literature and the Language Revolution* (London: Faber, 1972): 165.

26 George Steiner, *Language and Silence*: 104.

Chapter 5

1 Ian Hamilton, 'The First Life of Salman Rushdie', *The New Yorker*, 25 Dec. 1995–1 Jan. 1996: 92.

2 *Ibid.*

3 *Ibid.*

4   At the time of *Shame*'s publication in 1983 Zia was still in power. He died in an air crash in 1988.

5   *Ibid.*: 105.

6   *Ibid.*: 92.

7   W. J. Weatherby, *Salman Rushdie: Sentenced to Death* (New York: Carroll and Graf, 1990): 50.

8   *Ibid.*: 17.

9   Hamilton, 'First Life': 95.

10 *Ibid.*: 94.

11 *Ibid.*: 92.

12 W. B. Gallie, *Philosophy and the Historical Understanding* (London: Chatto and Windus, 1964): 9.

13 Hamilton, 'First Life': 96.

14 Weatherby, *Salman Rushdie*: 37.

15 David Wilson, 'Fable Minded', *The Times Literary Supplement*, 21 Feb. 1975: 185.

16 Peter Tinniswood, Review of *Grimus*, *The Times* 6 Feb. 1975: 8.

17 See Robert Towers, 'On the Indian World-Mountain', *The New York Review of Books* 28.14, 24 Sept. 1981. Reprinted at www.nybooks.com/articles/6913 (accessed January 2006).

18 Cheekily, Rushdie repeated this libel in *The Ground Beneath Her Feet* (1999) once he could no longer be prosecuted. See GBF, 281-2.

19 Katherine Frank, 'Mr. Rushdie and Mrs. Gandhi', *Biography: An Interdisciplinary Quarterly* 19.3 (1996): 245–58.

20 John Sutherland, 'Suddenly, Rushdie's A Second Division Dud', *The Guardian*, 3 Sept. 2001: Features, 5.

21 Roger Woddis, '*The Satanic Verses* Review', *New Statesman and Society*, 30 Sept. 1988: 4.

22 Hamilton, 'First Life': 106.

23 *Ibid.* Affection must have lingered, however, since the dedication 'R.D.' in Rushdie's 1987 *The Jaguar Smile* refers to Davidson.

24 Hamilton, 'First Life': 107.

25 Xavier Arguello, 'The Writer as Tourist', *New Republic*, 20 April 1987: 33.

26 *Ibid.*: 30.

27 *Ibid.*: 31 and 34.

28 *Ibid.*: 31.

29 Michael Massing, 'Snap Books', *New Republic*, 4 May 1987: 21.

30 *Ibid.*: 25.

31 Edward Said, 'Irangate', *The London Review of Books*, 7 May 1987: 10.

32 Daniel Pipes, *The Rushdie Affair: The Novel, The Ayatollah, and the West*, 2nd edn (New Brunswick: Transaction, 2003): 44 and 52.

33 *Ibid.*: 49 and 46.

34 Edward Said, 'Orientalism Reconsidered', in *Postcolonial Criticism*, eds Bart Moore-Gilbert, Gareth Stanton and Will Maley, Longman Critical Readers (London: Longman, 1997): 133.

35 Marianne's name was removed from *The Satanic Verses* to minimise danger to her after the announcement of the *fatwa*. The dedication in the Consortium paperback simply became: 'to the individuals and organisations who have supported this publication'.

36 Weatherby, *Salman Rushdie*: 129.

37 *Ibid.*: 130.

38 *Ibid.*: 150.

39 The *fatwa* is variously translated. This translation is taken from Weatherby, *Salman Rushdie*: 154.

40 *Ibid.*: 165.

41 *Ibid.*

42 William Nygaard, *The Price of Free Speech*, trans. Rosemary Fearn (Oslo: Scandinavian University Press, 1996): 21.

43 Tariq Ali and Howard Brenton, *Iranian Nights* (London: Nick Hern, 1989): i.

44 *The Rushdie Letters: Freedom to Speak, Freedom to Write*, ed. Steve MacDonogh, in association with Article 19 (Dingle, Ireland: Brandon, 1993): 9.

45 Weatherby, *Salman Rushdie*: 210.

46 MacDonogh, ed., *Rushdie Letters*: 149.

47 *Ibid.*: 157.

48 *For Rushdie: Essays by Arab and Muslim Writers in Defense of Free Speech*, ed. George Braziller, (New York: George Braziller Inc. 1994): ii.

49 *Ibid.*: 41.

50 Claire Messud, Review of *East, West*, *The Guardian* 7 Jan. 1995: 20.

51 See Ian Black, 'Rushdie Breakthrough', *The Guardian*, 15 Sept. 1998: 7.

52 Anon., 'The Lifting of an Unliftable *Fatwa*', *The Economist*, 3 Oct. 1998: 49.

53 Martin Amis, 'Rendezvous with Rushdie', *Vanity Fair*, Dec. 1990: 161.

54 D. T. Max, 'Manhattan Transfer', *The New York Times*. Reprinted in *The Observer*, London, 24 Sept. 2000: Review 2.

55 D. T. Max, 'Manhattan Transfer': 2.

56 Matt Thorne, *The Independent*, 'Rich Man's Blues', 26 Aug. 2001: Features, 15.

57 Sutherland, 'Suddenly': 5.

58 Charles Foran, 'Mad and Bad', *Far Eastern Economic Review*, 11 Oct. 2001: 81; David Gates, *Newsweek*, 'Raging Bull', 17 Sept. 2001: 68.

59 Boyd Tonkin, 'Fury! The Savaging of Salman Rushdie', *The Independent*, 7 Sept. 2001: Features 1.

60 Toby Clements, '*Fury*', *The Times*, 21 Sept. 2002: 20.

61 Tonkin, 'Fury!': 1.

62 This interview remains unpublished.

63 For Rushdie's comment see 'Muslims Unite!', *The Times*, 11 Aug. 2005: 19.

64 For a gripe, see Natasha Walter, *The Guardian*, Sept. 3, 2005: Review Section, 21.

65 Justine Hardy, 'Fall of the Tightrope Walker', *The Times*, August 27, 2005: Features, 9; and Suhayl Saadi, 'Storm in the Valley of Death: *Shalimar the Clown* by Salman Rushdie', *The Independent*, 9 Sept. 2005: Books, 22.

66 John Updike, 'Paradise Lost: Rushdie's *Shalimar the Clown*', *The New Yorker*, 5 Sept. 2005: 155.

Chapter 6

1 Jorge Luis Borges, 'The Thousand and One Nights', in *Seven Nights*, trans. Eliot Weinberger (New York: New Directions, 1984): 51.

2 See, for instance, *Fury*, in which it is observed that 'Golden age science fiction and science fantasy were … the best popular vehicle ever devised for the novel of ideas and of metaphysics' (F, 169).

3 Uma Parameswaran, 'New Dimensions Courtesy of the Whirling Demons: Word-Play in *Grimus*', in Fletcher, ed., *Reading Rushdie*: 37.

4 Rushdie shares an interest in Sufism with Lessing's *Canopus in Argus* series (1979–83). For parallels between *Grimus* and Carter's *Infernal Desire Machines of Dr. Hoffmann* (1972) see Ib Johansen, 'The Flight from the Enchanter: Reflections on Salman Rushdie's *Grimus*', in Fletcher, ed., *Reading Rushdie*: 31.

5 Gerardine Meaney, *(Un)Like Subjects: Women, Theory, Fiction* (London: Routledge, 1993): 69–70.

6 Natalie M. Rosinsky, *Feminist Futures: Contemporary Women's Speculative Fiction*, Studies in Speculative Fiction 1 (Michigan: Ann Arbor, 1982): 114 and 29.

7 *The X-Men* began life as a comic book series, written by Stan Lee and published by Marvell from September 1963 onwards, when both Saleem and Salman would have been sixteen, and at the height of their comic-book reading careers.

8 Robert Potter, *The English Morality Play: Origins, History and Influence of a Dramatic Tradition* (London: Routledge, 1975): 33. Potter is writing about medieval morality plays such as *Mankind* and *Everyman*. The application of this pithy summation of the medieval morality drama to *Midnight's Children* is revealing: Saleem, like Everyman or like Mankind, becomes, or believes he becomes, the human embodiment of a collective people. Unlike Everyman, however, Saleem is not a representative of all humanity, but only a particular kind of Indian experience in the late twentieth century. Rushdie's vision is therefore, unlike the anonymous Christians', non-universal.

9 Catherine Cundy, '"Rehearsing Voices": Salman Rushdie's *Grimus*', in Fletcher, ed., *Reading Rushdie*: 53.

10 Brennan, *Salman Rushdie*: 70.

11 *Ibid.*

12 Johansen, 'Flight': 24–5.

13 Parameswaran, 'New Dimensions': 43.

14 For Rushdie's uses of Farid ud-Din Attar's Sufi poem *The Confer-
    ence of the Birds* see Roger Y. Clark, *Stranger Gods: Salman
    Rushdie's Other Worlds* (Montreal and Kingston: McGill-Queen's
    University Press, 2001): 13–17 and 37–8; and Andrew Teverson,
    'Fairy Tale Politics: Free Speech and Multiculturalism in *Haroun
    and the Sea of Stories'*, *Twentieth Century Literature* 47.4 (2001):
    444–7 and 463–4. For Rushdie's uses of Dante's *Divine Comedy*
    see Clark, *Stranger Gods*: 37. Brennan also examines the associa-
    tions between *Grimus* and mystical or religious texts in *Salman
    Rushdie*: 71–8. The mysterious Liv, dressed in black in her house
    on the hill, is a familiar Gothic figure. Johansen also sees something
    of the gothic mad scientist in the character of Grimus (Johansen,
    'Flight': 28). There is a pastiche of the Russian novel in the scenes
    featuring the pre-revolutionary Russian aristocratic family the
    Cherkassovs. The scenes in the Elba Room replay a 'bad Western'
    (as the novel itself has it, G: 185). Norse mythology is heavily
    referenced in Grimus's godlike home, under the shadow of the
    Ash Yggdrasil. Finally, the figure of the powerful magician has
    significant parallels in Amerindian lore – as Johansen points out
    in 'Flight': 28–9.

15 Barthes, 'Death': 231.

16 In defence of the argument we might further note that Rushdie
    seems to have concealed, in the name of the 'Gorfs' from 'Thera' a
    direct allusion to the French theoretical tradition. The word 'Gorf'
    is an anagram of 'Frog'. 'Thera', meanwhile, points in the direction
    of both 'Theory' and, as an anagram, 'Earth'. The Gorfs of Thera,
    we may conclude, are 'Frog' or 'French' Thera-ists, and their ideas
    come not from some other-worldly place but from the all-too-
    familiar environs of Earth.

17 Ahmad, *In Theory*: 70.

18 Fredric Jameson, *Postmodernism: Or, The Cultural Logic of Late
    Capitalism* (London: Verso, 1991): 66.

19 T. S. Eliot, '*Ulysses*, Order, and Myth', *Selected Prose of T. S. Eliot*,
    ed. Frank Kermode (New York: Harcourt, 1975): 177.

20 Jean-François Lyotard, 'Answering the Question: What Is Post-
    modernism?', trans. Régis Durand in Lyotard, *The Postmodern
    Condition: A Report on Knowledge*, trans. Geoff Bennington and
    Brian Massumi (Manchester: Manchester University Press, 1984):
    81.

21 Avrom Fleishman, *The English Historical Novel: Walter Scott to Virginia Woolf* (Baltimore: Johns Hopkins, 1971): 15.

22 Harry Shaw, *The Forms of Historical Fiction: Sir Walter Scott and His Successors* (Ithaca: Cornell University Press, 1983): 20–1.

23 *Ibid.*

24 Ironically, Rushdie's description of *Midnight's Children* is offered in support of an argument that *Midnight's Children* does *not* represent a new form of historical fiction. The fact that this is precisely the form that most traditional historical fiction has taken seems to belie Rushdie's own argument abut his work.

25 Rushdie alludes to Scott at least twice in his writing. The first allusion occurs in *Midnight's Children* when Saleem, as a young man, visits the cinema to see the classic historical romance *Quentin Durward* (MC, 178); a film version of the 1823 novel. This event occurs, perhaps not accidentally, at about the same time that Saleem discovers his powers and sets out to become a recorder of his nation's history. It is also framed by Rushdie's semi-ironical suggestion that the recorder of history practises a kind of 'tourism-in-a-clocktower' (MC, 179). A second allusion to the fiction of Walter Scott in Rushdie's writing occurs in his short story, 'The Courter', in which the father of the young Indian narrator (a semi-autobiographical figure for Rushdie himself) rents 'a fancy address' for the family's stay in London: 'Waverley House in Kensington Court, W8' (EW, 182). The naming of the house may be, on one hand, ironic, if the novels of Sir Walter Scott are taken to represent the tradition of British writing that Indian narratives have arrived to complicate. On the other hand, it may be the case that Rushdie conjures the spirit of Scott in order to intensify the sense of cultural variousness that the story revels in by introducing a Scottish (not an English) arrow into the quiver.

26 Walter Scott, *Waverley*, ed. Andrew Hook (London: Penguin, 1972): 173.

27 Walter Scott, *Ivanhoe*, ed. A. N. Wilson (London: Penguin, 1982): 8–9.

28 Georg Lukács, *The Historical Novel*, trans. Hannah Mitchell and Stanley Mitchell (London: Merlin, 1962): 54.

Chapter 7

1 Zia's 'Islamisation' programme is characterised by legislation such as the 1979 Hadood Ordinance that reinterpreted rape as an act of adultery by the woman. Further legislation was also passed that made the legal evidence of two women equivalent to that of one man. See Inderpal Grewal, 'Salman Rushdie: Marginality, Women and *Shame*', in Fletcher, ed., *Reading Rushdie*: 136–7; and Sugata Bose and Ayesha Jalal, *Modern South Asia: History, Culture, Political Economy* (London: Routledge, 1998): 232.

2 Bhutto's heavy reliance on the military to shore up his regime, particularly his use of the army to forcibly suppress tribal insurrections in Baluchistan, effectively returned the army a measure of the power they had lost after their defeat in the 1971 civil war. It was, in addition, Bhutto's political corruption that led to the post-election street riots of July 1977 that gave Zia his chance to seize control of the state. See Bose and Jalal, *Modern South Asia*: 230–1.

3 The term 'conjoined opposites' is taken from *The Satanic Verses*, where it is applied to Gibreel Farishta and Saladin Chamcha (SV, 426). Its applicability to *Shame* shows that the Gibreel/Saladin duality in *The Verses* is anticipated in the earlier novel. We might also trace the device back to *Midnight's Children* in which the relationship between Saleem and Shiva is developed along comparable lines.

4 Marlowe, like Rushdie, fuses farce and tragedy. He also borrows from the medieval psychomachia.

5 As a daughter of the character who represents Zulfikar Ali Bhutto in *Shame*, it is logical to conclude that Arjumand Harappa, is an early caricature of Benazir Bhutto, prior to her Prime Ministership. Rushdie, on selective occasions, has denied this equation. In a 1987 interview with Sedge Thompson at San Fransisco State University he insisted (perhaps fearing a similar libel case to that which followed his characterisation, and naming, of Indira Gandhi in *Midnight's Children*) that Benazir Bhutto's belief that she was a character in *Shame* was misplaced (SRI, 85). Such denials, however, are disingenuous. Arjumand's biography, from her birth to her house arrest, parallels Benazir Bhutto's, and there are very considerable similarities between Rushdie's characterisation of Arjumand Harappa in the novel and his characterisation of Benazir Bhutto in his non-fiction – most prominently, his representation of both as having excessive attachments to their fathers to the point that they are willing to countenance corruption (see IHL,

57–8). In later interviews Rushdie has not exerted himself to deny the parallel. See, for instance, Hamilton, 'First Life': 105; and SRI: 131.

6 Ovid, *Metamorphosis*, trans. Mary Innes (London: Penguin, 1955): book VI, lines 578–9.

7 Lavinia's abusers have proved themselves 'craftier' than Tereus (II. iv.41) by cutting her 'pretty fingers off' (II.iv.42) as well as cutting out her tongue. William Shakespeare, *Titus Andronicus*, ed. Sonia Massai (London: Penguin: 2001).

8 Catherine Cundy, *Salman Rushdie*, Contemporary World Writers (Manchester: Manchester University Press, 1996): 53.

9 Grewal, 'Salman Rushdie': 140.

10 *Ibid.*: 139.

11 Ahmad, *In Theory*: 144.

12 *Ibid.*

13 Grewal, 'Salman Rushdie': 128.

14 Ahmad, *In Theory*: 145.

15 *Ibid.*

16 *Ibid.*

17 Grewal recognises that 'Sufiya's genocidal mimicry is meant to be a critique of patriarchal culture' because it seeks to 'change the present condition of women by showing how horrific the result would be if it remained unchanged'. According to Grewal, however, this critique fails 'because its horror can operate only by playing on a patriarchal fear of women and by showing the potential for destruction that is contained within women' ('Salman Rushdie': 138). If there is a legitimate feminist objection to the representation of women in *Shame* then it seems to lie here, rather than in the objection voiced by both Ahmad and Grewal that Rushdie fails to show women overcoming oppression.

Chapter 8

1 Frantz Fanon, *Black Skin, White Masks*, trans. Charles Lam Markmann (London: Pluto, 1986): 232.

2 Fanon, *Black Skin, White Masks*: 100. See also 223–4.

3 V. S. Napiaul, *The Mimic Men* (London: Penguin, 1969): 20; Samuel

Selvon, *The Lonely Londoners* (New York: Longman, 1956): 111.

4 The allusion to 'The Love Song of J. Alfred Prufrock' does a great deal of work here. On a superficial level Rushdie is borrowing some of the stuffiness of Eliot's Prufrock and giving it to Saladin. More profoundly, however, Rushdie manages to suggest, on the one hand, that Saladin is more Westernised in this outlook than his claimants might wish him to be, and, simultaneously, that he is in a better position to 'occupy', 'inhabit' and 'reclaim' Western tradition than he himself might wish to believe. See SV: 287.

5 Bhabha, *Location*: 224.

6 See Philip Engblom, 'A Multitude of Voices: Carnivalization and Dialogicality in the Novels of Salman Rushdie', in Fletcher, ed. *Reading Rushdie*: 301. The quotations describing aspects of the menippea are all taken from Bakhtin, *Problems*: 114–18.

7 Bakhtin, *Problems*: 115–16.

8 The first Brixton riot occurred on 11 April 1981, the second on 28 September 1985. In both cases rioters were responding violently to heavy-handed and discriminatory police tactics. On 23 April 1979 riots were sparked after protestors gathered to object to a meeting of the extreme right-wing National Front party at the Southall town hall.

9 Angel Gabriel is a direct translation of 'Gibreel Farishta' from the Urdu.

10 The four dream chapters are 'Mahound', 'Ayesha', 'Return to Jahilia', and 'The Parting of the Arabian Sea'. One of these sections, 'Ayesha', contains two distinct dream narratives, and two, 'Return to Jahilia' and 'The Parting of the Arabian Sea', are continuations of earlier narratives begun in 'Mahound' and 'Ayesha'. There are, therefore, three distinct stories that are intertwined in Gibreel's dreams, which later become scenarios for a trilogy of films planned by 'Whisky' Sisodia: *'Gibreel in Jahilia, Gibreel Meets the Imam,* [and] *Gibreel with the Butterfly Girl'* (SV: 345).

11 This episode, as Sara Suleri notes, is based upon the Hawkes Bay incident of February 1983 in which thirty-eight Shia Muslims led by Naseem Fatima 'walked into the Arabian Sea in the expectations that the waters would part' and allow them to walk to Basra. For a thorough reading see Sara Suleri, *The Rhetoric of English India* (Chicago: Chicago University Press, 1992): 202–5.

12 See Shabbir Akhtar, 'Art or Literary Terrorism?', in *The Salman Rushdie Controversy in Interreligious Perspective*, ed. Dan Cohn-Sherbok (Lewiston: Mellen, 1990): 7; and M. M. Ahsan, 'The

"Satanic" Verses and the Orientalists', in *Sacrilege versus Civility: Muslim Perspectives on* The Satanic Verses, eds M. M. Ahsan and A. R. Kidawi (London: The Islamic Foundation, 1991): 131–2.

13 The satanic verses follow directly from verses 19 and 20 that ask 'Have you considered al-'Lat and al-'Uzza and Manat, the third, the other'. They read (in Rushdie's transliteration of the Arabic) 'tilk al-gharaniq al-'ula wa inna shafa'ata-hunna la-turtaja', which is translated as 'These are the exalted females whose intercession is to be desired' (SV, 340). Rushdie's translation on this occasion uses the word 'females' because it reinforces his suggestion that Mahound's exclusion of these goddesses reflects the masculinist bias of the faith. However, other translations (and Rushdie's alternative translations) use either 'birds' or 'soaring ones' instead. See Akhtar, 'Art or Literary Terrorism': 7; and Ahsan, 'The "Satanic" Verses and the Orientalists': 132.

14 Ahsan, 'The "Satanic" Verses and the Orientalists': 132. This article was re-written and reprinted as a commentary on the Rushdie Affair, but it was first published in 1982 as a scholarly interrogation of the tradition, long before the appearance of *The Satanic Verses*.

15 Akhtar, 'Art or Literary Terrorism': 8.

16 Suleri, *Rhetoric*: 192. See also Jaina Sanga, *Salman Rushdie's Postcolonial Metaphors: Migration, Translation, Hybridity, Blasphemy and Globalisation* (Westport: Greenwood, 2001): 116–17.

17 *Behzti* was withdrawn by the Birmingham Repertory Theatre after demonstrations against its depiction of sexual exploitation and murder in a Sikh temple. One month later, The Christian Voice staged street protests against the BBC screening of *Jerry Springer: The Opera* by Stewart Lee and Richard Thomas because of its depiction of a mock crucifixion.

18 Salman Rushdie, 'Muslims Unite!' *The Times*, 11 August 2005: Comment, 19.

19 *Ibid.*

20 *Ibid.*

21 See Ahsan, 'The "Satanic" Verses and the Orientalists': 131.

22 Akhtar, 'Art or Literary Terrorism': 22.

23 Suleri, *Rhetoric*: 191.

24 *Ibid.*: 190.

25 *Ibid.*: 191.

26   *Ibid.*

27   *Ibid.*

28   *Ibid.*: 192.

29   *Ibid.*: 190 and 193.

Chapter 9

1   David Tushingham, 'Salman Rushdie in Conversation', Theatre Programme, *Haroun and the Sea of Stories*, dir. Tim Supple, National Theatre (Cottesloe) 1 Oct. 1998: 5.

2   Jawaharlal Nehru, 'Tryst with Destiny' (14 August 1947), in *The Penguin Book of Twentieth Century Speeches*, ed. Brian McArthur (London: Penguin, 1992): 234.

3   *Ibid.*: 237.

4   Rushdie admits the connection with Thackeray, but also insists that 'it's not all Thackeray. Another model for the character was Russia's Vladimir Zhirinovsky' (CSR, 195–6).

5   Aijaz Ahmad, *Lineages of the Present* (London: Verso, 2000): n. 346.

6   *Ibid.*

7   *Ibid.*

8   Rushdie knew that an Indian filmmaker had been violently attacked for a hostile representation of Thackeray, and published his novel anyway – perhaps disproving Marianne Wiggin's assertion that he is 'not the bravest man in the world'. See Amrit Dhillon, CSR: 169.

9   '[A] fascist spectacle, in the classic sense' according to Ahmad, *Lineages*: 166. See also Sunil Khilnani, *The Idea of India* (London: Penguin, 1999): 150–2; and Bose and Jalal, *Modern South Asia*: 227–8.

10   After the re-conquest of Southern Spain the Inquisition instituted a policy of religious cleansing that resulted in the expulsion or forcible conversion of Jews and Muslims. These expulsions are also echoed in the fate of Moraes, since his complex inheritance connects him to both the Jewish and Muslim faiths.

11   '[T]he story simply willed a happy ending,' Rushdie has observed. Initially he had planned not to bow to the convention, but he was 'suddenly struck' by the realisation that he 'couldn't impose

this modern sensibility on a story which was demanding a happy ending'. See Tushingham, 'Salman Rushdie': 5.

12 For my consideration of Rushdie's uses of fairy tales in this and other novels see my essay 'Migrant Fictions: Salman Rushdie and the Fairy Tale', in *Contemporary Fiction and the Fairy Tale*, ed. Stephen Benson (Detroit: Wayne State University Press, forthcoming 2008).

13 See Jonathan Greenberg, '"The Base Indian" or "the Base Judean"?: *Othello* and the Metaphor of the Palimpsest in Salman Rushdie's *The Moor's Last Sigh*', *Modern Language Studies* 29.2 (1999): 94; Justyna Deszcz, 'Salman Rushdie's Magical Kingdom: *The Moor's Last Sigh* and Fairy Tale Utopia', *Marvels and Tales: Journal of Fairy-Tale Studies* 18.1 (2004): 32; and Stephen Henighan, 'Coming to Benengeli: The Genesis of Salman Rushdie's Rewriting of Juan Rulfo in *The Moor's Last Sigh*', *The Journal of Commonwealth Literature* 33.2 (1998): 57.

14 See also Alexandra Schultheis's argument that 'Rushdie tempers [his] pessimism with the regenerative potential of the aesthetic' in 'Postcolonial Lack and Aesthetic Promise in *The Moor's Last Sigh*', *Twentieth Century Literature* 47.4 (2001): 570.

15 See Rachel Trousdale, '"City of Mongrel Joy": Bombay and the Shiv Sena in *Midnight's Children* and *The Moor's Last Sigh*', *The Journal of Commonwealth Literature* 39.2 (2004): 95.

16 *Ibid.*: 108.

17 The irrepressibly various life of Bombay continues, however, as Rushdie implies in his following novel, *The Ground Beneath Her Feet*, when he continues to reincarnate characters from earlier representations of the city. Aurora, for instance, is spotted at a Bohemian party delivering stinging set-downs. Saleem's aunt, Pia Aziz, appears at the same party, and Lord Methwold, also of *Midnight's Children*, has a substantial role to play throughout.

Chapter 10

1 Shaul Bassi, 'Orpheus's Other Voyage: Myth, Music and Globalisation', in *The Great Work of Making Real: Salman Rushdie's* The Ground Beneath Her Feet, eds Elsa Linguanti and Viktoria Tchernichova (Pisa: Edizioni Ets, 2003): 113.

2 Anthony Giddens, 'The Globalizing of Modernity', in *The Global Transformations Reader: An Introduction to the Globalization*

Debate, eds David Held and Anthony McGrew, second edition (Cambridge: Polity, 2003): 60.

3 For a concise summation see Manfred Steger, 'Is Globalization a New Phenomenon', in *Globalization: A Very Short Introduction* (Oxford: Oxford University Press, 2003): 17–36.

4 Stuart Hall, 'The Local and the Global: Globalization and Ethnicity', in *Culture, Globalization and the World-System*, ed. Anthony D. King (Minneapolis: University of Minnesota Press, 1997): 29. The observation is of course derived from Karl Marx.

5 Hall, 'Local and the Global': 28.

6 David Held and Anthony McGrew, 'The Great Globalization Debate', in Held and McGrew, eds, *Global Transformations Reader*: 5.

7 Hall, 'Local and the Global': 28.

8 *Ibid.*

9 *Ibid.*: 32 and 31.

10 *Ibid.*: 32–3.

11 *Ibid.*: 33.

12 *Ibid.*

13 *Ibid.*: 34–5.

14 *Ibid.*: 34.

15 Christopher Rollason, 'Rushdie's Un-Indian Music: *The Ground Beneath Her Feet*', in *Studies in Indian Writing in English*, vol. 2, eds Rajeshwar Mittapalli and Pier Paolo Piciucco (New Delhi: Atlantic, 2001): 144.

16 *Ibid.*: 146.

17 Bassi, 'Orpheus's Other Voyage': 111.

18 *Ibid.*: 113.

19 *Ibid.*

20 Hall, 'Local and the Global': 36.

21 This synchronic arrangement, to some extent, recalls that of Rushdie's first novel *Grimus*, which also engages in shifts between parallel dimensions. In contrast to *Grimus*, however, the parallel worlds of *Fury* are clearly rooted in known realities. Rushdie also uses this technique in *The Satanic Verses*.

22 Sarah Brouillette, 'Authorship as Crisis in Salman Rushdie's *Fury*', *The Journal of Commonwealth Literature* 40.1 (2005): 137–56.

23 *Ibid.*: 139.

24 *Ibid.*: 140.

25 Rushdie reworks the recent history of Fiji via Jonathan Swift, but it is still broadly recognisable. In 1999 Fiji's first democratic elections brought the Labour Party to power, representing the numerically superior but economically downtrodden Indian population. A coup the following year, organised by the Fijian businessman Georges Speight in the interests of the relatively privileged Fijian minority led to the deposition of the new Indian head of government Mahendra Chaudry. Speight's coup was ultimately a failure, but it did lead to the collapse of democracy on the island and the resumption of a military rule that favoured ethnic Fijians disproportionately. In *Fury* Solanka's girlfriend, Neela, is a descendant of Indian migrants to 'Lilliput-Blefuscu', a 'double speck in the remote South Pacific' (F: 156). Ethnic conflict on this island between the indigenous 'Elbees' and the 'Indo-Lilliputians' also culminates in a coup led by 'a certain Skyresh Bolgolam, an indigenous Elbee merchant' (F, 215), and Neela travels to 'Lilliput-Blefuscu' to fight on behalf of the doomed Indo-Lilly resistance.

Chapter 11

1 Brennan, *Salman Rushdie*: viii.

2 *Ibid.*: viii–ix.

3 *Ibid.*: 165.

4 *Ibid.*

5 *Ibid.*

6 *Ibid.*: 58.

7 *Ibid.*: 84–5.

8 *Ibid.*: 148.

9 *Ibid.*

10 *Ibid.*: 163.

11 *Ibid.*: 149.

12 *Ibid.*: 164.

13 *Ibid.*: 103.

14 *Ibid.*: 105.

15 Ghosh, *When Borne Across*: 20.

16 Ibid.

17 Ibid.: 8 and 5.

18 Ibid.

19 Booker, 'Midnight's Children, History, and Complexity': 283–4.

20 Ibid.: 284.

21 Ibid.: 286.

22 Baker argues that Ahmad employs 'a rather crude reflectionist model of the relation of literary form to economic forces' – an argument that might also serve as a response to Booker. He also contends that Rushdie's fiction, specifically The Satanic Verses, 'embodies the struggle … to envision or to anticipate a New, a utopian possibility, that is not merely a late capitalist ideological appropriation of a utopian discourse'. See Stephen Baker, The Fiction of Postmodernity (Edinburgh: Edinburgh University Press, 2000): 167 and 183.

23 Jaina Sanga, Salman Rushdie's Postcolonial Metaphors: Migration, Translation, Hybridity, Blasphemy and Globalisation (Westport: Greenwood, 2001): 4.

24 Ahmad, In Theory: 11.

25 Joel Kuortti, Fictions to Live In: Narration as an Argument for Fiction in Salman Rushdie's Novels (Frankfurt: Peter Lang, 1998): 31. Kuortti is, here, discussing Haroun and the Sea of Stories, but since it is not mentioned that this is an outcome that can be expected only in utopian fantasy fiction, this statement appears to describe Rushdie's thinking more generally.

26 Ahmad, In Theory: 124.

27 Ibid.: 138.

28 Ibid.: 139.

29 Ibid.: 127.

30 Brennan, Salman Rushdie: 144.

31 See Ahmad, In Theory: 27; and Georg Lukács, 'Realism in the Balance', trans. Rodney Livingstone, in Aesthetics and Politics: Debates Between Bloch, Lukács, Brecht, Benjamin, Adorno, ed. Ronald Taylor (London: Verso, 1980): 33.

32 Bertolt Brecht, 'Against Georg Lukács', trans. Stuart Hood, in Taylor, ed., Aesthetics and Politics: 82.

33 See Taylor, Aesthetics and Politics: 61–2. The articles by Brecht are included in this collection under the title 'Against Georg Lukács': 68–85.

34   Ahmad claims that whilst Rushdie can speak of himself as 'a man of the Left' on certain issues, 'racism, religiosity, dictatorship, empire', he is only left-wing 'in a general way' because he does not exist within a 'community of praxis [...] accepting and struggling with the risks and the restrictions and the suffering that such bonding often implies' (*In Theory*: 156–7). Such a demand for commitment, however, seems to conceal the commissar's demand for conformity, against which the whole spirit of Rushdie's fiction rebels.

35   Ahmad, *In Theory*: 69.

36   Dustin Griffin, *Satire: A Critical Reintroduction* (Kentucky: University Press of Kentucky, 1994): 24.

37   *Ibid.*

38   In this respect Rushdie's satire may be closest to that of Swift who, according to Griffin, 'reminds us that satire can be written "As with a moral View design'd" and yet not precipitate fixed moral precepts'. See Griffin, *Satire*: 26.

39   Ahmad, *In Theory*: 139.

40   Theodor Adorno, 'Reconciliation under Duress', trans., Rodney Livingstone, in Taylor, ed., *Aesthetics and Politics*: 167.

41   *Ibid.*

42   Bakhtin, 'Discourse': 26.

43   *Ibid.*

44   *Ibid.*

45   *Ibid.*

46   Kathryn Hume, 'Taking a Stand while Lacking a Center: Rushdie's Postmodern Politics', *Philological Quarterly* 74.1 (1995): 209–30.

47   *Ibid.*: 216.

48   *Ibid.*: 215.

49   *Ibid.*

50   *Ibid.*: 227 and 219–20.

51   *Ibid.*: 223.

52   Brouillette, 'Authorship as Crisis': 137–56.

53   *Ibid.*: 139.

54   *Ibid.*: 139–40.

55   *Ibid.*: 140.

Select bibliography

Books by Rushdie

East, West (1994; London: Vintage, 1995).
Fury (London: Jonathan Cape, 2001).
Grimus (1975; London: Paladin, 1989).
The Ground Beneath Her Feet (1999; London: Vintage, 2000).
Haroun and the Sea of Stories (1990; London: Granta, 1991).
Imaginary Homelands: Essays and Criticism: 1981–1991 (London: Granta, 1991).
The Jaguar Smile: A Nicaraguan Journey, 2nd edition (London: Vintage, 1997).
Midnight's Children (London: Jonathan Cape, 1981).
The Moor's Last Sigh (1995; London: Vintage, 1996).
The Satanic Verses (1988; Delaware: Consortium, 1992).
Shalimar the Clown (London: Cape, 2005).
Shame (1983; London: Picador, 1984)
Step Across This Line: Collected Non-Fiction 1992–2002 (London: Jonathan Cape, 2002).

Selected other works by Rushdie

'The Empire Writes Back With a Vengeance', *The Times*, 3 July 1982: 8.
'*Midnight's Children* and *Shame*', *Kunapipi* 7.1 (1985): 1–19.
Detailed listings of Rushdie's publications from 1975 to 1996 can be found in Joel Kuortti's *Salman Rushdie Bibliography* (see below).

Interview collections

Chauhan, Pradyumna, ed., *Salman Rushdie Interviews: A Sourcebook of His Ideas* (Westport, Connecticut: Greenwood, 2001).

Reder, Michael, ed., *Conversations with Salman Rushdie* (Jackson: University of Mississippi Press, 2000).

Selected Rushdie criticism and further reading

Afzal-Khan, Fawzia, *Cultural Imperialism in the Indo-English Novel: Genre and Ideology in R. K. Narayan, Anita Desai, Kamala Markandaya, and Salman Rushdie* (University Park: Pennsylvania State University Press, 1993).

Ahmad, Aijaz, *In Theory: Classes, Nations, Literatures* (London: Verso, 1992).

Ahsan, M. M., and A. R. Kidwai, eds, *Sacrilege versus Civility: Muslim Perspectives on* The Satanic Verses (Leicester: The Islamic Foundation, 1991).

Appignanesi, Lisa, and Sara Maitland, eds, *The Rushdie File* (Syracuse: Syracuse University Press, 1990).

Baker, Stephen, *The Fiction of Postmodernity* (Edinburgh: Edinburgh University Press, 2000).

Bhabha, Homi, *The Location of Culture* (London: Routledge, 1994).

Booker, Keith M., ed., *Critical Essays on Salman Rushdie* (New York: G. K. Hall, 1999).

Bose, Sugata, and Ayesha Jalal, *Modern South Asia: History, Culture, Political Economy* (London: Routledge, 1998).

Braziller, George, ed., *For Rushdie: Essays by Arab and Muslim Writers in Defense of Free Speech* (New York: George Braziller Inc., 1994).

Brennan, Timothy, *Salman Rushdie and the Third World: Myths of the Nation* (Basingstoke: Macmillan, 1989).

Brouillette, Sarah, 'Authorship as Crisis in Salman Rushdie's *Fury*', *The Journal of Commonwealth Literature* 40.1 (2005): 137–56.

Clark, Roger Y., *Stranger Gods: Salman Rushdie's Other Worlds* (Montreal and Kingston: McGill-Queen's University Press, 2001).

Cundy, Catherine, *Salman Rushdie*, Contemporary World Writers (Manchester: Manchester University Press, 1996).

Deszcz, Justyna, *Rushdie in Wonderland: Fairytaleness in Salman Rushdie's Fiction* (Frankfurt: Peter Lang, 2004).

Fletcher, M. D., ed., *Reading Rushdie: Perspectives on the Fiction of Salman Rushdie*, Cross/Cultures 16 (Amsterdam: Rodopi, 1994).

This work includes an excellent annotated bibliography of Rushdie criticism up to 1994.

Ghosh, Bishnupriya, *When Borne Across: Literary Cosmopolitics in the Contemporary Indian Novel* (New Brunswick: Rutgers University Press, 2004).

Gonzalez, Madelena, *Fiction After the Fatwa: Salman Rushdie and the Charm of Catastrophe* (Amsterdam: Rodopi, 2005).

Goonetilleke, D. C. R. A., *Salman Rushdie* (New York: St. Martins, 1998).

Gorra, Michael, *After Empire: Scott, Naipaul, Rushdie* (Chicago: University of Chicago Press, 1997).

Grant, Damian, *Salman Rushdie*, Writers and Their Work (Plymouth: Northcote House, 1999).

Grewal, Subir. www.subir.com/rushdie.html (accessed January 2006).

Hall, Stuart, 'The Local and the Global: Globalization and Ethnicity', in *Culture, Globalization and the World-System*, ed. Anthony D. King (Minneapolis: University of Minnesota Press, 1997): 19–39.

Hamilton, Ian, 'The First Life of Salman Rushdie', *The New Yorker*, 25 December 1995–1 January 1996: 90–7 and 100–13.

Harrison, James, *Salman Rushdie* (New York: Twayne, 1992).

Huggan, Graham, *The Post-Colonial Exotic: Marketing the Margins* (London: Routledge, 2001).

Hume, Kathryn, 'Taking a Stand while Lacking a Center: Rushdie's Postmodern Politics', *Philological Quarterly* 74.1 (1995): 209–30.

Khilnani, Sunil, *The Idea of India* (London: Penguin, 1999).

Kuortti, Joel, *The Salman Rushdie Bibliography* (Frankfurt: Peter Lang, 1997).

Linguanti, Elsa, and Viktoria Tchernichova, eds, *The Great Work of Making Real: Salman Rushdie's* The Ground Beneath Her Feet (Pisa: Edizioni Ets, 2003).

Mishra, Vijay, 'The Diasporic Imaginary: Theorizing the Indian Diaspora', *Textual Practice* 10.3 (1996): 421–37.

Nasta, Susheila, *Home Truths: Fictions of the South Asian Diaspora in London* (Basingstoke: Palgrave, 2002).

Pennycook, Alastair, *English and the Discourses of Colonialism* (London: Routledge, 1998).

Pipes, Daniel, *The Rushdie Affair: The Novel, The Ayatollah, and the West*, 2nd edition (New Brunswick: Transaction, 2003).

Said, Edward W., *Culture and Imperialism* (London: Chatto, 1993).

Sandhu, Sukhdev, *London Calling: How Black and Asian Writers Imagined a City* (London: Harper, 2004).

Sanga, Jaina C., *Salman Rushdie's Postcolonial Metaphors: Migration, Translation, Hybridity, Blasphemy and Globalisation* (Westport: Greenwood, 2001).

Sawhney, Sabina, and Simona Sawhney, *Twentieth-Century Literature*, Special Issue: Salman Rushdie, 47.4 (2001).

Smale, David, ed., *Salman Rushdie:* Midnight's Children / The Satanic Verses, *A Reader's Guide to Essential Criticism*, Icon Readers' Guides (Cambridge: Icon, 2001).

Suleri, Sara, *The Rhetoric of English India* (Chicago: University of Chicago Press, 1992).

Vishwanathan, Gauri, *Masks of Conquest: Literary Study and British Rule in India* (Delhi: Oxford University Press, 1998).

Weatherby, W. J., *Salman Rushdie: Sentenced to Death* (New York: Carroll & Graf, 1990).

Index

Note: literary works by writers other than Rushdie can be found under the author's name; 'n.' after a page reference indicates the number of a note on that page and page numbers in **bold** refer to main entries.